Engaged Spirituality

Bloomsbury Studies in Religion and Civic Culture

Series Editor: Richard Flory

Published in collaboration with the Center for Religion and Civic Culture at the University of Southern California (CRCC), the volumes in this Open Access series investigate the nexus of religion and public life. As CRCC has done since 1996, the series focuses on the ways that religious organizations and spiritual movements adapt and respond to the many challenges they face. Volumes utilize multiple disciplinary perspectives, both within and across volumes, and represent the range of perspectives of specialists at CRCC, including scholars, journalists, and faith leaders. The volumes address issues such as processes of institutional and organizational change in response to social, cultural, and political developments, religiously motivated efforts by individuals and movements to create social change, and the importance of "place" as a key variable in how organizations and individuals understand and conceptualize their role in the civic sphere. The books also provide resources to support faith and community leaders' efforts to understand how religion "works" in society and to improve the communities they serve.

Engaged Spirituality

Stories of Religious Resilience, Inspiration, and Pursuing the Common Good

Edited by
Ken Chitwood

BLOOMSBURY ACADEMIC
LONDON • NEW YORK • OXFORD • NEW DELHI • SYDNEY

BLOOMSBURY ACADEMIC
Bloomsbury Publishing Plc, 50 Bedford Square, London, WC1B 3DP, UK
Bloomsbury Publishing Inc, 1359 Broadway, New York, NY 10018
Bloomsbury Publishing Ireland, 29 Earlsfort Terrace, Dublin 2, D02 AY28, Ireland

First published in Great Britain 2026

Series design by Jade Barnett
Cover image: Water Rite © Noel Rojo, 2019

A catalogue record for this book is available from the British Library.

A catalog record for this book is available from the Library of Congress.

ISBN: HB: 978-1-3505-6346-9
PB: 978-1-3505-6345-2
ePDF: 978-1-3505-6347-6
eBook: 978-1-3505-6348-3

Series: Bloomsbury Studies in Religion and Civic Culture

Typeset by Integra Software Services Pvt. Ltd.

CONTENTS

FIGURES

CONTRIBUTORS

Athar Ahmad is a journalist and documentary maker whose work has featured across radio, television, and online. From presenting documentaries for the BBC, to examining the role of religion in the world today, Athar's work aims to shed a light on untold stories and perspectives. Athar is currently Program Director for the MA in Audio Storytelling for Radio and Podcast at University College London.

Ken Chitwood (Ph.D., University of Florida) is a postdoctoral researcher in the Study of Religion at Universität Bayreuth, Germany. He is also an Affiliate of the USC Center for Religion and Civic Culture, European Correspondent for *Christianity Today*, Senior Correspondent for Interfaith America, and Editor of ReligionLink, a premier resource for reporters writing on religion. His work has appeared in the *Los Angeles Times*, *The Washington Post*, *Chicago Tribune*, BBC Radio 4, Religion News Service, *The Times of India*, *USA Today*, *The Guardian*, *Foreign Policy*, *Houston Chronicle*, *New Lines Magazine*, The Conversation, Religion Unplugged, NPR, and elsewhere. He is the author of *The Muslims of Latin America and the Caribbean* (Lynne Rienner, 2021) and *Borícua Muslims: Everyday Cosmopolitanism Among Puerto Rican Converts to Islam* (University of Texas Press, 2025).

Innocent Eteng is a Nigerian journalist and media manager with years of experience in solutions-oriented reporting. He is the publisher of Nigeria's leading solutions journalism platform, Prime Progress, which he founded in 2021. He is also the founder and executive director of the Religion Journalism Foundation (in Nigeria), a nonprofit media organization reporting at the intersection of religion and society. Innocent has written for several global media, including *Yes Magazine*, *The Christian Science Monitor*, and *TRT World*.

Hebah Farrag is Associate Director of Grants at PATH, a leading homeless services provider in California. Farrag is the former Assistant Director of Research at the USC Center for Religion and Civic Culture (CRCC), where she managed a portfolio of research projects while pursuing her own research on religion and social change. Farrag has been widely quoted and has written for publications such as *The Berkeley Forum*, *On Being with Krista Tippett*, and *Forced Migration Online*. Farrag served as the project manager and research team lead (alongside Don and Arpi Miller) in the Spiritual Exemplars Project, a global initiative on engaged spirituality tasked with collecting 100 profiles of exemplary people working to promote human flourishing.

Richard Flory (Ph.D., University of Chicago) is Executive Director of the Center for Religion and Civic Culture at the University of Southern California. He is a sociologist whose research focuses on religion and social change, religious and cultural change, the role of faith groups in developing and maintaining civic society, and the religious and spiritual lives of youth and young adults. He has published several books, including most recently, *Religion in Los Angeles: Religious Activism, Innovation, and Diversity in the Global City* (Routledge, 2021) and *Back Pocket God: Religion and Spirituality in the Lives of Emerging Adults* (Oxford University Press, 2020).

Linda Freund is an independent multimedia reporter based in Barcelona, Spain. She recently served as a senior video journalist for *The Wall Street Journal* and a journalism fellow at the USC Center for Religion and Civic Culture (CRCC) and the Chaplaincy Innovation Lab at Brandeis University. Prior to this, she worked as a roving foreign correspondent, contributing reports from conflict zones across South Asia and East Africa. Her work focuses on emerging markets and the socio-economic origins of conflict and trauma.

Nalika Gajaweera (Ph.D., University of California Irvine) is a cultural anthropologist, specializing in the connections between academic research, community engagement, and public scholarship. Her work explores the intricate relationships between religion, race, gender, ethics, and social justice, drawing on research conducted in Sri Lanka and the United States. She is the Assistant Director of the Humanities Center at the University of California, Irvine.

Clément Girardot is a freelance reporter from France. His work covers emerging technologies, gastronomy, religion, underground culture, climate change, and historical memory. He is drawn to original narratives that challenge and captivate readers. His articles have been published by renowned outlets such as *Wired*, *Al Jazeera*, *The Guardian*, *Politico*, *Le Monde Magazine*, *Mongabay*, and more. In 2019 and 2023, he received the journalismfund.eu transnational European grant for investigative reporting. In 2016, he was awarded the Nicolas Bouvier Reporting Prize by the Geneva Press Club. Girardot also co-founded and worked as an editor for *Mashallah News*, an award-winning online media platform dedicated to the Middle East.

Kevin Douglas Grant is the co-founder and chief development officer of The GroundTruth Project, an award-winning nonprofit news organization that is building the future of local journalism from the ground up. GroundTruth is home to Report for America and Report for the World, service journalism programs that have partnered with hundreds of local newsrooms in twenty-one countries to create more than 600 reporting positions on critical public interest beats since 2017. Previously senior editor at GlobalPost, Grant has led reporting fellowships in fifty countries and published and spoken widely. He is an adjunct journalism professor at Georgetown University and has been a fellow at the Poynter Institute, International Center for Journalists and USC Center for Religion and Civic Culture.

Arpi Miller (Ph.D., University of California Los Angeles) researched different forms of immigrant organizing, exploring how skills and connections translate across arenas. Her case study featured Salvadoran American activists in the Los Angeles area. Arpi now lives in Colorado with her husband and two children. She balances her time between freelance research projects and both secular and faith-based immigrant advocacy and accompaniment as Director of ISAAC of Northern Colorado.

Donald E. Miller (Ph.D., University of Southern California) is the former Leonard K. Firestone Professor of Religion at USC and co-founder of the Center for Religion and Civic Culture. He is a sociologist of religion with an interest in global religious trends, new patterns of religious practice, and innovative organizational responses to cultural change. He is the author, co-author, or editor of eleven books and has received major grants from numerous foundations. He was the principal investigator for the "Spiritual Exemplars Project," supported by the John Templeton Foundation and Templeton Religion Trust.

Monique Parsons is a journalist and award-winning audio producer whose work has aired on NPR News, podcasts, and public radio stations nationwide. She is a graduate of Princeton University, Northwestern University, and Harvard Divinity School. A former Journalism Fellow at the University of Southern California Center for Religion and Civic Culture, she was managing editor of *Interfaith America Magazine* and, with historian Sarah Allaback, the co-author of *Green Gold: The Avocado's Remarkable Journey from Humble Superfood to Toast of a Nation*, published by Counterpoint Press in May 2025.

Magdaléna Rojo is an independent multimedia journalist covering global issues and human rights. She focuses on solutions and underrepresented voices. Originally from Slovakia, she has been working in the countries of the Global South for more than ten years now and is currently based in

Oaxaca, Mexico. Rojo's work has been published in *The New Humanitarian*, *The Context News*, *Deutsche Welle*, *Mongabay*, *Unbias the News*, *Atmos*, among others. She is an author of a narrative nonfiction book *Women Who Stay* (published in Slovakia in 2023).

Stephanie Saldaña is from San Antonio, Texas and has spent nearly two decades living and reporting from the Middle East. A graduate of Harvard Divinity School, she is the author of three acclaimed books. Her latest book, *What We Remember Will Be Saved: A Story of Refugees and the Things They Carry*, was awarded the 2024 Religion News Association's Excellence in Reporting Award for Nonfiction.

Priyadarshini Sen is an independent journalist based in Delhi. She's covered religion, politics, social justice, and environment widely across India, Asia, United States, Europe, and North Africa. She's currently working on her first book about religious nationalism in India and helping organize peace dialogues around the world. She's received several national and international awards for her work.

Shaina Shealy works as a Senior Producer for the public radio show and podcast "Snap Judgment." Her stories have taken her to a thorn forest in India, mushroom houses in the Rwandan hills, a home for retired movie stars in Myanmar, and an ice-cream shop in Gaza City. She lives with her family outside of Washington, DC.

Nick Street was senior writer at the USC Center for Religion and Civic Culture through his death in 2023. Nick worked with Cecil Murray on his memoir *Twice Tested By Fire: A Memoir of Faith and Service* and later developed an archive of 450 sermons from Murray's time at FAME Church in partnership with the church and the USC Libraries. Nick studied religious ethics at Oberlin College and the Candler School of Theology at Emory University. After a decade working as an editor in the world of scholarly publishing, he returned to graduate school at USC Annenberg, where he received an M.A. in print journalism. His writing on religion, science, sexuality, media, and culture has appeared in *The Wall Street Journal*, *Los Angeles Times*, *LA Weekly*, *Jewish Journal*, *Search*, *Religion Dispatches*, *Patheos*, and *The Revealer*. In addition to his role at CRCC, he worked as the managing editor of TransMissions, the website of the Knight Chair in Media and Religion at USC.

Megan Sweas is the editor and director of communications at the USC Center for Religion and Civic Culture. She led the journalism fellowship for "Spiritual Exemplars: A Global Project on Engaged Spirituality," awarding eighty grants to journalists to profile humanitarians around the world.

Sweas is the author of *Putting Education to Work: How Cristo Rey High Schools Are Transforming Urban Education* (HarperOne, 2014). She has written about social issues and religion for publications such as Religion News Service, *YES! Magazine*, *National Catholic Reporter*, *Tricycle*, *The Washington Post*, and *U.S. Catholic* magazine, where she served as an editor. She has journalism degrees from the University of Southern California and the Medill School of Journalism at Northwestern University.

Kimberly Winston has spent more than three decades covering religion for secular media. Her work has appeared in the *Los Angeles Times*, *The Washington Post*, and on the websites for NPR and Five-Thirty-Eight. For five years, she was a producer for and contributor to the public radio show "Interfaith Voices." She is a 1994 graduate of the Columbia Graduate School of Journalism and currently resides in Northern California.

ACKNOWLEDGMENTS

Whether as an ethnographer, journalist, or anthology editor, I am but a steward of stories. Thus, I am indebted to the range of storytellers who contributed to this public conversation about the role of religion in contemporary global society.

First and foremost, I want to thank Don Miller, who not only served as the Spiritual Exemplars Project's principal investigator but invited me to be this anthology's caretaker over a pile of pancakes in Fort Collins, Colorado. His leadership and guidance cannot be overstated, and I remain indebted to his keen intellect and capacious kindness. The same goes to the entire USC CRCC team, both past and present: Soraya Ahyaudin, Hebah Farrag, Richard Flory, Nalika Gajaweera, Brie Loskota, Arpi Miller, Napah Phyakul Quach, Najuma Smith, Nick Street, and Megan Sweas. I am particularly grateful to Don and Megan for writing a wonderful Foreword for this book. Additionally, I would like to thank Heather Choate Davis and the people of First Lutheran Venice, who hosted me as a Scholar-in-Residence in summer 2024, partnering with CRCC on a series of public talks titled "How Then Shall We Live?"

I was also immensely humbled and delightfully honored to have worked alongside a bumper-crop of talented journalists on this project, both those who contributed to this anthology and those who shared their stories elsewhere: in print, online, and via video or audio. I learned much from all of you about how to tell a good story. This book would not be what it is without you. I'd like to say a special thanks to members of our team who passed along the way, but who left an indelible mark on the project, this anthology, and our lives: Maria Emilia Martin, whose presence I was graced with as we discussed the concept of exemplarity at our initial project retreat in 2019; Julia Lieblich, who shared with me what it is to wrestle with the world's pain through the written word; and Nick Street, whose last conversation with me was about telling the story of exemplars with compelling clarity and care.

And what would this project be without the exemplars themselves? Specifically, I'd like to thank the exemplars who welcomed me into their homes, families, and lives: Muhammad Elgazzar, Ela Gandhi, Sonia Tinoco García, Azza Karam, and Alissa Wahid. I am also thankful to others whom I added at my sole discretion as "exemplars" in this book: Kezevino Aram,

Alan Bern, and David Rosen. They too invited me along, to pry into their life's work, and share their stories.

Thanks are also due to the wonderful team at Bloomsbury who welcomed this anthology as the first in a new series on Religion and Civic Culture. Cheers to Lalle Pursglove for directing the ship, as well as Sarah Skinner, Sophie Ruthven, Seb Claas, Clara Ferreyra, Anne Hunt, and Jane Fieldsend for being such a helpful crew.

Finally, to my wife Paula and my parents Sandy and Bob. Each of you, in your own way, have exemplified the best that religion and spirituality have to offer. Thank you for embodying goodness and grace in my life every day.

SERIES PREFACE

Drawing on scholarship from the Center for Religion and Civic Culture at the University of Southern California (CRCC), the volumes in this series investigate the nexus of religion and public life. As CRCC has done since 1996, the series focuses on the ways that religious organizations and spiritual movements adapt and respond to the many challenges they face. Volumes utilize multiple disciplinary perspectives, both within and across volumes, and represent the range of perspectives of specialists affiliated with CRCC, including scholars, journalists, and faith leaders.

CRCC's work has consistently found that spirituality that transcends oneself compels many people to be engaged with the grand challenges of our time. Religious and spiritual traditions provide both a moral vision for a more just world and the institutional and social capital required to create positive change in society. In keeping with CRCC's mission to produce empirical research on religion and to bring that research into conversation with faith and community leaders, the books in the series are intended to engage both academics and practitioners. The volumes will provide original empirical research on emerging trends on the power and role of religion in the public sphere. This research demonstrates how religion is shaped by, and in turn shapes public culture, politics, and discourse. The books will also serve as resources to support faith and community leaders' efforts to understand how religion "works" in society and to improve the communities they serve.

CRCC is committed to the idea that the world is enriched when people bring their religious, spiritual, and cultural values into dialogue with others, thus creating a more robust and inclusive public sphere. We hope that the books in the series will further engagement across religious, cultural, and political differences as the volumes reveal the common commitments of like-minded people of different faiths.

Richard Flory
Series Editor
Executive Director
USC Center for Religion and Civic Culture

FOREWORD

By Megan Sweas and Donald E. Miller

Journalists and researchers who focus on the intersection of religion and social change, as we do, have the privilege of meeting some of humanity's best. These are individuals who care deeply about their fellow beings, live in alignment with a high standard of morality, hold a vision of a better world, and have the skills and leadership to build that vision. These pages contain the stories of such "spiritual exemplars," as we have dubbed them.

Years before launching the project that led to this book, Donald Miller brought the Rev. Dr. Cecil L. Murray, our "prototypical spiritual exemplar" with him to Rwanda. They visited another extraordinary humanitarian, Jean Gakwandi, who took them to a meeting with a group of widows. Most had lost their families and been raped during the genocide. Speaking to the women, Rev. Murray pulled out a 5,000 franc note from his pocket. He proceeded to wad it up, throw it on the ground and stomp on it. Unraveling it again, he asked the women what it was worth. They replied, 5,000 francs, of course. Murray's point was clear. Regardless of how we've been stomped on, we, too, maintain equal worth.

For Don, it was an opportunity to witness a moment of healing, a moment Don knew was consistent with Rev. Murray's decades of ministry. Having witnessed how Rev. Murray brought economic justice to South Los Angeles, how Jean Gakwandi comforted his fellow survivors of the Rwandan genocide, how another exceptional person, Mama Maggie, served thousands of children in Cairo's slums, Don wanted to better understand such extraordinary people. He also wanted to share their stories.

"Spiritual Exemplars: A Global Project on Engaged Spirituality" is the culmination of Don's career traveling around the world on research projects and meeting exemplary people who shaped how he thinks about religion and moral responsibility. With funding from the John Templeton Foundation and Templeton Religion Trust, the USC Center for Religion and Civic Culture (CRCC) profiled 104 people, representing thirteen faith traditions and forty-two countries, through the project. A team of thirty-three journalists told these stories in *The New York Times*, *The Guardian*, *Al Jazeera*, *Christian Science Monitor*, Religion News Service, and more. The Spiritual Edge produced an award-winning podcast featuring two seasons of sound-rich audio documentaries, and we produced fourteen video profiles. This book brings together many of the stories, edited by one of the journalists who worked on the project. We hope the narratives within its pages will shape your thinking as well.

The project was unique—we might say exemplary—in both its subject matter and methodology (and we are grateful for the Templeton Foundation and Trust for funding such an innovative model). From a research perspective, it expanded upon a burgeoning field of research on moral exemplars, primarily undertaken in psychology and moral philosophy. Scholars leading this field ask why we should limit our understanding of human moral functioning by looking at the average person; rather, studying exemplars teaches us something about the full range of human potential. Somewhat surprisingly, the role of religion and spirituality is nearly absent in the literature on exemplars, even though several scholars note its prevalence among subjects that they have studied. In their classic text, *Some Do Care* (1992), scholars Anne Colby and William Damon examined twenty-three people who were identified as living truly extraordinary lives of moral commitment and action. They found that religious faith shaped the commitments and spurred the action of 80 percent of their sample.

William James argued more than one hundred years ago that religion and spirituality play a role in moral development and functioning. Studies have shown that James was correct, argues Lawrence Walker, a psychologist focused on moral development. Yet, he writes, "the field of moral psychology has nevertheless generally disregarded the significance of religion and spirituality in morality" (2003: 374). In fact, he goes on to say: "Within the discipline of psychology, the study of religion and spirituality has been considered anathema on a fairly consistent basis, either by a blanket denial of their importance in the daily lives of the vast majority of people or by a univocal focus on their negative manifestations" (p. 374).

With our project on *spiritual* exemplars, we built upon the work of philosopher Linda Zagzebski (2013), who argues that exemplars are foundational to moral theory. In other words, morality is and always has been defined in direct reference to exemplars. In her view, moral learning occurs through a process of *admiration* of exemplars, both living and dead, and *emulation*—attempting to be like them. We encounter these "saints" through narratives as well as direct contact. It is in their embodied expressions that we understand what it means to love, care, forgive, be grateful, and create lives filled with purpose, honesty, diligence, and other virtues.

Yet many of our examples of morality remain historical figures. We look to the lives of saints, bodhisattvas, or yesterday's exemplars to understand what it means to live according to higher principles, but after their death, the tendency toward hagiography can distort the lives of even the best of us, concealing struggles and faults. For our project, therefore, we wanted to focus on living individuals, from all around the world and multiple faith traditions. Hebah Farrag, then CRCC's assistant director of research, analyzed lists of prize winners, humanitarians, and notable religious leaders to help us better understand the category of "spiritual exemplar" and define it. Based on a set of criteria, Hebah compiled a list of 450 living individuals inspired and sustained by their religion or spirituality to advance human flourishing, and would go on to manage the project's research and liaise with the 104 exemplars profiled.

Meanwhile, Don approached Megan Sweas, a journalist and CRCC's director of communications, to ask how to best capture the stories of 100 such individuals and share them with non-academic audiences. Could journalists tell those stories? Megan had recently traveled to Italy on an International Reporting Project fellowship, reporting about how the Catholic Church was responding to Pope Francis's calls to hospitality amidst a surge of migration. From Rome to Naples to Sicily, she met Catholic sisters who embodied both a soft compassion and steely resolve in their efforts to protect victims of human trafficking. They were challenging international criminal networks, legal structures that penalized victims, and institutional indifference within the church, all while providing young women with care, safety, and a future. Certainly, these were stories of "spiritual exemplars." Building on her experience, CRCC set up a similar fellowship for journalists with some key differences. We asked the journalists to embed with one exemplary individual for a week, getting to know them, their organization, and their communities on a level rarely afforded to journalists. The journalists had editorial control over their final product, but they also shared their interviews with the exemplar with CRCC's research team, who read and coded them for common themes.

When we opened applications for the fellowship, Megan had a particular religion reporter in mind for the project: Ken Chitwood, the editor of this volume. At the time, Ken was finishing a doctorate in religion, straddling the worlds of journalism and academia, just like the project. Ken's journalism experience influences his approach to ethnography and storytelling, while his academic background grounds his reporting. Ken was one of 350 journalists who applied to this fellowship, and his application stood out. Indeed, through the course of the project, he produced thoughtful stories, profiling five exemplars despite pandemic restrictions. He also embraced the "life story" interview guide that we offered to the journalists as a tool to use to talk to the exemplars. The approach went on to influence his reporting on other significant individuals, many of whom he has included in this book.

From the beginning of the project, we wondered what we would learn from our unique methodology of using journalists as data collectors and storytellers within a larger academic project. Little did we know that Ken was asking the same question. When Ken sent us a short blog post he wrote reflecting on the idea of "ethnographic journalism," we asked him if he would like to explore that idea further. He responded that he had thousands more words on the subject saved to his computer. Ken eagerly agreed to an additional role of surveying, interviewing, and conducting focus groups with his fellow journalists. He wrote articles and gave conference presentations about how the project shaped the journalists' approach to their craft and how journalistic storytelling can make academic research more accessible. It was a natural progression, therefore, to ask him to compile this volume featuring the storytelling that emerged from the project.

Ken has expertly selected representative stories from the project and brought them into conversation with one another, all framed by his own insights on religion and storytelling. One of the key insights we gained from the exemplars' stories is that while spirituality inspires and sustains their humanitarian work and activism, the work also influences their spirituality. Likewise, you will also read in the following pages how reporting on exemplars has influenced journalists. Ken calls his approach "ethnographic journalism," but the late radio reporter Maria Emilia Martin called her work on the project "spiritual journalism." Just as Rev. Murray did for the women in Rwanda, exemplars push all of us to see the inherent dignity in all people. No matter our religion or belief system, their examples challenge us to uphold our own values.

On a final note, it is important to consider the global context in which this project took place. Within a year of launching the fellowship, we experienced a global pandemic, racial justice protests, Brexit, and the crackdown on democracy movements in Hong Kong. As we write today, conflicts rage in Ukraine, Palestine/Israel, Sudan, and elsewhere. The United States is rethinking its role in the world and renegotiating its economic relationships. The United States and many other countries have made significant cuts to development budgets, humanitarian aid, and even assistance to their own poor. Meanwhile, the impacts of climate change are increasing, from the floods that ravaged exemplar Ida Puliwa's communities in Malawi, to the destructive wildfires that destroyed Don Miller's house in Altadena, where we had met to discuss ideas emerging from the exemplars project.

It would be easy to fall into despair in the face of personal and global adversities. The news must cover these bleak realities, but the goal of our project and this book is to inspire you to imagine an alternative world and, at a personal level, risk being an agent of change. Exemplars are countercultural, running against the streams of consumerism, isolationism, and supremacism. They step into the most challenging of situations—into towns infected by Ebola, into the lives of gang members, into global climate negotiations.

As research team member Arpi Miller beautifully described,

> They are in so many ways unstoppable, acting in deep love for the communities they are a part of, refusing to accept the status quo, swimming upstream and taking immense risks that many of us could never imagine. And yet, at the same time … exemplar's work contexts are pressure cookers that nudge them over and over toward spaces of radical release and surrender.

During volatile times, their stories demonstrate how we can confront the great challenges of our time with a spirit of peace and even joy. In these exemplars, we hope you may find people that you can both admire and emulate.

Megan Sweas
Editor, "Spiritual Exemplars: A Global Project on Engaged Spirituality"
Director of Communications, USC Center for Religion and Civic Culture

Donald E. Miller
Principle Investigator, "Spiritual Exemplars: A Global Project on Engaged Spirituality"
Professor Emeritus, University of Southern California

References

Colby, Anne and Damon, William (1992), *Some Do Care: Contemporary Lives of Moral Commitment*. New York: Free Press.
Walker, Lawrence J. (2003), "Morality, Religion, Spirituality—the Value of Saintliness." *Journal of Moral Education* 32 (4): 373–84.
Zagzebski, Linda (2013), "Moral Exemplars in Theory and Practice." *Theory and Research in Education* 11 (2): 193–206.

Introduction

Telling Good Stories

I woke with a start to the rumble of my smartphone on the bedside table. It was 5:03 a.m. in İnönü, a neighborhood nestled in Istanbul's eastern hills. My colleagues were on the phone, calling for proof of life. "Are you okay?!" they asked. Groggily coming to and sharpening my senses, given the tone of their queries, I replied, "Yes. Yes, I'm fine." Then, one of them said, "Good, good. We just wanted to check. We got a somewhat cryptic, message from Elgazzar last night."

Elgazzar. In Arabic: "the butcher."

I was in Istanbul to profile Elgazzar as part of the Spiritual Exemplars Project. The goal of the project, sponsored by the University of Southern California's Center for Religion and Civic Culture, was to better understand how religious values and spiritual practices inspire and sustain social action. The subjects included a nun who performed the first Buddhist same-sex wedding, a Jewish lay leader who served more than 2 million meals to food-insecure college students, a priest who helped rescue 150,000 distressed refugees in the Mediterranean Sea, a Buddhist who served more than 400,000 people in 400 Sri Lankan villages, and a Latina convert who founded the first shelter for Muslim migrants at the U.S./Mexico border. Their lives, whether inspired by African Religious Traditions, Bahá'í precepts, Protestant ethics, Humanist altruism, or Indigenous spirituality, were meant to exemplify some of humanity's highest shared values in pursuit of the common good.

Elgazzar was one of those exemplars. The night before the phone call, I ate dinner at Elgazzar's home, near Yeditepe University where he taught trauma surgery in the school of medicine. Though Elgazzar was a butcher by name, he was renowned as a war zone surgeon, saving countless lives on both sides of conflicts in Yemen and Syria, Sierra Leone and Libya, South Sudan and Egypt. He trained the famed White Helmets—a humanitarian group of over 3,000 men and women working to save lives and support communities in areas affected by the war in Syria—on how to perform emergency first aid. When he lived in Cairo, he rushed to Tahrir Square at the height of Egypt's crackdown against its revolution in 2011 and had his own life threatened while trying to save lives during Sierra Leone's civil war in 2000. He was a hero. A savior surgeon. A spiritual exemplar.

Given all that, why were my colleagues concerned? Fearful that Elgazzar's humanitarian work had put me in the sights of Egyptian security forces? Before I can share why, and what happened, I want to start with the story of stories themselves.

The power of a good story

At the 2023 Oscars ceremony, the theme for the evening's speeches was the "power of story." Actors and moviemakers talked about stories shaping us, how they open a window into the soul, and provide hope in the midst of turbulent times. Performer Ke Huy Quan, who won Best Supporting Actor for his role in the film *Everything, Everywhere, All at Once*, even shared a bit of his own story as he accepted the award, saying, "my journey started on a boat. I spent a year in a refugee camp. And somehow, I ended up here on Hollywood's biggest stage. They say stories like this only happen in the movies. I cannot believe it's happening to me." We love a good story like Huy Quan's. Or, for that matter, the one told through movies like his. A riveting testimony. A whodunnit or compelling memoir. A tale told by the fireside. A ripping yarn.

But why? Why are we moved by stories? What is, after all, the "power of story?" Might there be something to learn about truth-telling and newswriting, religion and spirituality, *through* story? Stories, or at least the good ones, reflect the drama of human existence. The recognition that something is wrong or strange or not quite right. Then, the desire to fix it, to resolve the tension, to make things better and bring the arc to climax and completion, restoration and fulfillment. Stories do not always end well, nor do they always end cleanly. But the best stories, the ones that stick with us and influence our lives over time, involve struggle and often end in some surprising or unexpected way.

In 1979, Californian Joan Didion published a collection of essays that typified what was called the "New Journalism"—a style of newswriting more reminiscent of long-form nonfiction than traditional reporting. Still fact-based, but interpolated with subjectivity and immersive imagery, Didion's writing not only featured powerful stories about Black Panther party meetings, experiments with entheogens, and recording sessions with The Doors in 1960s Los Angeles, but her own psychological journey as a journalist. More than information or exposition, Didion's stories were just that: narrative accounts that took the reader somewhere, rather than just telling them some*thing*. In the opening sentence of the essay "The White

Album," Didion underscored why readers found her stories so unputdownable and why, in turn, she felt compelled to write them. "We tell ourselves stories in order to live," she wrote, "we interpret what we see, select the most workable of the multiple choices. We live entirely … by the imposition of a narrative line … to freeze the shifting phantasmagoria which is our actual experience."[1] The "imposition of narrative," Didion writes, is like a sacred canopy,[2] holding the anomy and chaos at bay, projecting meaning onto the incomprehensible universe, and encouraging us to hope things will work out just fine—even, or especially, if we are not sure they will.

With these words, Didion hit on what this book is all about: a good story. At its heart, this book is a testimony to the power of telling good stories. But with an unexpected twist. Or you might say, a surprise ending: That telling good *religion* stories advances vital conversations around some of the most critical issues of our time. In the crux of the late-modern, beset as it is with humanitarian crises and internecine conflict, polarized politics and the retreat of democracy, hate speech and misinformation, environmental degradation and deadly global diseases, economic disparity and debates around gender, cultural identity, and education, we need good *religion* stories. In a world so often divided, torn apart by what seems insurmountable tensions, religion stories told across traditions remind us to break through our own narratives, or those of "our people," and listen for a while to the story of humanity as a whole. Those kinds of stories not only connect us, they help us rediscover who "we" are in the process. Narratives, especially in the hands of quality storytellers, provide both a degree of significance to individual lives and a through-line of truth for our shared existence. They also preserve the memory of deeds across time, enabling the actions of others to become sources of inspiration for the "gap between past and future," as German American historian Hannah Arendt put it—that is, models to be imitated, and, if possible, surpassed.[3]

With that in mind, this book draws on profiles of spiritually engaged humanitarians written by reporters to help us better understand global religion and its entanglement with issues of worldwide concern, such as inequality, conflict, and climate change. Moreover, these journalistic profiles also help us better imagine the many "tomorrows" religious actors are actively trying to create across the world.

During the Spiritual Exemplars Project, team members realized they were not only gaining insights about how spiritually engaged humanitarians understand their lives and work, but about how religious values and spiritual practices inspire and sustain social action on a larger scale. This book is an outgrowth of that process, taking readers on a journey to meet people doing extraordinary work and to share their life trajectories, traumas, and triumphs. As a testament to the project's hybrid academic-journalistic format, these stories make a point as well. They are not explicitly scholarly ruminations on themes of religion, activism, exemplars, or spirituality. Instead, this book leads with the premise that we cannot address the world's most intractable issues and advance human flourishing without telling the stories of religious actors around the globe inspiring hope, fostering resilience, and contributing to the common good. Thus, this book does not attempt to provide an overarching theory about spiritual exemplarity, engaged spirituality, or good/bad religion. Instead, convinced that the best argument for change can be found in an irresistible story and the best story can prove an irresistible argument, it is a narrative-driven attempt to expand readers' minds, nourish their souls, and cultivate fresh ways of bringing about real change in a world that seems to be spiraling out of control.

Of course, good stories are founded on facts. News, as well as academic research, revolves around concrete details, specific circumstances, and verifiable data. We could not have news without the core journalistic value of following facts where they lead. Anything else is an adventure in missing the point of news. Journalists who know their stuff, however, take the facts they collect, the quotes they source, and the substantiated reports they gather to help the reader make meaning beyond *just the facts*. A newswriter may start with a posture of searching, rather than knowing. They may write with the who, what, when, where, why, and how at the forefront of their mind. But, with a bit of creativity and imagination, they can then shape a story—a retelling of what is, with an aspiration to what could be. I believe we find ourselves in such stories. The feelings and thoughts we did not know the names of. Places we have been to but forgot. People we have seen but still do not understand. Stories teach us about the world and our place in it. They teach us to grow into the people we want to become. Stories are metaphors for life, helping us make meaning. They open us up and crack us open, enable new questions and fresh responses, empower our creative capacities, and unlock our capacity for greater empathy.

That is what this book is about. It is about stories that not only relate the facts of exemplars' lives or tell us about the world as it is but prompt us to imagine how it could be. They revolve around the recognition that something is wrong or strange or not quite right. Then, the desire of an individual or group of people to fix it, to resolve the tension, to make things better—with a bit of personal transformation along the way. Finally, a tale of resolution or a takeaway with a view to the work still to come. The stories do not always end well, nor do they always end cleanly. In fact, you could even say the stories do not end, as the problems persist, and the conflicts continue. After all, "a story," wrote scholar Katherine McKittrick, "cannot tell itself without our willingness to imagine what it cannot tell"[4]–or, perhaps, *what it has yet to tell*. The work remains, even if some of the people profiled in this book have passed away or the problem persists. Regardless, each story contains within it more than facts, but a kernel of truth. The kind of truth that transcends. That communicates. That tells a story.

But who, pray tell, is an exemplar?

Every story has a beginning, a middle, and an end. The hinge point is a moment of conflict, a time of transformation that gives meaning to what precedes it (rising action and tension) and what follows (resolution and denouement). This book's story stretches back to November 2018, when the Center for Religion and Civic Culture (CRCC) launched the Spiritual Exemplars Project[5] with the aim of better understanding how extraordinary people are driven by religious beliefs and spiritual practices to provide humanitarian care—to accompany children orphaned by AIDS, fight oil companies in the Arctic, perform surgery in the midst of war, or save migrants from certain death in the desert or at sea. Whether such individuals are Buddhist, Muslim, Christian, or do not adhere to any particular tradition but remain spiritually active, we wanted to explore the role religion plays in motivating people to commit their lives to humanitarian work and to see what place practices like prayer and meditation have in sustaining those individuals' *engaged spirituality*.

The goal was to capture the narratives of 100 such individuals and tell their stories in such a way as to not only inform *but inspire*—challenging readers to emulate the life-giving commitments of the spiritual exemplars themselves. Rather than simply hold them up as saints that few can relate to, we wanted to tell exemplars' stories in all of their complexity and struggle, doubts and tensions. This led the team to adopt a hybrid approach combining journalistic investigation with academic research. Collectively, over thirty journalists told 104 exemplars' stories through eighteen podcast episodes with *The Spiritual Edge*, eleven documentary videos across multiple platforms, and the publication of more than 115 articles in publications like *The New York Times*, *The Guardian*, *Al Jazeera*, *Christian Science Monitor*, *Harvard Divinity Bulletin*, *New Lines Magazine*, as well as at outlets like Religion News Service and Religion Unplugged.

Before the popular publications and award-winning podcasts, the journalist fellows gathered with researchers at USC in May 2019 for orientation. Sitting around the table with journalists, munching on a hummus and cucumber sandwich, one of my colleagues quipped that she had been reporting on religion for more than two decades and never, in her experience, met someone she thought was exemplary. Her exclamation was more than a lament over the state of human depravity and double-standards or a critique of religion and its adherents. It was also a fundamental question the hybrid team of social scientists and reporters had to wrestle with. These award winners, volunteers, luminaries, and leaders—for all the good they seem to do—are they really, truly, exemplary? And, if that is the case, what makes them so and what might we learn from their lives and work?

For the most part, when exemplarity research has touched on spirituality, it has centered on the nature, structure, psychology, and lived development thereof.[6] Reviewing the literature, the CRCC team felt exemplar research represented an underutilized approach to studying the role religion plays in motivating people to commit their lives to humanitarian work and how spiritual practices sustain exemplars in the challenges they face. We therefore adapted the exemplar methodology to contribute to a public conversation about the role of religion in contemporary society and develop a subfield within exemplar research on the role of religion and spirituality in humanitarian work.

As intimated above, and as educational psychologist Kendall Cotton Bronk wrote, "the exemplar methodology is a sample selection technique that involves the intentional selection of individuals, groups, or entities that exemplify the construct of interest in a highly developed manner."[7] In this instance, our research intentionally focused on rare individuals, not necessarily in terms of their acts and characteristics, but as Bronk put it: "in the intensity with which they demonstrate those particular characteristics." Accordingly, examining exemplars' lives was meant to reveal what the upper ends of religious and spiritual engagement look like in the context of exemplars' own biographies and their concomitant struggles, doubts, and tensions. The aim was not only to understand exemplarity better, but to explore the exemplars' hopes and needs, the philanthropic and humanitarian contexts within which they work, and the potential of journalistic storytelling to help us make sense of them.

By doing so, the idea was to glimpse not only *what is* but also *what might be possible* with regard to work on varying issues of global concern. As Bronk noted, the study of exemplary individuals is crucial to understanding how it is that they have grown and developed into such dedicated and commendable models of service—and how "more typical individuals" might follow in their footsteps (or not). In other words, if exemplars characterize the leading edge, perhaps their lives can be generalized and imitated. For instance, if you and I manage to act in an exemplary way from time to time, these individuals seem to do so consistently and to great effect. How then, by looking at their lives in nuanced detail, might we bridge the gap between our irregular altruism and their steady, successful commitment to doing good?

With this theoretical orientation in place, the challenge became identifying the right individuals. For this project, the nomination criteria specified they must be (1) a living individual anywhere in the world;[8] (2) inspired and sustained by spiritual values, beliefs, or practices; (3) who committed their lives to significant impact that advances human flourishing, broadly defined; (4) are admired and emulated by others within and beyond their community; and (5) respect all human rights, such as those defined by the Universal Declaration of Human Rights. They could be public luminaries, political figures, influencers, artists, philosophers, explorers, pioneers in their fields, contemplative heroes, or the "extraordinary ordinary"—those who work on a small, local, or unnoticed scale. In line with previous studies,[9] the decision to use relatively vague nomination criteria and to include both journalists and their publics as nominators in the process was intentional. The research team was concerned that relying solely on their own expertise to nominate or to use more prescriptive nomination criteria might unnecessarily narrow the conception of who counted as a spiritual exemplar. Thus, the team sought to identify exemplars who reflected more popular conceptions of religious and spiritual excellence. Following these criteria, the team built a database of exemplars for potential profiles. The aim was to construct a collection that reflected the world's diversity, taking race, gender, sexual orientation, geography, and religion into account. Culling awards lists and research on faith-based organizations as well as soliciting pitches from journalists working on the project in addition to nominations from the public, the team constructed a database of 450 individuals across sixty-four countries.

In the end, 104 individuals were profiled. This final list was impacted by a variety of factors, including conversations with the journalists about the "pitchability" of the profiles to newspapers, magazines, radio programs, and podcasts; the travel limitations put in place during the course of the Covid-19 pandemic; and adjustments as the team noted how the list was skewing in one direction or another. For example, midway through the project, I was asked to profile more Muslim women in the Global South, in order to counteract a bias in the profiles completed at that point (mid-2020) toward Catholic and Protestant Christians, men, and North America. Thus, my next three profiles were on Azza Karam, an Egyptian Muslim woman working in interreligious dialogue and development; Alissa Wahid, a Muslim woman leading interreligious dialogue and helping address civil unrest in Indonesia; and Sonia Tinoco García, a Latina convert to Islam who opened the first shelter for Muslim migrants along the U.S./Mexico border.

Because of these intentional choices and course corrections, the project's geographic, gender, age, and religious distribution was broad. Though the sample still skews toward the United States (due in part to Covid-19 restrictions and the fact that most of the journalists were based there), forty-two countries are represented in the sample. Nearly 20 percent are from Africa (roughly equal to 19 percent of the global population overall), 21 percent from Asia, including the Middle East (compared to nearly 59 percent), 12 percent from Europe (compared to 9 percent), and 8 percent from Latin America (equal to the region's global share). Of those forty-two countries, the United States, France, Nigeria, Palestine/Israel, and India were those most represented. On gender and age, there was also good distribution, with 57 percent of the exemplars being women, 42 percent male, and 1 percent non-binary. More than half are between thirty and sixty years of age, which contradicted our speculation that the list might skew older, given that exemplars are generally recognized later in life. Nonetheless, a full 44 percent are above sixty years of age and just 3 percent are under thirty.[10] The profiles' religious distribution is also wide-ranging, with thirteen different faith traditions represented, including African Religious

Traditions, the Bahá'í Faith, Buddhism, Catholicism, Protestantism, Eastern Orthodoxy, Hinduism, Humanism, Indigenous Religions, Islam, Jainism, Judaism, and Old Norse Paganism.

Project researchers and journalists did not settle on a single definition of "religion" or "spirituality" during the project. Moreover, the labels used for traditions were not always accurate or all-encompassing. For example, when speaking of African Religious Traditions in Patrisse Cullors's story, the label is sometimes too broad, without due appreciation given to the rich variety of traditions, practices, and locally inscribed experiences such an umbrella term may unnecessarily flatten. At other times, the terms were too narrow. Take, for example, terms like "Hinduism" or "Hindu," which have proven notoriously difficult to define. In recent years, Hinduism has been treated as a religion, described as a way of life, or critiqued as a construction of colonialism.[11] In this book, such labels fall flat when trying to encapsulate the spiritual perspective of someone like Ela Gandhi, who says she is "inspired by Gandhian values," invoking the spiritual path and teachings of her grandfather, Mahatma Gandhi. Raised in Gujarat in a family that followed a form of Vaishnavism—one of the major Hindu traditions—Mahatma Gandhi later identified as a Sanatani Hindu, incorporating aspects of the Vedas, Upanishads, Puranas, and other religious texts and scriptures into his teachings and practice. Along the way, Gandhi spoke of how his perspectives were also inflected by interactions with Christian and Muslim interlocutors, as well saying he was heavily influenced by Jainism in his youth. Classifying Ela Gandhi as "Hindu"—or even as a follower of a "Hindu tradition"—seems a stretch and does not match her self-understanding or identification. Elsewhere, when Stephanie Saldaña profiles Huda Abu Arqoub and Jacques Mourad in Syria, one is ostensibly Muslim, the other Syriac Catholic. But as Saldaña's profile shows, these labels are insufficient to describe the "interreligious identity" each has developed, given their respective life experiences and encounters.

Thus, led by our ethnographic and journalistic commitments and convinced that religion does not exist separate from the public worlds within which these exemplars live, we followed their self-identifications, practices, and perspectives as they inform, and are informed by, those worlds. Rather than treating religion as some *sui generis* tradition *out there* or belief system or feeling *within us*, this book is oriented around religion's entanglements with the political, social, affective, embodied, and material contexts within which religion and the religious (or any number of its descriptive synonyms: faith, belief, devotion, worldview, or spirituality) is made manifest in the lives of its practitioners and communities. Rather than dogmatically stick to one label or definition over another, this book lets the dissonance speak to, or perhaps resonate with, the reader and their own understandings of the diversity of religious traditions, practices, and communities in the late-modern world.

Moreover, this book does not focus on exemplars' religious experiences nor try to explore and explain things like mysticism, transcendence, or ecstasy. In other words, rather than framing spiritual exemplars as those, "concerned with the self as the subject of religious commitments, traits, religious aspirations and religiously inspired ideals,"[12] this book looks at how spiritual exemplars address shared social concerns and societal challenges. Although the chapters that follow reveal how individual exemplars wrestle with personal problems and practice a variety of disciplines as a means of spiritual formation, inspiration, and sustenance, the focus is on the end result of these personal journeys—their impact on the communities and contexts around them. That is because we found the exemplars' theology, philosophy, or worldview is not divorced from their political, cultural, or economic context. Instead, the ways they believe or feel or have faith are deeply embedded within their local contexts as well as broader communal, national, regional, or transregional networks. Furthermore, though their practices include a variety of ritual and devotional pieties—prayer, meditation, corporate worship/rituals, retreat, etc.—which give them a sense of inspiration, hope, renewal, sustenance, or that reframe their work within cosmic registers, there was something very "this-worldly" about their approach to religion and spirituality (e.g., finding God in the people they serve).

Consequently, if we were to follow the school of thought that defines religion by its salient features (e.g., leaders and divine beings, key texts and scriptures, predicaments and problems, worldviews and ultimate orientations, lived ethics, morals, and practices, institutions and infrastructures, and societal concerns),[13] this book places more emphasis on the *latter* characteristics in that list (i.e., lived ethics, morals, and practices, institutions and infrastructures, and societal concerns) than on the former. Therefore, this book does not try to resolve the differences between religion and spirituality's respective features and delineations as discussed across a range of literatures. Nor does it make an overarching claim about religion and/or spirituality based on the narratives in this book. Nevertheless, I believe it points to how people of varying religious identifications and practices can, and do, contribute to a world of constant arrival and fresh possibilities. We can thus imagine, and perhaps begin to embody and enact, other kinds of futures in and through the beliefs we hold dear and the practices we foster in our attempt at living our own forms of engaged spirituality.

Following previous uses of exemplar methodology,[14] we relied on semi-structured interview protocols to collect life history and case-study data. The team developed a list of sample interview prompts, which the journalists used and adapted as they saw fit in the field. The questions were organized around themes such as inspiration (e.g., what originally attracted or motivated you to work for social good?), sustenance (e.g., what helps you with resilience in the face of—or in the wake of—stress and fatigue?), reciprocal effect (e.g., how did your understanding of the work evolve over time?), shadow side (e.g., what have you sacrificed for this work?), and influential individuals and institutions (e.g., what kinds of practical support do you receive? Did any mentors help guide you along the way?). In addition to these thematic questions, journalists were also encouraged to conduct a life-history interview (or interviews), asking exemplars to recount the "chapters of their life" with follow-up questions about significant experiences, turning points, evolving insights, challenges, and poignant memories not mentioned elsewhere.

Through the interviews, subsequent profiles, data coding, and initial analysis, both researchers and journalists found the exemplars' lives compelling. At the same time, we reflected on how their lives were not blameless, nor were they always outstanding or wholly remarkable. They were sometimes quite ordinary in their manner, simple in their lifestyle, or perhaps even repugnant with pride or in their attempts to control their narrative and public image. They had egos and shortfalls, conducted themselves in seemingly contradictory fashion, and could disappoint those they served—or those who profiled them.

On the one hand, this was quite surprising. Though their lives were normal in many ways, these were also exceptional individuals, whose conduct differed from that of "typical" people and who broke through to do good in a way that was significant and sustainable. How then, could we discover that their lives were not nearly as fine and faultless as one might hypothesize? On the other hand, our understanding of their daily struggles and shadow sides showed us that they are, after all, *simply human*. This is quite encouraging, if you think about it. Instead of showing exemplarity to be the domain of particular individuals, we found that exemplarity can be found in many unexpected places and embodied by a wide array of otherwise unexceptional individuals. For example, we found that there are multiple pathways to humanitarian work, often prompted by a search for meaning and purpose or some experience (a crisis, trauma, political situation, or economic circumstances) within an exemplar's community. Therefore, rather than some inherent trait or special character, what made these individuals stand out is the way they recognized, acknowledged, or applied a moment, a sense of higher purpose and calling, or that something different in their lives by paying attention to it, fostering it through spiritual practices, grounding it in their personal religious narratives, and continuing to pursue it through holistic resilience and gritty perseverance.

Thus, we suggest, spiritual exemplarity is context bound—by history, culture, geography, politics, class, embodied realities, etc. This was underscored by the fact that whether or not an individual was recognized as exemplary or not was a consequence of their influence and local power, their role as a public or private figure or influencer, what country they lived and region they worked in, what position they occupied in their respective religious, social, or political community, whether they were male or female, inclusive or exclusive, and a whole host of additional, contingent factors. In other words, we found through listening to their stories that exemplarity is best understood as a function of religious, social, political, and economic context rather than any inherent quality or set of values, beliefs, or practices.

All of this made their stories that much more compelling. If exemplarity is not the sole reserve of the religious or spiritual elite and there are many ways of acting altruistically, then perhaps typical people—like you and me—might be able to make more of an impact than we can presently imagine. What if, to put it another way, we too are the *ordinary, extraordinary*? And what if letting the stories of these individuals speak for themselves might help us all seek alternative futures and create the communities of care we dream of? What if all we need is a *different kind of story* to make the world a better place? A good story, about ordinary, extraordinary people of religious conviction and spiritual inclination, doing what they can with what they have been given to make a tangible difference? That is why, in the end, we decided to let the journalists tell the stories and to let the stories speak for themselves.

On "do-gooders" and telling good religion stories

Nonetheless, as intimated above, the risk of a project bringing together scholars and journalists became evident from the onset. Would the tensions between the norms, aesthetics, and ethics of sociological research and journalism prove too much? How could journalists not only tell stories, but act as data collectors helping a team of sociologists and ethnographers collect an archive of information about positive social change on issues ranging from climate change to human rights, poverty to gender equity? It turns out, they would do so by doing their jobs well.

In the orientation meeting, CRCC's researchers said they were not interested in "saintly" stories or Pollyannish portraits. Instead, they wanted well-rounded features, based on solid journalistic practices—fact-finding research, interviews, and verification. These stories were not meant to be excessively cheerful or optimistic, but real-life representations of what it means to confront the world's most intractable issues, including burnout and trauma, personal failures and foibles, loneliness and loss—what we in the project called the "shadow side" of humanitarian work. In effect, the journalists were charged to tell good stories. Some of the profiled characters in this book, for example, are flawed. Sometimes their motivations are contradictory, even confusing. Sometimes, their work falters, fumbles, or fails.

As the project's principal investigator Don Miller wrote, news coverage of religion is often cynical, focusing on corruption, abuse, and other justifiably negative elements within faith communities.[15] Though critical coverage is warranted, and necessary, this project focused on people who dedicate their lives to human flourishing in all its forms, promoting positive social change. We did so out of an interest to better understand why people would commit themselves to a life of radical engagement with issues of justice and equity, often at considerable personal cost. Furthermore, we wondered if sharing their stories with various publics through journalistic profiles might not only reveal their motivations, practices, and perspectives, but also inspire such action by those who read or otherwise encountered those stories. In other words, although "negative coverage of religion by the media is necessary and useful because it provides a critique of ... religion that is corrupt and authoritarian,"[16] this book's focus on *good* religion stories—exploring what it looks like for religious actors to address evils ranging from genocide and torture to spiritual abuse and everyday inequality—provides hope, perspectives to ponder, and guidance for the road. It does not make the case that religion is inherently "good." It does not advocate that religion is, has been, or will be a force for good in the future. Spiritual exemplars still deserve interrogation. There is still a responsibility to tell the story of religious actors behaving badly. But this book tells a more complicated story through narratives of individuals living out their faith in contexts across the globe, finding substance and motivation for the benefit of the world. After all, that is exactly what good journalism should do: tell a more complicated story.

Hence, the research team sought journalists willing to tell these stories, sending them around the world to report on them first-hand. Although, as previously mentioned, the Covid-19 pandemic limited travel and in-person access, many journalists spent numerous days, if not weeks, with their subjects, interviewing, observing, and participating in the individual's home, community, and work context. In the vein of ethnographic, literary, or solutions journalism (see below), this first-hand, intimate experience with the exemplars not only had a personal impact on the journalists themselves but made for a different kind of narrative than that often found in religion-related news.

With that in mind, each of this book's chapters focuses on a different aspect of contemporary human experience, chronicling individuals' efforts to fix what is wrong, with an eye toward how others might find solutions in their stories. Blending reporting, analysis, and personal commentary, this book includes writing from journalists and researchers from the project on how exemplars are addressing a wide variety of urgent global concerns, including cultural empowerment, education, environmental justice, gender and sexual equity, health care, humanitarian aid, human rights, interreligious dialogue and peace-building, and socio-economic development. These categories are further broken down into specific issues. For example, the section on human rights deals with both racial justice and immigration; the section on gender equity on LGBTQI+ empowerment and sexual violence. These categories are slippery, of course, and often overlap in the stories told—for example, with cultural empowerment often playing a significant part in Indigenous peoples' advocacy for environmental justice. Furthermore, the individuals profiled often take a holistic approach to their work, seeing education, health care, and economic support as inherently intersectional. Readers can, of course, read the chapters straight through. But given the nature of the exemplars' works, and the project itself, readers are also encouraged to jump around to different topics, stories, and narratives as they might prefer.

Either way, and although readers may not walk away believing in *karma* or the afterlife, the power and humanity of these portraits will inspire and inform, helping them see how articles of faith, religious practices, and spiritual commitments can help us all reimagine the way we engage the tangible, troubling realities of our shared existence. As one person at a public presentation about the research reflected: "These stories help us not be depressed or discouraged about the state of the world but inspired to take a more positive attitude toward our shared challenges."

In the face of this century's growing challenges, it is evident that our world needs new systems of care—structures that transcend divisions of race, class, caste, gender, nation, religion, ability, sexuality, or political orientation. As pandemics and calamities related to the climate crisis threaten lives and our collective survival; as human flourishing falters instead of flowering; as the delivery of quality aid, education, and health care is challenged by the demands of global capitalism; as human suffering on massive scales continues to confront us in the media; and as human divisions appear to grow ever deeper, these stories highlight humans across the globe trying to build such systems of care and foster new communities of compassion. Their paths are all different. Their callings too. Their work on our shared planet's most pressing issues is not yet finished. But together, the chapters of their lives stand as testaments to the power of a good story to help us get there.

From California to Cairo: My journey to a good religion story

I joined the project in early 2019. After hearing about the call for applications, I knew the project was a perfect fit. I had been working as a religion newswriter for several years and my interest in religion emerged out of the very place the project was based: Los Angeles, California. Much to my mother's chagrin, my family relocated from a quaint bedroom community in the San Francisco Bay Area to the seemingly chaotic mass of California's "big city" in 1993. I was eight years old. Who I am today was significantly shaped by the megacity's multi-ethnic reality and the tensions and hybrid creations it produced, from the unrest and social protest following the outcome of the

Rodney King Jr. trial to the cultural productions of its assorted bohemians, *fronterizos*, and border walkers.[17] In particular, I was touched by the religious assemblages that were viscerally visible on the streets of the last megalopolis to emerge in the relentless pursuit of American frontier, vividly experiencing its borderland verisimilitudes, and fundamental ambiguities within my own social networks. In high school, my friends identified with a range of heritages, from Iran to Italy, Korea to France, Sweden to Mexico. They were evangelical and Catholic, Wiccan and Buddhist, agnostic and Jewish, Protestant and Muslim. Raised in a rather-conservative, evangelical Lutheran household with tenuous connections to a mixed-European heritage, I had the opportunity to learn about religious and cultural traditions other than my own through my relational networks and everyday interactions with friends, family, and neighbors. Through these everyday relationships, I witnessed—and was tangibly influenced by—the "shifting mosaic"[18] of Los Angeles's religious and cultural miscellany alongside the magnetic swirl of its vibrant beauty and wicked injustices and inequities.

The CRCC's own origin story emerged out of the same context. As the conflagrations of the Los Angeles uprising began to subside in 1992, a number of civic, corporate, and interreligious coalitions were formed to heal the deeply divided city and to address the underlying social problems that had provided tinder for the firestorm of protest. The founders decided to research the role faith groups placed in the public square following the social unrest, documenting how congregations and other faith-based organizations (FBOs) sought to unify the city following the upheaval. One of their principal interlocutors—and collaborators—was the Rev. Cecil Murray who, in the words of contributor Megan Sweas, became CRCC's "in-house exemplar." Murray, who is profiled by Nick Street and Sweas in this book, served as a reference point for what "engaged spirituality" looks like for the CRCC team. Since the aftermath of 1992, and through the engaged spirituality project, CRCC has been dedicated to advancing the understanding of religion and society at multiple scales, supporting faith and community leaders in becoming full partners in the work of positive social change.

To me, it seemed our trajectories were intertwined, and the chance to partner with CRCC researchers was a chance I could not pass up. So, I applied. As part of my application, I was asked why I was interested in the project. I wrote:

> Religion and spirituality matter. They motivate us. They move us inwardly and outwardly and move with us across the globe. Throughout the annals of time and over vast geographic boundaries, religion and spirituality have helped humans express their deepest questions, confront some of the most critical issues of life, and influenced virtually every human society, civilization, or culture since the dawn of human history.

And yet, despite their ubiquity and importance, religion and spirituality are still relatively misunderstood in public narratives. Even if they are valued, there remains a blind spot in our critical understanding of how religion and spirituality function in the lives of some of humanity's most inspiring individuals and compelling communities.

After more than a decade reporting on religion, I am convinced that if we want to understand our world, we must pay attention to the role religious actors play in shaping values, addressing the complexities of the human condition, and informing behaviors and policy in changing circumstances. Not only will this allow us to better appreciate the human condition and apperceive its highest shared values, but it might improve the possibility of addressing some of humanity's most urgent shared challenges. Although the foundations of modern religion are shifting and spirituality as we have long known it is undergoing daily transformations, neither shows any signs of going away. Religion and spirituality will remain tenaciously important and will continue to impact human societies for the foreseeable future, playing a role in addressing the world's most intractable problems—both for good and for ill. As Azza Karam, former Secretary General of Religions for Peace International likes to say, "we should not be talking about whether religions matter, but *how* they matter."

My work, whether academic or journalistic, has always focused on these facts. Whether reporting from New Zealand, South Africa, Kenya, the United Kingdom, Germany, Palestine, Georgia, or Indonesia—or Houston, Texas, Gainesville, Florida, and Phoenix, Arizona—my writing has been geared toward addressing and ameliorating the worst effects of religious illiteracy.[19] Thus, the Spiritual Exemplars Project presented a prime opportunity to continue that work and shine light on how religion and spirituality function in the lives of exemplars and their communities in a diverse array of places and from multiple points of view. As a journalist fellow on the project, I profiled five "exemplars": Muhammad Elgazzar (Muslim, Egypt), Ela Gandhi (Ghandian/Hindu, South Africa), Alissa Wahid (Muslim, Indonesia), Azza Karam (Muslim, Egypt/the Netherlands/United States), and Sonia Tinoco García (Muslim, United States/Mexico). In addition, the project inspired and informed several other profiles I worked on in recent years, including the likes of Alan Bern (Jewish, United States/Germany), Kezevino Aram (Hindu, India), and David Rosen (Jewish, Israel/Ireland). Encountering and profiling these exemplars helped me explore the highs and lows of human values, the wide range of religious values and practices that inform humanitarian efforts, and the stunning diversity of exemplary work being done in the concrete contexts of individuals and their networks in, across, and between various geographies. This book includes several of my profiles and reflections on what I learned about the power of telling good religion stories in advancing vital conversations on critical issues of global import.

Ethnographic religion journalism

I was not, however, alone in this story. In addition to the CRCC research team, I wrote alongside more than thirty talented reporters on their own professional and personal journeys. This book reflects their storytelling prowess and personal trajectories of transformation. Through a series of focus groups with my fellow journalists at the conclusion of the project, I heard about what attracted them to the work and how their experience changed the way they report the news. They defined their reporting on the project in various ways: as ethnographic journalism, solutions journalism, literary journalism, and even "spiritual journalism," which speaks to the personal impact reporting such stories can have on the journalists themselves.

The journalists' stories and reflections reminded me of what Ed Simon called the "New Religion Journalism." Resonating with the New Journalism of Didion and others in the 1970s and 1980s, this kind of religion reporting employs narrative nonfiction to interrogate a reporter's own perspective, "against the backdrop of wider issues, where authors frequently insert themselves into the story in a manner in which more traditional 'God beat' reporters wouldn't."[20] That comes with both promises and pitfalls, productive tensions and generative frictions. While it can bring renewed pleasure to the practice of storytelling, it can also present challenges when taking the story to the market and attempting to offer a unified narrative. Furthermore, it calls into question personal binaries between theism and atheism, the secular and religious, public and private, good religion and bad, as well as professional, conventionalized ideas about what journalism should and should not be. By not fitting neatly into our ideas about journalistic ethics or a reporter's relationship to the field and their interlocutors, this kind of storytelling also complicates the genres and categories we often force "good" (or "proper") journalism into. When journalists are immersed in the personal lives and context of their interlocutors—or the story itself—they must wrestle along an equilibrium between stylistic concerns and conventions, loyalty to the public and to their interviewees, as well as their own opinions and beliefs.

Such complex narratives can be hard to tell. Each journalist in the project shared how they found it difficult to pitch, place, and get these stories published in secular news outlets. They shared how both the amount of nuance and texture these stories required and the perception that these "do gooders" are not necessarily "newsworthy," proved challenging when pitching to editors and other gatekeepers at major publications and platforms. Nonetheless, journalists were able to publish in an array of outlets. Their stories were not about the usual characters of money, power, and scandal (not that these were willfully ignored), but they did involve conflicted characters and the messy realities of trying to do good in a world that feels on fire. The exemplars were, and are, flawed people—addicted to adventure, self-motivated and self-aggrandizing, stubborn and arrogant—and their profiles also reflect the "shadow side" of humanitarian work.

In the end, their work resonated with a public yearning for "good religion" stories—reporting that is riveting, with a focus on religion as a key aspect of the narrative. Though it may not have been easy, these stories evoked and inspired, provoked and challenged. In the words of one reader who commented on my story about Sonia Tinoco García and her work at the U.S./Mexico border: "this is writing that makes a layperson like me really care about something that I didn't seem to care about or ask questions in a way that I never thought to ask, or answer questions in a way that I never even thought to approach." This book tells this story too, showcasing not only the journalist's writing, but the process they went through to tell it. Whether profiling spiritual exemplars, sharing their own journey, or sometimes combining the two, this book is a testament to the power of telling good stories.

As we discovered throughout the process, to write such stories, there is often no substitute for "being there," as Kenneth Woodward put it.[21] Woodward, longtime religion editor at *Newsweek*, argued that religion coverage in the media should increasingly move from "event to immersion"—or, we might say, from incessantly and repeatedly focusing on "hard" news (e.g., facts, figures, events, individuals, or incidents that are considered to be timely and consequential to people locally, regionally, nationally, or internationally) to more features-based journalism, which demands contextual exposure, in-person interviews, and sitting with a story over a much longer period of time.

Such a shift, I suggest, would parallel the reporting featured in this anthology, which critically unpacks the social, political, economic, and cultural conditions out of which religious actors decided to act. Religions are not monochrome, clear-cut entities. Their edges are blurred. Each faith tradition is made up of diverse, complex, and sometimes diametrically opposed constituencies. Thus, when covering such complex stories as Israel/Palestine, immigrant deaths in the Mediterranean Sea, or conflict trauma surgery in Syria, journalists need to "be there." Woodward argued that, when done at a distance, religion reporting can feel more like a "research project" than a story assignment. Critiquing reporters whose "world is confined to the computer screen in front of them,"[22] he encouraged newswriting done intimately, written by those "embedded" as reporters in the field, and with richly interwoven narratives of embodied experience or flesh-and-blood realities.

Of course, not all newswriters are afforded the opportunity or resources to take deep dives into religious actors' lives and contexts or to tell their stories in depth via long-form features, podcasts, or documentary shorts. These projects and formats often involve—and even demand—something akin to fieldwork and participant observation along with the journalists' usual stock and trade of interviews and fact-finding. The Spiritual Exemplars Project, however, offered just such an opportunity as it allocated resources so that reporters could visit, interview, and profile "exemplars" that were roughly representative of global religious diversity.

The result is akin to what is sometimes called, "ethnographic journalism"[23]—or "anthro-journalism."[24] Journalist and anthropologist Anne Kirstine Hermann used this term to highlight the use, and importance, of fieldwork by journalists. She argued:

> [a]t a moment in time when multiculturalism poses evident challenges to the press and media trends require more contextual reporting, ethnographic journalism emerges in American feature journalism. Analyzed holistically, this genre is characterized as the employment of immersion strategies adopted from social science for distinct storytelling purposes.[25]

These methods, however, transform conventional journalistic epistemology, changing it through practice. For example, whereas journalists might value fact and event-driven stories, ethnographers would prefer interpretive, holistic, and theoretical approaches. Or, where journalists might see their role as being detached narrators loyal to the public, ethnographers would see themselves as immersed, empathetic, participants who are loyal to their interlocutors. Although Hermann recognized how these modes and mechanisms are based on ideal types, they do speak to the divergent tendencies between the norms, ethics, and aesthetics of the two fields. Hermann suggested that ethnographic journalism could emerge as a form of mediation between the two, and, in turn, help address weaknesses in both—whether that be some of the ethical conundrums or positivistic assumptions that journalists are wary to wrestle with or the disconnect between ethnographers' jargon and public understandings of the very issues researchers seek to elucidate.

This suggestion helped order some of my thoughts and reflections as I considered what I learned as a journalist fellow who happens to be an ethnographer working on a project where both are involved. It also prompted me to consider what that might mean for religion newswriters' and ethnographers' shared desire to explain, illuminate, critique, and examine religious socialities, actors, leaders, and institutions. At the end of the project, we organized a survey of the journalist fellows, as well as three follow-up focus groups with sixteen of the journalists involved in the project. I also conducted an additional four interviews with journalists who were involved in the project or have employed an "immersion" approach to reporting on religion stories.

After sharing a bit about the stories themselves (e.g., a story about an Iraqi cook delivering meals to those still recovering in Aleppo, Syria; a story about a Buddhist monk who trains CEOs in meditation and mindfulness techniques as a way to peace, but also to boost their productivity; a story about a former child soldier in Rwanda who now works with children who have experienced trauma in conflict situations), reporters were asked a series of questions related to their work, specifically about: (1) Storytelling and the story's impact on their self-and/or professional life; (2) aspects of research and ethnography in comparison with journalism; and (3) shaping/placing stories about exemplars in the real world.

On storytelling and the story's impact on their self and professional life, journalists shared several reflections:

1. That this kind of reporting was simultaneously "soul-filling" and "draining."
2. They struggled with the balance between journalistic ethics and being involved in the life of their interlocutors (e.g., with gifts, personal affect, class, gender, and religious differences and/or similarities).
3. They struggled at times with the divergent affective tendencies at work when they were of a different faith [or no faith] than their interviewees.
4. The stakes, they said, were higher than with less immersive stories and assignments.
5. They felt more invested than with other stories. This led them to reflect more intentionally, and critically, on their own positionality.

More specifically, one journalist said, "I went with the plan to stay on the sidelines, like normal. But then I arrived at the meditation center and the guy was like, 'No, you need to participate.'" Another reflected, "The question of 'who are you responsible to?' is a dilemma to work around. I felt responsible to the exemplar during the process and then later, more responsible to the public as I wrote."

Regarding aspects of research and ethnography in comparison with journalism, the journalists felt that this was, "just good reporting." They used a range of language to describe and define the kind of reporting this required, including immersion reporting, literary journalism, anthro-journalism, slow journalism, solutions journalism, deep journalism, and embedded reporting. Regardless of what they called it, journalists felt, "this kind of journalism" helped with certain issues but complicated others. Journalists said that while it helped with reporting on "third rail" issues (e.g., abortion rights or sexuality, political conflicts, etc.), addressing trauma, bringing more marginalized and unnoticed stories to the fore, and deconstructing the process of journalism itself, it also introduced dilemmas around responsibility and engagement with the subject(s) involved. One journalist said the "relationship between subject and journalist is so much more in-depth" by "inviting you to stay with people; to see in reality what life is like." Agreeing that this kind of work was much more "ethnographic in principle," one pair of journalists said they already applied practices from anthro-journalism in their work and that this project allowed them to further solidify and refine their approach. Another, who had not done such in-depth work before, said, "ethnographic journalism invites a kind of revolution in covering religion, particularly religion and headline-grabbing, difficult issues." They continued, saying, "this kind of reporting and writing allowed me to get beyond stereotypes and soundbites ... allow[ing] me the time and space to really dig into people's stories."

In effect, the journalists on the project came to appreciate the value of more ethnographic approaches to reporting as a means to tell richer, more nuanced, and better stories. Though certainly not approaching the depth of multi-year or multi-sited research, their reporting took on the characteristics of quality ethnography: ensuring craft in execution according to qualitative measurements of exposure (i.e., direct contact with field and interlocutors, number of hours spent talking to respondents), cognitive empathy (i.e., the degree to which the researcher is able to interpret and critically empathize with those observed and interacted with), heterogeneity (i.e., the diversity of people and places visited and engaged with), palpability (i.e., how concrete the data is), and follow-up (i.e., how the researcher responds to questions and problems that arise during the course of field research and/or interviews).[26] They also said such stories offered hope, too, for journalists like themselves. One journalist shared that as a way to cope with and counterbalance all the stories of pain and suffering and destruction and violence she reported—many about how religious actors, communities, and institutions were the source of such things—she would "seek stories of resilience and perseverance—often tied to faith." She added, "these inspiring tales, however, take a little longer to develop than hard news about tragedy and terror."

At the same time, when it came to shaping, placing, and publishing stories, journalists found that ethnographic journalism could also come with limitations and present other challenges. In general, journalists felt it was difficult to get these stories (a) published or (b) published in a way that respected the process of reporting they went through. Some shared particularly onerous editorial processes and outright conflicts with editors. Others shared how editors welcomed these kinds of stories and let them "report the story as it was." Outside of editorial relationships, journalists found the process of writing generally enjoyable, if sometimes difficult to manage, given the amount of interview material and experiential data involved. One journalist said in the focus group, "it's hard to whittle so much down and get it on paper. Particularly hard to sell it to editors because the story isn't 'newsie.' The best I could do was try to tie it to some kind of hard news."

Even so, journalists overall felt that, though they would love to do more in-depth, ethnographically informed reporting in the future, the main issue holding them back is resource related. Without further support from publications, grant-making institutions or foundations, or fellowship opportunities such as that with CRCC, they felt their ability to do such reporting would be severely limited. Ethnographic journalism simply costs too much in terms of time, money, and bandwidth.

Following the project, interviews with journalists, and focus groups, I was swayed to believe that the "deep hanging out" that ethnography requires allows for journalists to explore how people craft their own selves, their sense of belonging, and their larger communities in the context of everyday life. The resulting stories help us walk away with a richer apperception of contemporary human life and how ideals, dreams, and actions are made manifest by people situated differently according to their contexts gendered, economic, and social orders. Moreover, it offers an opportunity for journalism to dive deeper into the diversity, complexity, and dynamism of how human lives intersect with religion, generating new questions about how we understand "religion" in the first place.

Also important to consider is what the practice of "ethnographic journalism" might bring to the ways we communicate research findings. According to Hermann, whereas ethnographers often structure according to their data, journalists structure the data according to their story; ethnographers inform, but journalists inform with a broader range of publics in mind; ethnographers aim for expertise (often using insider language and jargon), journalists aim for accessibility; ethnographic writing is complex, journalistic writing simplified; ethnographic writing is systematic and analytic, journalistic tends to be dramatic and descriptive. With this in mind, this book lets the structure, style, and language of journalism speak for the data of social science.

In this way, it may further prompt us to reconsider how we *tell about society*.[27] This project, and this book, started with data, evidence, and ideas. It collected observations through life history interviews and journalists' "deep hanging out" with the exemplars in the context of their everyday lives. It then uses those data as evidence, to demonstrate how spiritual exemplarity not only exists, but may be replicable. As sociologist Howard S. Becker explained, this kind of knowledge about society can be shared and interpreted through different forms of telling—fiction, films, photographs, maps, mathematical models—many of which remain outside the boundaries of conventional social science. In this project, we chose to present the data/evidence in the form of *journalistic stories*. These stories are qualitative reflections of somebody's life, somebody's experience. Different kinds of people, doing different kinds of work. All data. But instead of representing them in a table with numbers or an infographic, we turned the numbers into stories, the tables into tales of an exemplar's life, in all its complicated beauty, messy wonder, and sometimes-audacious hope. As much as possible, we let these stories speak for themselves, exist as evidence of exemplarity at work in the world, and point to ways we might advance vital conversations on the most critical issues of our time.

Therefore, rather than telling readers what they are supposed to learn or see in the data, journalists in this book let the characters speak for themselves, effectively putting the story (and the argument) "in their mouths"—or in their own words. In this way, the stories reflect the hybrid nature of the project, featuring narratives written by journalists and social scientists who pursued alternative ways of doing either ethnography or journalism in traditional fashion. Thus, readers will see elements of the project's blended, ethnographic journalism in each of the chapters, creating together a compelling case for religion and spirituality's role in making better futures possible. The stories are nuanced and textured, locally focused with an eye to the global nature of the issues concerned, filled with both fact-based reporting and interpretive, qualitative analysis and reflexivity. In this way, these are not only powerful stories, but compelling arguments—for new approaches to journalism, for a wider appreciation of how actors motivated by religion and spirituality are making an impact across the globe, and, perhaps, for how we might all work toward building a better world. Together, they show how the best arguments make for good stories and the best stories make excellent arguments.

Ethnographers can, at times, over-theorize their interlocutors' input, insights, and interventions. Journalists do not have the time, space, or inclination to do so and generally follow the principle of "show, don't tell" in letting their interviewees make the points for them. That means they offer relatively little in terms of interpretation or gloss and instead, let the characters tell the story to the reader. Social scientists of many kinds might learn from this and, while properly situating their interlocutors' comments in proper theoretical and lived context, "put the story in their mouths." They might, in fact, follow journalist Walt Harrington's suggestion to watch for a contemporary action line that will make the story more dramatically coherent and compelling to the reader.[28]

In turbulent times, we need those kinds of stories. We need *good* stories. We need *exemplary* stories. Such stories are not great only because of the specific cast of characters involved but because they teach us something about what it means to be human. Reflecting the variability and inconstancy of human experience, they are marked by curiosity, not certainty. They are humble and exploratory. They not only speak to a world that is, but a world that could be. And though the stories in this collection come from particular Muslims and Jews, Christians and Buddhists, they offer something compelling to people of all kinds. They have something to teach us about being better than our worst selves, leaning into the constant process of becoming, and looking for a place to belong and make a difference. Hearing these stories makes us feel less alone. Hearing these stories makes us feel more human. And hearing these stories pushes us to ask hard questions of ourselves and our world. While the question of how the narratives of our times will end remains in limbo, the stories shared in this book help us imagine how they *could* resolve. And those possible futures—or, we might say, endings—inspire and bring us hope in the midst of uncertainty.

The good, the bad, and in-between

Nevertheless, we all know that religious actors do not always do good. They are not always exemplary. They have often caused great systemic and individual harm. And instead of contributing to workable solutions, they have actively worked to cause, exacerbate, and prolong the problems we share and face. In other words, religious people, institutions, and structures have a shadow side. Which brings me back to "the butcher"—Elgazzar.

As is probably already clear to you, Elgazzar did not put me in danger in any way. In fact, I ended up not only interviewing him over a week in Istanbul but traveled with him to Egypt where I spent Eid al-Adha—the feast of the sacrifice—with him, his two sons, and family friends outside Alexandria. We went site-seeing together, laughed together, and dined together multiple times. He brought me along to the mosque for Eid prayers, we played soccer with his sons Omar and Youssef in the heat of the afternoon along the beach, went swimming at his villa in Borg El Arab, and I was there when the cow was slaughtered for the Eid sacrifice, witnessing Elgazzar truly embody his name, telling the *actual* butcher what cuts to make with his surgeon's eye for precision.

As I write in Elgazzar's profile, the man was, "disciplined, dignified and driven by a resonant desire to save those on the brink of death." During our conversations over the course of three weeks, he told me his hopes for his boys, his own plans for the future, and his fears—especially his paranoia about the Sisi government sending spies after him (hence the concerned messages he sent to colleagues on my first day in Istanbul). I also learned how Elgazzar first thought of medicine as a means to save his mother from a terminal illness. Not able to save his mother, he went on to save countless more lives as a renowned and award-winning war surgeon on both sides of conflicts in the Middle East and Africa.

But he still had a shadow side, you might say—as we all do. He was prideful, with a deep desire to control the narrative about his life and accomplishments. His mood could change on a dime, as he cut me off mid-interview or left me to stew in my hotel room for multiple days without responding to any of my WhatsApp messages if I probed too far or challenged his narrative. His family told me he was addicted to his work, often sacrificing time with his family and ignoring their pleas for him to not go back into the fray of war and strife to perform surgeries. After I published the long-form profile, he tried to log in with not one, not two, but *three* fake accounts to comment on how "amazing" a person this Elgazzar man must be … not knowing that his real name showed up on the back end of the publication's website.

I share the good, bad, and in-between of Elgazzar's story to remind us how religions—and the religious actors who make them what they are—are not monochrome. They are not all good or all bad. They are not clear-cut entities or one-dimensional characters. They are atoms and molecules and bits of dusts and stars and muck and mess and foibles and failures like us all. Appreciating exemplars' good, bad, and in-between helps us lean into the humanity of their stories. Because when we tell a good story, a compelling story, we tell a more complex story—about individuals and communities both near and far, but also about all of us. About what it means to be human, to look below the surface and the epiphenomena and the usual stories we hear in the media to appreciate what it means to be a human being shaped by religious beliefs, communities, practices and actions. We *need* those stories. And we need storytellers to tell them. Because when we tell these kinds of stories, the world becomes a more interesting, textured, dynamic, hopeful, honest, and true place. At least, that's what I've found in telling these stories.

For all of my complicated relationship with Elgazzar, for all his pride and paranoia, I was honored to tell his story. To share how he is just one of the many religious actors in this world pursuing the common good. His son Youssef saw it too. The younger of his two sons, Youssef sent me a WhatsApp message in June 2022, nearly three years after I first met Muhammad Elgazzar and his family in Alexandria. "Hello Mr. Ken," he wrote, "I wanted to inform you that my father passed away due to coronavirus. Thank you, for telling his story."

After receiving the message, I wrote back to Youssef sharing my condolences and passing along what peace I had to give. Then, I revisited the story I wrote about Elgazzar, reading about his contributions to the common good—his work to bring life in the midst of violence and war, destruction and death, which eventually led to his passing as he sought to serve those infected with Covid-19. As I read, I saw a quote from his other son, Omar, which I wrote down one evening at the family's home. "I am proud of [my father]. He inspires me. He inspires others," Omar told me. "He is an example to us. To serve those who need help. To save lives no matter what. Whatever I do today, I do because of him." I hope that in sharing the stories in this anthology, you are inspired too.

1

Human Rights and Humanitarian Aid

People's resilience is tied to their will to live,
to their will to survive, which is deeply spiritual.
PATRISSE CULLORS (IFÁ PRACTITIONER)

Each Christian must denounce social injustice.
MARGUERITE BARANKITSE (CATHOLIC)

My feeling of oneness with all informs my desire
for justice and has roots in my Hindu upbringing.
SUNITHA VISWANATH (HINDU)

When I die, when it's my time, all I'm going to
leave behind is the good things I do.
SONIA TINOCO GARCÍA (MUSLIM)

Introduction

Human rights violations and international crises are *de rigeur* in daily news. For good and for ill, an ongoing crisis or fresh report about the latest international injustice inundates our news feeds, populates our front pages, and threatens to drown us in dread during our morning doom scroll. But in this chapter, the stories turn the focus away from "bleed-and-lead" coverage toward more solutions-oriented reporting. Though definitions differ, solutions journalism focuses not only on the present problem at hand, but how people in various contexts are responding to social issues, advocating for human rights and addressing humanitarian situations, seeking to elucidate how and why responses are working or not working in specific contexts, gleaning what can be learned for similar issues in other parts of the world. In other words, it is reporting that describes the situation as it is, complicates simplistic narratives, and offers possible resolutions through the story of the individuals, institutions, or initiatives involved.

For example, Patrisse Cullors, as profiled by Hebah Farrag, is an American artist, activist, and co-founder of the Black Lives Matter movement, who co-created the *#BlackLivesMatter* hashtag in 2013. Advocating not only for racial equity, but for prison abolition and LGBTQ+ rights, Cullors combines critical theory, inspiration from global social movements, and input from Ifá, a West African divination system originating within Yoruba religion, in which Cullors is ordained. In Farrag's telling, Cullors believes the personal is political, the political is personal, and *everything is spiritual*. For her, then, abolition becomes a spiritual discipline. That perspective helps call into question the forced binary between so-called "secular" political projects and religious activism. Instead, Farrag's contribution shows the two to be intertwined, mutually imbricated in questions around human rights, dignity, and equity—as well as attempts at resolving them by activists like Cullors.

Or, covering the efforts of an Italian priest trying to save as many people seeking asylum across the Mediterranean Sea as he can, Linda Freund finds herself questioning the process and practice of journalism itself. On the one hand, Freund offers a textured take on one of the most pressing humanitarian challenges of our time: The forced movement of people across borders across the globe. On the other hand, her contribution is a personal exploration of her own reporting process and the ethics of capturing asylum seekers with her camera in the field. Freund's solutions-oriented approach not only explores how an exemplar is upholding human rights and addressing a humanitarian crisis, but how reporters themselves might uphold those same rights and not, intentionally or accidentally, exacerbate the crisis they set out to cover.

From Sri Lanka, Nalika Gajaweera profiles an exemplar involved in what some might deem more traditional forms of humanitarian aid: Kushil Gunasekera. As a young boy, Gunasekera felt compassion for the people of his ancestral village in Seenigama, who lacked the facilities to realize their potential. Finding success in business, he started Foundation of Goodness in 1999, which has provided medical, educational, vocational, and recreational facilities to thousands of inhabitants in numerous villages free of cost. Fueled by what Gajaweera calls "a karmic worldview," Gunasekera believes the more he gives, the more he will have to give. Such perspectives not only expand our notion of humanitarianism and philanthropy beyond the bounds of Western Christian norms, but also the limited pie philosophical hindrances that often hold people back from doing good with what they have.

Finally, I profile the "savior surgeon," Muhammad Elgazzar. I explore his efforts to save lives on both sides of battlefields in conflict zones across Africa and the Middle East and delve into some of his psychological and spiritual struggles along the way. Not only was Elgazzar a man of intense pride, he was also a bit of an addict—someone who struggled to stop serving, fueled not only by the Quranic injunction to save a life to save all humanity (5:32), but also the adrenaline pumping in his veins any time he entered a "hot zone." Though his family begged him multiple times across the years to not return to the front lines, Elgazzar admitted to me that he would in a heartbeat, if given the chance. His story reminds us that humanitarian exemplars need not always be exemplary in all aspects of their life. As each of these profiles show, while exemplars are motivated by a sense of compassion, a desire for justice and equality, feelings of empathy, selflessness, hope, courage, and humility, they also struggle with an array of challenges: burnout, corruption, loneliness, vicarious trauma, and compromised family relationships. This is what we in the project called the "shadow side" of engaged spirituality.

These profiles also highlight two other elements of engaged spirituality that will reverberate and resonate throughout the anthology: That there are multiple pathways to humanitarian work and various values that inspire, motivate, and sustain it. There is no single pathway, or even common causeway, to humanitarian work. Some of the exemplars feel a sense of calling, pursue humanitarian aid work as part of their own search for meaning, or rise up in response to a particular social need in the communities, nations, or regions. In this chapter's cases, for example, the desire to do something for other humans emerges out of the exemplars' own personal history, sense of crisis, or personal trauma (e.g., Gunasekera's village life as a child or the loss of Elgazzar's mother).

Despite the distinctions in their individual stories, the humanitarian actors in this chapter share common objectives. Grounded in perspectives from international human rights law and spiritual maxims to love and care for the neighbor, their goal is to alleviate suffering and protect lives, livelihoods, and people's dignity. Their responses, in general, are intended to address acute cases when these standards are violated, but can also be geared toward systemic injustice, structural inequalities, and long-standing issues in particular contexts. They are also resilient individuals with a sense of gritty perseverance. In the face of immense personal, spiritual, or physical challenges (even threats to their lives or those they love), each of the exemplars in this chapter embodies a sense of "holistic resilience," with which they seek to dismantle structures of injustice that require them and their communities to be resilient in the first place.

As readers will discover, that resilience is also grounded in spiritual practices that renew them for the difficult work ahead. Though practices varied from tradition to tradition—Catholicism and Ifá divination, Buddhism and Islam—each exemplar in this chapter employs a combination of disciplines to inspire and sustain their work: things like prayer, meditation, and mystical experience as well as an ongoing inspiration from, and engagement with, the precepts and scriptures of their faith. Though the solutions-oriented approach of these stories does not explicitly point in such a direction, the fact that spiritual disciplines are so central to these exemplars' work might make us wonder whether a robust and resilient spirituality might be part of the solutions-based approach to some of the greatest humanitarian crises of our age.

Often framed as shared problems requiring "secular" solutions beyond the work of religious institutions, the stories in this chapter remind us how religious actors—grounded and sustained by their own spiritual perspectives and practices—are already, and must be in the future, part of the solutions. There are, of course, issues of personal moral conviction, public health and other matters that can become points of divergence. Moreover, religious actors can be responsible, or at least share the responsibility, for violence, inequality, and civic discord. Nonetheless, these stories remind us that when it comes to asylum seekers' rights, racial injustice, serving and protecting the vulnerable, and numerous other issues of global justice, secular human rights groups and religious actors often find common cause. Thus, this chapter helps illustrate that if there are solutions to be found for some of our greatest crises, they will need to involve religious actors drawing on their own repertoire of spirituality to pursue them.

"Abolition Is a Way of Life"

Patrisse Cullors (African Traditional Religion/United States)

By Hebah Farrag

The first time I wrote about the work of Patrisse Cullors[1]—award-winning activist, best-selling author, acclaimed artist, and globally recognized organizer—it was 2015.

Cullors co-founded the Black Lives Matter movement (BLM) alongside two other Black women, Opal Tometi and Alicia Garza. The movement, which began on July 13, 2013—the day of the acquittal of George Zimmerman—who killed an unarmed Black teenager named Trayvon Martin, has been, at times, characterized as angry, leaderless, and godless.[2]

Its origins tell a different story, however. It was on that same day in July that Alicia penned a post on Facebook she called, "A Love Letter to Black People"[3] in which she declared, "We don't deserve to be killed with impunity. We need to love ourselves and fight for a world where black lives matter. Black people, I love you. I love us. We matter. Our lives matter." To this, Cullors added the now iconic hashtag: #BlackLivesMatter. The rest, they say, is history. Since its inception, BLM organizers have expressed their political demands within a founding spirit of love through an emphasis on spiritual healing, principles, and practices in their racial justice work. Since its inception, it's been mischaracterized in multiple directions.

In 2015, I was compelled to get my longtime friend on record about the spiritual impetus behind her work. In part, I wanted to share Cullors's story because I couldn't understand why the movement was consistently labeled as "secular" in both the media and academy.[4] To me, religion played a key role in the movement, but it was being largely ignored—as if it were invisible. But if you looked, spiritual perspectives and practices suffused the movement: protesters, clad in white, burning sage across militarized police lines; young activists chanting the names of those who had been violently murdered while pouring libations in front of courthouses, invoking ancestors' spirits; the creation and maintenance of sacred spaces, like altars and murals, that honored victims of state violence while providing places for communities to connect, grieve and heal; the use of plant medicine and ancient modalities like reiki[5] and acupuncture to relieve and heal those at the front lines of protest movements.

How were so many observers missing the spiritualty infusing almost every aspect of the movement for Black lives? To be fair, the non-normative can be hard to see. Luckily, I had a different vantage point.[6] The first time I wrote to Cullors, it was 2003. I was responding to an introduction she had sent me, getting my email address from a mutual friend after meeting at a poetry reading hosted at the 24th Street Café in Los Angeles's West Adams district. We became lifelong pen pals, getting to know her as Patrisse, and corresponding regularly by email, first as young budding activists and organizers trying to make sense of political theory, later as young women of color trying to navigate the travails of everyday life. It was from this perch, an insider's location, that I came to appreciate Patrisse's unique political orientation.

The political as spiritual: The evolution of an abolitionist

"Do we fight for our rights or fight for our souls, which comes first, political work to change the conditions or spiritual work to heal the wounds? but we really need both ... political or spiritual? why have we made these entities separate? How do we merge them? I want to merge them."

It was May 2005 when I received this email from Patrisse. Over the intervening two decades, I watched as Patrisse merged the political with the personal and spiritual, in a framework she defines as "abolitionist." I also watched as abolition became her way of life.

When Patrisse founded her first grassroots organization in 2011, Dignity and Power Now (DPN) in Los Angeles, she intentionally intertwined political advocacy with healing justice, community health, leadership development, and art.[7] Since 2013, BLM chapters and affiliated organizations have committed to spiritual principles, such as "healing justice"[8]—which uses a range of holistic approaches to address trauma and oppression by centering emotional and spiritual well-being—and "transformative justice,"[9] which assists with creating processes to repair harm without violence. "For centuries," Patrisse told me, "the way we are allowed to commune with the divine has been policed; in the movement for Black lives, we believe that all connections to the creator are sacred and essential."

Patrisse spent her time in Covid-19 lockdown working on Black health access, creating a "Care not Cages" platform and suing the Los Angeles County Sheriff's Department on behalf of inmates being denied testing and treatment. As a person ordained in Ifá, she also led meditations, that continue to this day in the form of abolitionist meditations that allow participants to better imagine the future while advocating for self-care, mental health awareness, healing justice, and art activism.

FIGURE 1.1 Patrisse Cullors, alongside collaborator and co-founder of the Crenshaw Dairy Mart noé olivas, pictured during an Ifá ceremony at the opening of their show "Freedom Portals" at the Charlie James Gallery in the Chinatown Neighborhood of Los Angeles on March 4, 2023. Courtesy of Hebah Farrag.

In the 2020 Measure J campaign, which successfully divested 10 percent of Los Angeles city's unrestricted general funds (estimated over $400 million per year) away from prisons and police and toward community health and alternatives to incarceration, Patrisse successfully stewarded a multi-sector coalition centered on "reimagining LA" toward a "care first vision." In a 2023 collaboration with the University of California, Los Angeles's Fowler Museum entitled "Free Us," Patrisse highlighted Yoruba sacred arts and African Traditional practices in an exhibition inviting audiences to "investigate their relationship to Christian supremacy and anti-African bias" as a "mirror" to help all "fulfill [their] destinies."

Whether in her political, social, or artistic work, Patrisse has woven together three core inspirations over her career: her personal experience at the hands of the state, her spiritual commitment to liberation, and healing alongside her political and historical acumen. Reminiscent of American feminist Carol Hanisch's groundbreaking essay "The Personal is Political," which is often referred to as an emblem of second wave intersectional feminism, connecting gender equity with civil rights and other social justice movements,[10] Patrisse's framework corrects longtime critiques within both civil rights and human rights-based approaches. At the same time, it is an expression of what Patrisse has always seen as a sacred duty in her life: To ensure that all people can live with dignity, including herself.

Human rights for all

Most human rights defenders utilize the law to advocate for victims of abuse. Accordingly, international human rights law (IHRL) is often viewed as a set of protective principles (or norms) meant to enshrine in law the basic inalienable rights of every human being; the right to life, equality, freedom from torture and slavery, freedom of movement, thought, religion, and association. Codified in international instruments like the Universal Declaration of Human Rights (UDHR), much criticism has been lobbed at human rights-based frameworks, lamenting their unenforceability or issues related to cultural relativism and universality. Human rights frameworks have often been critiqued as Western interventionism, used against non-compliant non-Western states by nations who are rarely held accountable for their own crimes.[11] What happens when some are exempt from "the law" and escape accountability, many ask?

Patrisse has long realized that those considered human rights violators and those dubbed human rights protectors could often be interchanged. As described in her 2018 memoir, *When They Call You a Terrorist: A Black Lives Matter Memoir*, Patrisse's community was often targeted by the criminal justice system, including her brother and father. In her memoir, Patrisse describes the torture systemic in LA County Jail through the experience of her own brother Monte's abuse.[12] Based on the Mapping Violence Project's statistics, there have been 672 people killed by police in the United States as of July 15, 2023.[13] According to the Los Angeles Police Department (LAPD) 2023 officer-involved shootings and critical incidents database, forty-one of those people were killed by the LAPD.[14] Keenan Anderson, Patrisse's baby cousin, a 31-year-old father and educator, was the second person to be killed by the LAPD at the start of 2023. He was tasered multiple times by officers responding to a minor traffic accident on January 3. Instead of offering care at a moment of crisis, Keenan died after his contact with the LAPD.

Human rights violations are not things that happen only in faraway places. The work of activists like Patrisse, who has spent her life working to hold the U.S. government and law enforcement accountable for state-sponsored crimes against Black Americans, highlights an approach that assumes the system is broken and must be fundamentally rebuilt. This radical approach to the pursuit of human rights has not gone unnoticed, as the 2021 Nobel Peace Prize nomination for the Black Lives Matter movement can attest to. Patrisse not only fights for justice for families, like her own, who have been harmed at the hands of law enforcement and subjected to state-sponsored violence, she recognizes the limitations of fighting solely to change, add, or reform legal systems. That is why she prefers to abolish them while providing healing spiritual care for communities in the process.

More law, more rights?

In the human rights community, there is an oft quoted saying: "does more law mean more rights?" Most often, the answer to that question is an emphatic *no*. As Patrisse writes in *An Abolitionist Handbook*, in reference to those who worked to abolish slavery, "abolitionists didn't say let's just make slavery *better* (through legal reform). 'Let's get them better shoes and dentures and clothing and fewer beatings and better hours on the plantation and the right to marry and keep their babies.' No, the system had to be abolished." There is "no halfway mark," she says, to ending slavery.[15]

Patrisse's abolitionist philosophy views legal victories, the creation of new rights or enforcement mechanisms, as one tool in the pursuit of human dignity and equality. The ultimate goal is to provide spaces for spiritual healing and care for community in a march toward a world where police, prisons, surveillance, and courts are no longer needed. "Abolitionist practice is about establishing a system that is rooted in dignity and care for all people," she says, "A system that does not rely on punishments as accountability."[16] In order to achieve this goal, which is difficult for most people to even imagine, Patrisse argues we must make abolition akin to a spiritual practice and train ourselves to live in a way that does as little harm as possible: to Earth, our families, relationships, friendships, organizations, houses of worship, and congregations. "If we create an economy of care," Patrisse says in an interview with Maxine Wally of *W Magazine*, "that means we individually, and in our interpersonal relationships, are caring for each other—but also it means our institutions are built to care for each other."[17]

Creating "economies of care"

Providing "economies of care" as she calls them, is evident in all Patrisse does. Starting in 2011 with DPN, known for its work on mass incarceration, Patrisse embedded a Director of Health and Wellness as part of its organizational model. When asked why, Patrisse explained:

> The Director of Health and Wellness is both for the health and wellness of the community and for the organization and the people in it. It's not just about changing policy, it's not just about changing lives, it's about changing our culture and it's about changing how we fight. We can change policies all day but if the fight to get there was full of trauma, was replicating oppressive dynamics and abusive dynamics, then what is the point?

For Patrisse, the goal has never been to build a "by any means necessary movement," a slogan popularized by the Black Panthers. Instead, BLM has always been a movement that deeply investigates what is the *best* means necessary for *all* Black lives to matter.

This focus on care and healing is especially important because of the toll human rights work takes on its defenders: humanitarian aid workers, frontline responders, human rights advocates. Each calling is known for its notoriously high rates of burnout, breakdown, and suicide.[18] Less reported, however, is how often human rights advocates and civil rights defenders are targeted as a result of their advocacy. In the Spiritual Exemplars Project's sample of 104 faith-inspired humanitarians, over 40 percent of the sample experienced trauma related to their justice work or had been directly attacked or targeted for working to advocate for others' rights. Some, like Father Jacques Mourad, a Syrian priest who worked to defend civilians from ISIS, was captured and tortured. Others, like Rosalina Tuyuc, Guatemalan human rights defender, had her family threatened violently for her actions. Others encountered threat of imprisonment, like Scott Warren, who was placed on trial for providing water to immigrants traveling across the United States' southern border. Patrisse herself has been contacted by the FBI on numerous occasions due to legitimate threats on her life, aside from the vicarious trauma she has lived seeing violence inflicted on her family by law enforcement. After the killing of her cousin in early 2023, Patrisse pursued legal consequences and reform, demanding an end to the cops on traffic stops policy and winning a rare "out of policy" ruling from the Los Angeles Board of Police Commissioners in October 2023.[19]

But Patrisse wanted more. She wanted healing and turned to her faith once again, this time through her art. In her show, "Freedom Portals," mounted at the Charlie James Gallery in the Chinatown Neighborhood in Los Angeles, Patrisse displayed artworks composed of framed sections of black-and-white patterned vintage 1950s "mud" cloth, revered in the Malian tradition. Each section of the cloth is embroidered with cowrie shells in a pattern reflecting the Odù, sacred Ifá verses used in divination, they were titled after. These Odù, or divine verses, are a central feature of Patrisse's Yoruba religious practice. As she told *The New York Times*,

> These works come from a place of deep grief for me, of wanting so badly for the world to be different. I kept thinking, what can I make that will help me? Ifá is the practice that I go to when I'm in my lowest moments. I feel like an Odù takes care of me, but it also takes care of the collective, of the community.[20]

At the opening of her show, a crowd gathered around a *Babalawo* and *Iyanifa*, an Ifá priest and priestess, affectionately called *baba* and *iya* as they blessed the gallery with a ceremony. The crowd chanted *Aśe*, a Yoruba term, defined by the priest leading the chant as "it shall, it must, come to pass." It also means power, "the ability to make things happen." He asked the crowd to repeat *Aśe*, as he called on the names of those that had lost their lives to police violence. Many in the room contributed names of their ancestors as those witnessing chanted, connecting each to one another. The priest and priestess invited Yoruba deities into the unified space with offerings of tobacco and rum, the ringing of bells and chanting of prayers and incantations. Patrisse's personal search for meaning and healing had once again turned into a collective ceremony for healing. The political, once again personal. The political, once again spiritual.

"What a Priest Taught Me about Telling Refugee Stories with Dignity"

Mussie Zerai (Roman Catholic/Italy)

By Linda Freund

"I think I survived for a reason. To be a voice for the voiceless," Solomon Asefa told me as he gazed out upon the Mediterranean Sea. These were the very waters where, in 2013, he narrowly escaped a shipwreck off the coast of Lampedusa, Italy, a primary European entry point for migrants, mainly coming from Libya and Tunisia. And in 2023, the Eritrean was ready to be that voice. Fresh from his shift as a bus driver in Avesta, Sweden, Asefa joined Eritrean Catholic priest Mussie Zerai and me, a video journalist, on a Zoom call. I pressed "record."

"The reason I am sharing my story is that the challenges and hardships many of us face when we come [to Europe] may be similar for all Eritreans," Asefa said. His hope is to dispel the myth that refugees crowding boats en route to Europe have some kind of moral injury—that their journey is a choice rather than an act of survival. As Asefa continued, Father Zerai offered support in Tigrinya, their shared language. "You put your life 100 percent on the line when you cross," he told Zerai. "But Father, the cruelty I faced. [The Eritrean military] tied my hands with iron bars, and they hung me up in a dirty place. They tortured me day and night. They did this just for a normal thing, for little infractions or challenges."

Father Zerai listened intently. "You were not a stranger to them," he told Asefa. "You were not even an enemy; you were their brother. You want to know what they said to me when I said, 'I am your brother?' and 'Why do you beat me like this?'" Asefa recounted. "They said 'Shut up. We don't have a brother like you.' Their lack of humanity and ruthlessness was ..." Asefa paused. "I was near death, barely able to breathe. [My captors] were eating and drinking on top of me. They just laughed and sneered while I was dying in front of them." Zerai replied, "Our home country, our families, our beloved home. These are the challenges that made us leave our homeland to live in a foreign country. You survived and today you are telling the story. How many of our brothers and sisters did not get this opportunity? How many of our brothers were buried in some backyard and left there?"

"Yes, yes very true," Asefa said. A moment later, he chuckled. His one-year-old son, donning a Harvard sweatshirt and a gummy smile, popped into the frame, playfully blowing kisses to both Zerai and me. "You see, Linda," said Zerai, addressing me in Italian, "*This* is the story."

Refugees aren't the crisis

Zerai's words were a punctuation mark in what turned out to be our multi-year conversation about reporting on refugees with dignity. The forced movement of people across borders across the globe is proving one of the most pressing humanitarian challenges of our time. In 2022 alone, over 100 million people were displaced due to conflict, violence, human rights violations, and climate change, as reported by the United Nations High Commissioner for Refugees (UNHCR).[21] The future of refugees crossing the Mediterranean Sea into Europe is more uncertain than ever before. European Union (EU) nations, along with other sovereign territories across the globe, overwhelmed by the increasing number of asylum seekers and the assumed economic burden, are adopting more restrictive refugee policies.

Journalists bear a responsibility to cover this story, but portraying vulnerable groups sensitively poses a complex challenge. For three years, I worked on a documentary profile of Father Zerai,[22] known as the refugees' "guardian angel." In 2003 an American journalist wrote the priest's phone number on the walls of a Libyan detention center. Since then, Zerai's cell phone has become an unofficial crisis hotline. To date, Zerai has received thousands of emergency calls from distressed people on the move, dialing his number from wrecked and sinking vessels in the Mediterranean Sea. "When I receive a call the destiny of those people is in my hands because they are at the mercy of the sea, often aboard crumbling dinghies or vessels," Zerai told me from his residence in Rome, Italy. "I ask myself 'Can I do it? Will I have enough time to save them, to rescue them? Will the rescue boats arrive in time?'" Zerai said he's helped save more than 150,000 lives since 2011.[23] "I personally know a lot of people whose lives were saved by calling you," said Ethiopian Abu Kurke, whom Zerai helped. "Seriously, I can't thank you enough."

The documentary's focus quickly broadened beyond the priest himself, connecting me to a global network of refugees Zerai has assisted. As the project progressed, the priest asked that refugees' rights and dignity be protected in the production. Catholic social teaching, I learned, is anchored in the concept of dignity as the cornerstone of a moral society. Violating a person's dignity is tantamount to violating their very essence. For refugees who have already endured trauma and loss, preserving their dignity becomes an imperative act of compassion. Documentaries, especially those involving survivors who volunteer to share their stories, demand a delicate approach that acknowledges the potential for re-traumatization. In production meetings with fellow producers, Salem Haile and May Tsehay, we often asked, "How will telling this story serve and support both the people who endured these traumas and the public learning about these issues for the first time?" And, more troubling, we wondered, could the real crisis not be refugees but the narratives we tell about them?

Departing from the same old story

But producing a documentary about refugees that isn't extractive or doesn't add fuel to the fire of an already inflamed media narrative requires more than well-intentioned questions. It demands a departure from conventional storytelling formulas and the stereotypical idea of what it means to be a journalist—even if it risks alienating potential media partners.

For example, a global news outlet expressed interest in commissioning the documentary, but with one condition: I film Father Zerai actively working with newly arrived refugees in Italy that he had rescued. The priest refused. "My duty is to protect the dignity and rights of the vulnerable and weak," he told me. Bringing a camera in at such a fragile time might make a refugee feel compelled to perform their pain, especially if they believe their asylum status is at stake. Given this power imbalance, how could we guarantee consent?

It was as if the priest had shined a light on my journalistic blind spot. I agreed with his position. When I told the news team we wouldn't document the new arrivals, it surprised them. A good documentarian, after all, splinters the camera into their subjects' lives, capturing high-stakes or challenging moments followed by redemption. It's a formula I often adopted in my decades as a video journalist. But adhering to it with Father Zerai would reinforce a narrative he aimed to shatter. Too many refugees' stories center on victimhood, with cameras fixed on transit centers, camps, or the plight of new arrivals. They emphasize the impossibility of the situation and the burden of the crisis, depicting newcomers in challenging, weakened, or compromised situations. This inadvertently glorifies the activists assisting them, while denigrating the refugees themselves.

The current refugee predicament, driven by political instability, persecution, resource scarcity, and climate change, is a massive geopolitical problem. But, intentional or not, valorizing activists in video reports risks creating a misleading feel-good loop that gives viewers a false sense of progress. This can sometimes oversimplify the issue when the truth is that *we all* participate in policies that make refugees in the first place—from support for authoritarian regimes to blocking humanitarian visas.

I explained this, and more, to the media outlet. Their question: But Father Zerai supports refugees during life-or-death moments. Could we still effectively tell his story without showing him actively doing this? My answer: Yes. We would amplify the voices of people he's helped, those who chose to share their stories and have had time to process their trauma. People like Solomon Asefa, who could reflect on his journey from a position of empowerment. After weeks of radio silence, the media outlet finally agreed to collaborate.

Telling their own stories

"[Refugees] are in charge of telling their own stories," wrote Stephanie Saldaña, a fellow journalist contributor to the Spiritual Exemplars Project.[24] "We don't have the right to ask them more than they offer on their own about the events that happened," she wrote me in an email. Instead of asking refugees "tough" questions, the stereotypical trait of a good journalist, Saldaña is more selective. "There were many questions I chose not to ask," Saldaña said. "For me, these silences and gaps are also part of the story." Later, Saldaña shares the unasked questions in her writing.[25] "By noting it in the text, I'm also trying to model the way that we live in conflict, in which there are many uncomfortable silences, stories that go untold, and things that remain unsaid."

When Solomon Asefa shared his story with Father Zerai, he did so on his own terms, guiding the conversation. This, interestingly, created space for his own inner conflict to emerge. Asefa realized his heart was filled with simultaneous wanting and rejection. He wants to be a "voice for the voiceless," but admitted it's equally "devastating to be the one who has to survive and the one who has to remember." This is the real stuff—the divergent affective tendencies inherent in being human. It also makes for a better, more compelling story.

Asefa's story was heavy but familiar to Father Zerai, who offers daily spiritual support to people on the move across Europe. After the Zoom call, Zerai retreated to his chapel, where he found solace in prayer—inhaling deeply and closing his eyes as tranquility embraced him. "If you don't have broad shoulders, if you don't have strong footing, which for me is my faith and prayer, the risk is huge. Even the risk of ending up in some psychiatric clinic is real," Zerai told me.

Documenting without dehumanizing

Later that week, I reviewed the footage of Zerai in prayer. I began to think about the ethics of the image itself when telling a survivor's story. In *Film and Genocide*, an anthology of essays about how films and documentaries represent genocide and ethical practices and forms of witnessing,[26] Marsha Orgeron writes about soldiers turned amateur videographers who

FIGURE 1.2 Father Mussie Zerai giving mass to Eritrean Catholics in Zurich, Switzerland. Courtesy of Linda Freund.

documented the atrocities of the Holocaust. Sergeants like Joseph Bernard Kushlis who took 8mm film of Ohrdruf, the first Nazi camp to be liberated by U.S. forces.

I was shown footage of the liberation at an early age. It was my parents' way of having me bear witness to our traumatic heritage (my Jewish aunts perished in Auschwitz and my grandfather was killed in a death camp in Poland). I also learned, at a young age, how the visual document, when captured intentionally, had the power to hold war criminals accountable and direct future attitudes and policy. In Kushlis's case, he didn't just haphazardly document the mass graves. He humanized the dead by capturing footage of "a single body or two in a fashion that tends to them as individuals," Orgeron wrote. Most importantly: He never trained his lens on the living. Kushlis respected the survivors' dignity.

To be sure, sometimes a story about refugees merits footage of overcrowded migrant centers, in order to document the limitations of the facilities, or to question whether a country, for example, has the economic resources to handle the influx. But there are still opportunities to be intentional, even with such shots. Do we need close-ups of weeping and disheveled faces to best tell this story? Do we need to show cramped dinghies packed solely with single men, feeding into the stereotype that refugees are a dangerous, homogeneous wave of male energy? What if, while showing select images, we acknowledged the multiple dimensions of the people involved? Boats in the Mediterranean aren't packed with exploiters or born criminals. Most carry fathers, mothers, babies, doctors, artists, and engineers who are escaping perilous situations.

"There's a lot of work we need to do in reframing that," said Ravishaan Rahel Muthiah, Communications Director at the Joint Council for the Welfare of Immigrants, in a July 2023 panel discussion.[27] "Many had flourishing lives back home, but due to human rights crises, wars, climate change, or other factors, they were forced to move. In some cases, they find themselves in worse circumstances than before."

"We must rebel against toxic narratives," journalist Katy Fallon added. "They dehumanize human beings which has a direct link to policy and human rights abuses.[28] It leads people to think you can do things like watch people drown because you don't see people as humans."

There is no better way to rebel against toxic narratives than to disrupt the journalistic model itself. If Father Zerai hadn't imposed limits on me during the documentary production, I would never have questioned the extractive way I was working. To follow his lead made me uncomfortable, at first. It marked a departure from a journalist's professional habit to call the editorial shots and document everything. But it was indispensable, especially as I don't share the same cultural background as the groups I often report on.

Journalists are communicators. We share facts, circumstances, verifiable data. We use this information to hold the powerful accountable, challenge lies, expose inequalities, and make sense of the world. Yet, what if it became commonplace for us to seek insights directly from the people at the heart of our stories on how to genuinely convey their narratives? What if journalists strove, not just to respect the dignity of their subjects but to be transformed by it? How might this approach reshape the stories we tell? How might it in turn, shape the world we live in?

"The More you Give, the More Will Be Yours to Give"

Kushil Gunasekera (Buddhist/Sri Lanka)

By Nalika Gajaweera

"I want to be one of the nicest human beings that this earth has seen," Sri Lankan Buddhist philanthropist Kushil Gunasekera told me in an interview early in 2020.

I've known Kushil for years, so I'm no longer surprised when he makes such bold pronouncements about his life goals. From the naming of his humanitarian organization as the Foundation of Goodness, to its organizational mission of promoting "unconditional compassion," bold claims of moral excellence are fundamental to Kushil's understanding of himself as a Buddhist humanitarian.

At first glance, Kushil's ambition to be one of the nicest human beings may seem overzealous or even audacious. Yet, such a gloss would overlook Kushil's passionate and earnest desire to cultivate and perfect his spiritual vocation of generosity. Take for instance the time when, facing severe personal financial duress, Kushil used the last remaining credit on his credit card to pay the college fees for three children of a woman he hardly knew. Facing financial bankruptcy, he had mortgaged his home for a personal loan. He was not deriving a salary from his organization, for he believed that relying on charitable contributions given to an organization primarily to serve poor beneficiaries was akin to deriving a "profit" from others' misery. Taking financial benefit from humanitarian work, he felt, tainted the purity of his intention of unconditional compassion. At the outset of his charitable work, Kushil supported himself and his daughters from the proceeds of the sale of his lucrative sugar import business. Yet, over the years, those resources had run dry.

It was in the midst of this significant financial uncertainty that he received a phone call from a widow in Sri Lanka who needed urgent financial help.

The woman's husband had died suddenly, and she found herself struggling to pay for the final semester of her children's education. Someone she knew who had heard of Kushil's altruism had suggested she reach out to him for help. "I told her, 'Look, your problem is far worse than mine, I have one month to worry about my next payment, and I can somehow sort that out, you go ahead and pay this now,'" he recalled. "At that moment, there was a fire that was burning within her, and I was able to just put it out." He said to me once, "you know, this has happened to me many times. It's a miracle. Every time I want to do something good, money has come from somewhere."

In this, Kushil reminded me of the phrase, "When you give more, you get more." But he lives by another phrase: "The more you give, the more will be yours to give." Social change-making through humanitarian work is a field that for the most part is centered on a secular moral discourse; that is, the focus of the work is on ending social injustice, affirming equality, and advocating for fundamental human rights. Yet, amid the aid world's landscape of good works, there are also individuals and groups who engage in these efforts out of motivations that are not reducible to liberal humanist reasoning and who undertake this type of work as a kind of spiritual vocation.

Kushil Gunasekera's life history makes for a provocative point of departure to explore the idea of doing good as a spiritual vocation, demonstrating how certain individuals pursue externally directed acts of "doing good" as essential to their own spiritual self-making. In Kushil's case, as a Buddhist, his social work is a personal spiritual vocation that involves cultivating a karmically moral subject around generosity. It is a meritorious vocation that he sees as spanning multiple samsāric lifetimes.

Many Western Buddhists have often struggled with the doctrines of karma, rebirth, and spiritual merit. In my more recent research among meditation-centered communities of converts to Buddhism, I have consistently noted a reluctance to take these aspects of the tradition seriously, with many of my interlocutors commenting on the incompatibility of such ideas with their own interpretation of Buddhism. Indeed, many Buddhist converts dismiss these more orthodox teachings as cultural accretions that have little apparent relevance to twenty-first-century lives. Kushil's story, I suggest, may encourage Western Buddhists turning to the tradition as a source of moral inspiration to explore how other Buddhists elsewhere have considered the complex ideas of karma, rebirth, and merit as foundational, rather than peripheral, to the ethics of compassion in Buddhism.

"Pure" intentions

"Pure intentions do attract divine blessings," Kushil told me. We were standing on the verandah of his ancestral home in the southern coastal village of Seenigama, Sri Lanka. The salty breeze of the Indian Ocean drifted over us, and the sun shone brightly. The home was now the headquarters of the

Foundation of Goodness, the humanitarian non-governmental organization that Kushil founded more than twenty years ago. The house was ravaged by the 2004 Indian Ocean tsunami, in which Kushil himself was swept up, yet luckily survived, when so many others did not.

I was meeting Kushil again after ten years. I had first met him when I studied the Foundation of Goodness for my dissertation on Buddhist humanitarian responses to disasters in Sri Lanka. Today, the foundation is a million-dollar-a-year organization with more than 400,000 beneficiaries in 400 villages around the island of Sri Lanka. With the Covid-19 pandemic just beginning to hit the island nation, and as an organization that relies significantly on personal charitable contributions and corporate philanthropy from Europe, the foundation was surely experiencing fallout from the crisis. Given the uncertainty, I asked Kushil how the organization was managing.

Indeed, Kushil confirmed, the situation was less than optimal; many of their donors had withdrawn from scheduled fundraising programs. Yet, despite the anticipated challenges, Kushil maintained a characteristic optimism. He shared the story of the disappointing rejection his organization recently received for a proposal to fund a new project. But a fortuitous encounter with an influential figure helped raise the entire budget for the project during a single fundraising event. For Kushil, the episode was confirmation of his conviction that good deeds done with pure intention are "divine work" inevitably rewarded by a moral universe.

To be sure, for Kushil, the "divine" nature of this work has little to do with an appeal to heavenly intervention; rather, it resonates with a sense of aligning one's action with a moral universe. He later explained,

> I'm a Buddhist, so I'm not driven by gods, and I don't go asking for help from gods, but I feel if you are generous, if you are virtuous, and if you have inculcated wisdom, I think unseen divine beings who are probably at a higher plane may be helping you, looking at your karmic actions, and showering blessings on you. You have to be pure. You have to be generous. You have to be virtuous.

During my fieldwork, I had met other Buddhist employees at the NGO who held similar views—that their philanthropic work consisted of performing good karmic actions. Manoj, a 20-year-old from the local community and one of the NGO's youngest employees, expressed this view the most clearly. "We all have a certain *cétana* (intention) in our mind, and that is to help and to be of assistance. Our only expectation is to help someone, and this is our one happiness," he once told me in Sinhalese as we chatted over lunch one day. "If according to this pure intention we continue working, and if this work is good, yet this organization still breaks down, that would also mean that the Buddha's teaching is itself a lie. We know this won't happen, because we have seen time and again that Kushil receives donations from somewhere." Like Kushil, faith in a karmic worldview is central for Manoj in motivating good deeds.

Among my Sri Lankan Buddhist interlocutors working in the field of humanitarianism, this karmic worldview emerged as a notable undercurrent in the NGO's activities. It shapes how Kushil and other Buddhists at the NGO navigate uncertainties and challenges that are fundamentally secular in nature, from organizational sustainability to philanthropic fundraising. In international development today, programs are designed with what is considered a sustainable approach, to prevent "dependency" on foreign aid. Indeed, a central question that many international donors have raised with Kushil about his foundation is how the organization hopes to sustain itself without charging even a modest fee for its services to the community. Kushil and his staff, like Manoj, frame the problem of organizational uncertainty in a strikingly different way: Actions inspired by moral intention are karmically good acts, which inevitably produce merit. Their karmic capital is just as good, if not better and more moral, than monetary capital as the foundation for organizational sustainability.

Indeed, as Buddhist studies scholar Maria Heim argues, "In a world radically causal through the mechanisms of karma, it is difficult to consistently deny or overlook that spiritual and practical rewards follow from moral action and that they have a part in guiding human morality."[29]

Samsāric habits

Kushil told me that the imperative to give was something he had felt strongly since childhood. He vividly remembers, when he was about ten years old, sitting with his family at the dining table and seeing a poor man begging at the front gate of his parent's home in Seenigama. Kushil abruptly got up from the table and walked with his half-eaten lunch plate to give it to the man. His mother intercepted him and prepared a fresh plate of food for Kushil to give the man. "He (the man) was thrilled, and I was joyous to see him eating it with such pleasure," Kushil recalled. Kushil shared this story with me during my first interview with him in 2008. The story is one that he has recounted to me time and again over the years, and each time he seems to relive the state of joy he experienced at that moment in his young life.

Although a native of Seenigama, Kushil spent most of his youth away from the remote village, attending a boarding school in Colombo. This was a privilege only a few people from the village could afford; his father was a lawyer, and his mother's family-owned cinnamon groves in Seenigama. They were one of only two families in the village with middle-class wealth in an economically impoverished region of the country. The time Kushil spent in Seenigama during school holidays, away from the relative wealth of

Colombo, made an indelible impression on him. "[E]ach time I would come back to the village for holidays," he said, "I used to get tutored from all these bright kids, who were more skillful and extremely capable of doing good things, but just because of the lack of exposure and their disadvantaged backgrounds, they are not getting ahead in life."

Since the period of Dutch colonialism, Seenigama and the surrounding coastal regions had been one of the main producers of quicklime (calcium oxide), which is used in the construction industry. The village families also relied for their livelihoods on the environmentally destructive practice of coral mining, which provided a steady source of income for poor families but offered young people little opportunity for growth.

Spending his time with these youths in their own homes as a teenager and comparing his own life to theirs, Kushil felt embarrassed by the privileges he enjoyed as a middle-class Sri Lankan. He recalls how, while his poor peers earnestly studied in the dark under the glow of the kerosene lamp, he returned to a home lit by electricity. "I ... felt embarrassed," he recalled. He often gave away his clothes and would sneak snacks from his home to give his village peers. "I used to feel really sorry," he said. "I would give what I had; I think to the extent that my mother was beginning to feel I was bringing in too many people asking for food."

Academic success was not something Kushil pursued in his youth, and he is unabashed at having barely passed the tenth grade. For the most part, he spent his youth playing cricket, the favorite national sport of Sri Lanka, and later played for premier cricket clubs in the country. He leveraged these athletic accomplishments to get his first job in sales. With a charismatic and sociable personality, Kushil was a natural salesman, particularly adept at selling luxury cars. Even as a young adult figuring out his professional path in Colombo, and later in the Middle East, he found himself being pulled back to the people of the village. "I always had this feeling of trying to uplift the spirit and the background of the poor people who exist around [me]," he said. "I really thought one day I would have the means to basically be able to share and give opportunities to these people. So fortunately, I had that quality of compassion ingrained in me."

This notion of "ingrained compassion" points to a subtle Buddhist logic of karma and rebirth that is foundational to Kushil's idea of himself: that the experience of compassion in response to another's pain is a quality that is inherited from past rebirths and generated from past actions, what Buddhists in Sri Lanka call "*pera purudu*" (past habits). When I asked Kushil where he felt such qualities come from, he explained:

> I think from my past actions, over samsāric journeys, as we believe in karma we can't cultivate it overnight. I mean, you can, by seeing others in misery, but I think I have always had that quality of gifting and giving and sharing ... seeing others' miseries and feeling like I *need* to do something for them. I think that probably comes from doing good deeds and merit in the past—maybe in previous births—as a habit.

Continuing to cultivate a past-life habit of giving is central to a Buddhist worldview. Indeed, in the Theravada tradition in particular, *dāna*—or giving—is the foundation of spiritual development. Among Buddhists in Sri Lanka, generosity is the essential attribute of a virtuous person, for it is intimately connected to the core activity of the Buddha's path: the elimination of greed, hatred, and the delusion of ego—the belief that the "self" that I experience is somehow separate from the world around me. For Kushil, therefore, being generous is the central expression of his Buddhist commitments, a vocation that he sees as spanning multiple samsāric lifetimes.

Cultivating karmic seeds

Along with his work building a lucrative import business, Kushil established his reputation and social capital in the cricket world. He first volunteered for the national cricket committee, then was a chief administrator for the national World Cup team. He eventually took up the prestigious role of managing Muttiah Muralitharan, the world-record-setting Sri Lankan cricket legend.

Throughout his career, Kushil kept returning to his home village and seeking ways to be involved in charity. In retrospect, he views this continued returning as a manifestation of the original inspiration he felt during his childhood. "I guess I have that vision I want to do something for my village, and I planted that seed very firmly in my system." Kushil's seed-planting metaphor is common among Sri Lankan Buddhists, who often describe doing good as a karmic seed that yields merit—the fruit of one's effort and intention—often exponentially. As some of my Sri Lankan interlocutors put it to me, quoting the Pali verse, "*Cetanāham bhikkhave kammam vadāmi*," which loosely translates as, "If intentions are good, karma will ensue accordingly." In Kushil's case, this sense of universal karmic law animates his understanding of how his organization developed.

Reflecting on the Foundation of Goodness's beginnings, Kushil recalled the early days, when he would go into a school and see the lack of even the most basic requirements. He saw "kids not wearing shoes to school, taking one book to write eight subjects, without proper square meals, with parents who didn't have electricity or water in their houses." "I will just have to address these one by one," thought Kushil, "and as I began to do that, I found that kindness kept on multiplying. And I realized that the best way to lay a strong foundation was to create a charity." And multiply it did. The business sector and world of cricket that Kushil worked in offered him opportunities to expand his charitable activities. Sri Lankan cricket celebrities approached him and said, "Look, we love to do charity, but we don't know how to do it, and we like the way you're doing it, so can we join in?" Kushil sees the attraction of other philanthropists to his efforts as a natural consequence of his original intention.

In 1998, with a growing network of contributors, Kushil began to informally establish a charitable organization in Seenigama based out of the ancestral home of his parents. Recruiting the assistance of local youth volunteers to carry out the work in his absence, the welfare center distributed educational scholarships to rural students, offered English lessons and computer training to youth, defrayed medical costs for the elderly, and provided electricity, water, and sanitation in the homes of impoverished families.

In the midst of these developments, the 2004 Indian Ocean tsunami struck the eastern and southern coastline of Sri Lanka, killing more than 30,000 people. Seenigama was in one of the most devastated regions. Nearly every household lost someone. In fact, Kushil was present when the tsunami arrived on the morning of December 26. He was inaugurating a new education program that morning, and he and his community volunteers were among the hundreds who fled the wave of wreckage driven inland by the tsunami. They ran for safety to higher ground, sheltering at the same local village temple where Kushil's mother had taken him as a child.

The international aid response to tsunami victims in Sri Lanka was unprecedented. Kushil, drawing on his personal and professional networks, was well positioned to mobilize donors and volunteers to support reconstruction of his village. He provided essential supplies such as clothing to survivors, then rebuilt or repaired more than a thousand homes, as well as the village school. His organization was formalized as an official development NGO. The family home where Kushil first felt the intention to help his village became the center of operations for a multitude of development initiatives.

Until that time, Kushil had spent much of his energy growing his business, with charitable work taking a secondary role. The tsunami in 2004 was a turning point. Faced with the unprecedented challenge of rebuilding most of a village from scratch, as well as the additional challenge of meeting donor expectations, Kushil poured all of his energy into his philanthropic work. Three years into the endeavor, with the first phase of redevelopment complete, he sold his business to fully commit his time to the foundation.

Today, the organization boasts more than thirty community development programs in Seenigama and twelve other community development facilities, called Village Heartbeat Centers, across the island, including the north and east regions devastated by decades of inter-ethnic war. These centers offer free medical and psychological health resources, computer courses, English training, and preschool for vulnerable communities suffering from economic hardship as a consequence of war and natural disaster.

In Seenigama and other locations around the country, Kushil's organization also partners with public schools to use their athletic facilities—a swimming pool, cricket stadium, volleyball courts, or gym, for example—to offer fitness opportunities to rural youth. The sports programs concentrate on the mental, physical, and social health of youth participants as a way to develop their life skills. Every year, the foundation's Sports Club produces young athletes who represent Sri Lanka in national sports championships. Most recently, the foundation has been engaged in relief efforts responding to the needs of communities and hospitals in rural areas affected by Covid-19.

Cultivating a community of practice

Kushil's philanthropic commitments have prompted others to emulate his generosity in surprising ways. When Kushil was in a financial crisis—having spent nearly all of his money, credit balances, and assets to support the foundation—an affluent friend who had heard of his struggles came to his rescue. Kushil recalled what his friend told him:

> He said to me, "I couldn't have done what you did. You let go of your family house to the Foundation of Goodness. You had a lucrative business, which you also gave away for the good of other people. And here we are, earning so much money, and we still can't do what you did. So, you are my role model, and therefore I am going to give you this sum of money to settle any debts you have. And anything else you need; you only have to ask me, and everything is yours."

Since then, his friend has been Kushil's quiet patron, first rescuing him from his debts, then supporting him with monthly expenses. "So, from that time, I have never looked back, and he has continued to support me," Kushil said. When I asked Kushil—the philanthropist now the beneficiary of another's philanthropy—whether he was surprised at the fortuitous turn of events, his response was as I expected: "I think the making of that merit of doing good comes back to you," he said. "It is once again the philosophy that what you put into this universe is what you get back. So, I can't say I am surprised. *Kohin hari enawā*."

"*Kohin hari enawā*"—"It will come from somewhere"—is a Sinhalese turn of phrase I have heard Kushil use many times to refer to the fortuitous interventions that have rescued him or his organization in reciprocation for good deeds committed. It is not an uncommon idea among Sri Lankan Buddhists. Indeed, others who have worked with Kushil in the NGO shared this confidence. The foundation's social welfare programs are managed by salaried staff who come from the communities they serve. Speaking with the staff, I was often struck by how they assume their work has beneficial karmic effects on their own lives. One staff member described this phenomenon in the following way (translated by the author from Sinhalese): "The more we give through compassion, our problems are also somehow solved, without hindrance. That's how we understand it. We cannot rationally explain it that this happened as a result of that. Nonetheless, because we help them, something, somehow, solves our problems."

The idea of karmic return effected by "something, somehow" suggests the ineffable spiritual power of doing good. Indeed, in Sinhalese, karmic merit is sometimes figuratively described as a force ("*balaya*") metaphysically following an individual, bringing well-being and fortune. Like Kushil, some employees suggested that they felt that it was the "karma balaya" of their own past actions that guided them to the foundation so that they could "work in the way of merit," as one person put it. Within the Buddhist framework of karma, karmic returns are not guaranteed in this lifetime; indeed, their manifestations are uncertain and unknowable. Yet, for many contemporary Buddhists who inhabit this worldview, the unknowable-ness of karma does not foreclose the possibility that karmic returns can manifest in this life. For Kushil and those who work with him, there is deep faith that efforts to do good can produce a sense of divinity or transcendence in the lives they are living now.

Sow seeds that bear fruit

A few miles north of Seenigama, heading toward the southern town of Galle, the highway cuts through numerous small villages, making a sudden sharp bend to skirt the edge of the island's coastal belt. To the right are the warm waters of the Indian Ocean that invite surfers and tourists from the world over. But on the inland side of the highway, for miles on end, is a landscape of enormous destruction left behind by the 30-foot tsunami waves that struck these sleepy fishing communities. The tsunami occurred seventeen years ago, yet hollowed-out structures still stand among new developments, reminding one of that fateful day when more than thirty thousand Sri Lankans died.

Approaching Seenigama, there is a discernible shift in the mood and landscape. Suddenly, in contrast to the miles of ruin and vacant coastal countryside, Seenigama presents itself as a small yet bustling village. Apart from a bright blue billboard, erected by the Foundation of Goodness at the major intersection of the village, proclaiming "Seenigama: A village in the wake of a wave," there is little evidence that Seenigama was one of the most devastated villages on the coast, where every household lost at least one member of the family, and many lost far more. A series of "tsunami homes"—two-story buildings housing family-owned fruit stands, food shops, and mechanic stalls—line the short stretch of Galle Road. The Devol Devale—a temple (*devale*) for the indigenous Sinhalese god Devol, which miraculously survived the tsunami unscathed—is the proud spiritual and cultural center of the area.

During my research on post-tsunami recovery in Seenigama and the surrounding area, I heard many of the village locals express their thanks to the foundation and the efforts of Kushil and foreign donors in aiding the recovery and reconstruction of the village. One mother shared with me her perspective on the tragedy and the ensuing development aid. Her comment underscores how, as a Buddhist, she—like Kushil—sees her life as an element in an interconnected karmic moral universe. "The tsunami destroyed everything, and that was perhaps our karmic fruit (*karma pala*)," she said. "We had been mining for coral and that destroyed our environment. The tsunami was a return for that bad karma. But now we have recovered, and maybe it was our good karmic fruit for Kushil to be born in this small village, to come to our aid and help our village recover and rebuild."

Many Theravada Buddhists in Sri Lanka similarly see themselves situated within a larger cosmic moral universe shaped by their own karmic actions, moving through various levels of rebirth in samsāra, depending on their previous merit. For Kushil, this view translates into a moral imperative to engage in humanitarian work as a vocation spanning multiple lifetimes, efforts he regards as eliciting both spiritual and practical rewards and moving him toward what Buddhists call liberation by cultivating the ethos of "letting go."

A year has gone by since I last met Kushil. The pandemic has been unrelenting in its impact on poor and marginalized communities in Sri Lanka, yet Kushil and the Foundation of Goodness have been equally unwavering in their commitments to the communities they serve, despite uncertain funding for their projects. For Kushil, all it takes to face such challenges is a present-moment awareness of the moral exercise in generosity, grounded in an ethos of impermanence. Indeed, the goal is not to create a foundation that lasts forever (so common in Western philanthropic foundations), but rather to channel all the money and resources to those who need them. And to keep doing that right up until it all runs out. "I have lived in the present, put my best foot forward, and trusted that to shape and build the future," he told me. "What's past is gone, and I just want to make sure that my vision materializes by doing the best I can right now."

"A Butcher by Name"

Muhammad Elgazzar (Muslim/Egypt)

By Ken Chitwood

In the city of learned philosophers and a world-renowned library, named after Alexander the Great—I head west toward Borg El Arab to meet Dr. Muhammad Elgazzar, who could be considered a torch bearer for the legacy of Alexandrian medicine. My car passes numerous pick-ups going in both directions, carrying a menagerie of bovine burdens. Today is Eid al-Adha—the feast of the sacrifice—and these are the chosen beasts for ritual slaughter. Remembering the story of how God commanded Ibrahim to sacrifice his son Ismail as a test of faith, Muslims slaughter an animal on Eid al-Adha, recalling Ibrahim's sacrifice and the importance of submission to the God's will. It is hard to count how many cows I see on my 45-minute drive, but I estimate around sixty. My driver, Ahmed, tells me that a cow costs around fifty-five Egyptian pounds (around US $3.25) per kilogram.

I arrive in Borg El Arab and join Elgazzar and his two sons there to sacrifice their family's cow and have it butchered for *fattah*—a traditional dish of rice, pita, and beef. According to the Sunnah—the life and traditions of the Prophet Muhammad—one-third of the animal goes to families who paid for it, another third goes to those less fortunate, and the final third to friends, extended family, and neighbors. The Elgazzar cow, presently fighting the group of men seeking to subdue it before slaughter, cost around 26,235 EGP (about US $1,583), split between seven families. Elgazzar makes his way to the front of the pressing crowd with the head butcher and three assistants. They stretch the cow's neck out with a blindfold over its eyes and its appendages pulled aside by ropes. With a single move and an exclamation of "Allahu Akbar!" the butcher and Elgazzar make the deadly cut. The slice is silent, swift, and the blood spills out quickly. It looks like a poorly made corn-syrup concoction from a 1950s American war movie. Unreal and yet, visceral. Elgazzar appears unaffected by the process. After a few minutes, the cow breathes its last and hangs from a chain, to be butchered over several hours. Elgazzar comments on the anatomy of the beast with the precise eye of a doctor and gives suggestions to the butchers as they make their cuts.

Tiring of the butchering process, we both step outside for some fresh air. As the heat of the day intensifies, I ask Elgazzar about the ironic juxtaposition of wielding a knife to take a life, compared to his usual use of knives to save them. "These are completely different," he says sternly, "But I would always prefer to save the life, always."

Disciplined, dignified, and driven by a resonant desire to save those on the brink of death, Elgazzar—whose surname ironically means "the butcher" in Arabic—first thought of medicine to save his mother from a terminal illness. Not able to save his mother, he went on to save countless more lives as a renowned and award-winning war surgeon on both sides of conflicts in Yemen, Syria, Sierra Leone, and South Sudan.

Adventure stories and chicken surgeries

In many ways, Elgazzar was a normal Alexandrian child. He liked playing football, he read adventure stories and listened to the radio. In other ways, he stood out. Mr. Mohammed Rashad, one of his childhood teachers, told me, "He was always exploring, asking questions, and reading more than he needed to." Elgazzar saved money to buy books and magazines to create a library for himself and his friends. His favorite books were adventure stories: Rin Tin Tin, Mickey Mouse, and the local Egyptian favorite "King

Adventure." By primary school, Elgazzar began to explore the possibility of practicing medicine, reading books with titles like, "human beings, microbes, and disease," he said.

Two pivotal moments would cement this burgeoning desire for future medical service. While just six years old, Elgazzar's mother fell sick with colon cancer. Able to do little to stop it, she appealed to the young Elgazzar to become a doctor and save her life. There was not enough time. Elgazzar's mother eventually died. This "put into my mind that I have to be a good doctor and a good surgeon," he said. Thus motivated, at just eight years old, Elgazzar performed his first surgery. "We were raising chickens and ducks. One day, I found one of the young chickens lying down on the ground and crying. The intestines were spilled out on the floor." Feeling sympathy for the chick, he said, "I ran inside, brought needle and thread, and sat down to hold it in my hand. I pushed the intestines back inside and stitched the skin back together. I put it on the ground, and it started to run normally, as if nothing happened."

However, while his books had motivated him toward medicine, he had yet to study *peritonitis*. Peritonitis, the inflammation of the membrane that lines the abdominal cavity, is typically caused by bacterial infection. "I returned after one or two hours and the chick had died," said Elgazzar, "I did not know the reason at the time. But later, when I studied medicine, I learned what it was. I vowed then, never again," he said. At that moment, at eight years old, Elgazzar decided to become a surgeon, to save lives instead of watching them slip through his hands.

Fighting corruption along the Upper Nile

Egyptian medical schools tend to follow the "French model," which is made up of six years of undergraduate medical education, followed by a full-year internship program before graduates obtain a license to practice as general practitioners. There is also a compulsory period of "national service." Most top students choose to serve in the city they trained in, pick the best hospitals, and strive to stay on track for later post-graduate specialty training.

As his professors talked to him about which hospital in Alexandria he might serve in, Elgazzar had another idea. He wanted to go to Abu Simbel, a frontier town on the border with Sudan in the province of Aswan. Lying some 1,400 kilometers from Alexandria, Abu Simbel is literally on the other end of the country, just about as far up the Nile as any Egyptian could go for "national service." Elgazzar's professors and mentors tried to dissuade him, urging him to avoid the city, renowned at the time for corruption and crime. Undeterred, Elgazzar made his way to Abu Simbel via a 24-hour train ride winding its way parallel to the Nile. Why did he want to go? Perhaps motivated by the exploits of the childhood heroes he read about in books and magazines. "I liked adventure," he said. "I wanted to see other communities, to see how they are living, how they are working. I did not want an easy time, I was interested to face struggles and to solve them, to discover another part of the world."

At first, things went relatively well. Put in charge of a large hospital at the age of 25, Elgazzar was pleased to lead—to have the opportunity to make a difference and work with a team. It did not take long, however, for Elgazzar to meet resistance. Within the first month, Elgazzar was asked to sign off on the destruction of a large amount of beef that was supposed to be delivered to the local Land Reclamation Company. Sniffing more than spoilt beef, Elgazzar investigated the situation. What he discovered was that the beef had not been purchased and the company was getting paid for beef, and its destruction, that never existed in the first place.

Elgazzar refused to sign. Then the pressure piled on. The local health inspector, hospital staff, advisors, and friends all encouraged him to sign the paper and continue with the good work he was doing at the hospital. But Elgazzar stuck his feet in the Upper Egyptian sands and refused to budge. "In the end, I found myself fighting alone," he said. He soon discovered that saving lives in places like Abu Simbel sometimes meant being more than a doctor. Increasingly under pressure and fearing for his career, Elgazzar decided to go back to Alexandria to finish his national service.

"Whoever saves a life, it is as if he had saved all mankind"

After a stint in Alexandria as a private surgeon and some time working on the border between Libya and Egypt, Elgazzar found himself tired of day-in, day-out medical work in his hometown. Wary of the difficulties he faced in Abu Simbel, he still yearned for adventure.

In 1994, Elgazzar got his chance. Two and a half months before wrapping up his residency in Egypt, the Arab Medical Union (AMU) called him to serve one month in Yemen, where there was an ongoing civil war. Elgazzar immediately accepted. The youngest of the team, Elgazzar not only got the adventure he desired, but experiential wisdom from older colleagues from Jordan, Syria, and Egypt. The fighting was intense and brutal. Performing trauma surgery in a conflict zone for the first time, the learning curve was steep. "When you work in emergency, it's different from working with cold cases. You receive a casualty, and he is about to lose his life or not depending on your maneuvers. If you do it for him, you save his life. If not, you lose it," said Elgazzar.

He found the work immensely rewarding, much more so than any financial gain he could earn in Egypt. Solidifying this sentiment was a religious rationale he received from one of his senior surgeons. A colleague shared a verse from Surah Al-Ma'idah in the Quran to him: "whoever saves [a life], it is as if he had saved mankind entirely." This, Elgazzar said, was a critical turning point in his life. It was the beginning of his humanitarian work. And he was hooked.

Of malaria and machetes in Sierra Leone

While his fellow residents were polishing their résumés and preparing to apply for top hospitals in Egypt, Elgazzar packed his bags and departed for West Africa with his newly-wed wife, Rahab. Their mission was to serve in the town of Makeni, Sierra Leone, another country amid civil war.

After an attempted coup in 1991, various factions in Sierra Leone fought for control. The conflict lasted eleven years and left over 50,000 dead. Elgazzar arrived in January 1996 with Rahab, just months before a new government was to be formed, to serve as a general practitioner, surgeon, and gynecologist. They met misfortune as soon as they arrived. Elgazzar fell sick with malaria, there were rumors about spirits living in their home, and then, there were complications with Rahab's surprise pregnancy and their child died. The Elgazzars were devastated. And yet, between sickness, speculation, and their own personal suffering, the mission was successful. Tumors were removed, babies delivered, and the community stood in awe of the work that Elgazzar was doing. He was respected by patients and colleagues alike.

Then, in May 1997, looting, rape, and murder swept over the country in the vacuum of power left after years of fighting. Elgazzar's community was not spared. Not willing to take their chances, they fled through the bush across the border to Conakry, the capital of Guinea. There, their first child was born—Omar. Returning to Sierra Leone after six months, Elgazzar was now a father, a husband, and a respected community surgeon. Despite a difficult start, things seemed to be coming together and the humanitarian life he always dreamed of coming to fruition. "We spent about four months safely without any troubles. We lived normally," said Elgazzar.

"Then, all of a sudden, the national army collapsed, and the rebels attacked our hospital." It was chaos. But with dispassionate efficiency, Elgazzar grabbed their passports, the keys to their Land Rover, and a machete, one of the weapons of choice by the very rebels he sought to escape from. At the gate of their complex, the rebels confronted them and demanded their vehicles, money, and identification. With a gun to his head, Elgazzar attempted to negotiate with them. As he hashed things out, he recognized the leader of the rebels, a man he treated just weeks before. "I told him, 'I saved you, why are you doing this to us?'" said Elgazzar. With that, they dragged Elgazzar back to the home and abandoned him there with his loved ones, a fellow Arab family, and his machete. Now, instead of wielding a surgeon's knife, he clung to the "cutlass" in his hand as the only means of saving the lives of his wife, neighbors, and child. Elgazzar, the butcher, the surgeon, the father, the humanitarian. In that moment, it was a confusing mix of a doctor's oath and a father's commitment, conflict and chaos, life and death.

Still, Elgazzar remained laser-focused on protecting his family. Like a surgeon treating a trauma patient on the gurney before him, Elgazzar judged the situation dispassionately and did what he had to do. "Even when the bullets passed next to me, I didn't feel anything," he said, "and then I told myself, I have to be the hero, to solve it." Tearing through the bush for two straight days, Elgazzar and his family finally made it to the Guinean border. Fifty others fled along with them. Out of money, lacking documentation, physically decimated, and emotionally debilitated, the Elgazzars boarded a plane back to Egypt.

On the flight home, his wife continued to suffer. "When the captain turned on the microphone to make an announcement, she would jump. During sleep, when the air-conditioning turned on, she screamed," he said. Elgazzar's wife was suffering from PTSD—post-traumatic stress disorder. After two and a half harrowing years in Sierra Leone, Elgazzar was not sure he was up to the life of humanitarian work. He wondered if his wife would ever fully recover. He wondered if his son would be permanently scarred. He wondered if he would ever have the heart to leave Egypt and serve again.

Healing on the *hajj*

Upon their return, Elgazzar went back to work to try and rebuild their lives in Alexandria. His wife, however, could not return to "normal." He turned to Allah and begged him to cure the both of them. Just three weeks after they returned to Egypt, Elgazzar bought tickets to go with his wife on the hajj pilgrimage, a once-in-a-lifetime obligation for all Muslims who are physically and financially able to undertake it. "I was thinking how to fix the situation, how to cure it, like a spiritual surgeon," said Elgazzar.

Since he was a little child, Elgazzar had taken a disciplined, measured, and surgical approach to life and its obstacles. See a problem, treat the problem. Malaria? Get the right medicine. Death and chaos all around you? Find a way out. Whatever the situation, there was always a way that Elgazzar could solve the problem. Yet, as he watched his wife perform the peregrinations of the pilgrimage, pray with abandon in the desert, and receive the soul-healing balm that they believed only submission to Allah could give, he came to appreciate the limit of his own capabilities. "You have to know your limits," he said, "just as I realized I could not save my mother or that chicken, I realized I could not clinically treat people in certain circumstances. They need something more, some spiritual support." He concluded, "sometimes, all you can do is pray to Allah." It would be almost two decades before he was able to apply those lessons in the field of humanitarian medical work again.

Saving lives on all sides in Syria

Following Sierra Leone, Elgazzar took a 15-year break from international humanitarian work and medical missions. He opened his own clinic in Alexandria, worked in the community, served at hospitals in the Persian Gulf, and continued to serve the people of his own community. "I had a very good salary, very good position," said Elgazzar. "But" he said, "I wanted to go back again."

Then, when Syria devolved into conflict, the Arab Medical Union called on Elgazzar to serve from 2013 to 2014. Later, he worked with the International Committee of the Red Cross (ICRC) in 2015 in South Sudan and then in southern Syria and Jordan, offering training to doctors, medics, and volunteers working in cities such as Damascus and Aleppo. From 2016 to 2018, Elgazzar worked with the United Nations and World Health Organization in Gaziantep in southern Turkey to offer guidance to Syrian surgeons and doctors on trauma operations and chemical warfare.

In 2013, he arrived at the Arab Medical Union field hospital in the north of Syria. While trying to evacuate the wounded from Aleppo to their field hospital, Elgazzar risked his own life yet again. This time it was not machetes and small arms fire, but a carpet-bombing. "Bombs came from everywhere in the sky, all around us, there was nothing we could do, nowhere we could go." During his service in Syria, he lost two colleagues: one driver and one nurse.

Regardless of the threat to their lives, Elgazzar and his team treated Syrian soldiers and rebels of all stripes. "We would have two or three from the regime side, some from the opposition," he said:

> but we showed no discrimination. We would come from the hot zone with [the] wounded—abdomen, chest, ears, vascular, brain surgery, every kind of trauma—we would operate on them, sometimes up to ten hours. It did not matter who they were. It does not matter if they are "good" or "bad" people, we must continue in all the communities, all countries, all the lives. You can't just treat the "good," because the bad keep showing up too.

Elgazzar had taken his time to heal, two decades worth. In that time, he had come to a place of peace about those he treated. Regardless of religion, nationality, or deeds done, Elgazzar believes they should be given proper medical treatment. "Everyone should live, everyone should be helped—it does not matter who they are or what they have done. If I can save a life, I will save it."

Between home and the "hot zone"

For all his success, Elgazzar also faced more than his fair share of adversity. He relayed to me stories of fighting off both bats and stints of loneliness while serving with the Red Cross in South Sudan, facing discrimination from a colleague because of his Egyptian background and Islamic faith, as well as ongoing tensions over serving in the field versus settling with his family in Egypt, where he knows they want him to be.

The travel, uncertainty, and danger to their husband and father has all taken its toll on Rahab and their children. "One time I came home on leave and as I was walking out the door, my son Omar held on to my hand and cried, 'Please don't go back,'" Elgazzar said. "And another time, 'Baba, stop. We want to be with you. We are feeling alone.'"

His son, Omar, does not remember these feelings of fear and of hanging on to his father's hand. Nor does he remember the trauma of Sierra Leone, where he was only four months old at his father and mother's side during the rebel attack. Instead, he remembers pride. "I am proud of him. He inspires me. He inspires others," Omar told me at the dental clinic in Alexandria he opened with his father's help. "He is an example to us. To serve those who need help. To save lives no matter what. What I do today, I do because of him."

The call "between home and 'hot zone'" pulls Elgazzar in multiple directions. "Sometimes I miss my family," he said, "And when I get home, with my family, I am happy again. But then the next opportunity that comes, I am called to go." Above all, Elgazzar feels called by Allah. "He gave me the body that moves. He gave me the brain that received the medical education. He gave me a strong heart that is never afraid and can perform under fire," he said.

FIGURE 1.3 Muhammad Elgazzar, the "savior surgeon," poses for a portrait at Yeditepe University in Istanbul, Türkiye. Courtesy of Ken Chitwood.

For Elgazzar, this is the sum of his religion. "The Quran is not coming from Allah just to be read," he said. "Religion is your behavior. It's not just theory, not just for reading. It's your life. It is not enough to see pain and feel sad. You must do something about it," he said. "That is my religion."

Looking back on his service in Egypt, Yemen, Sierra Leone, Syria, and South Sudan, Elgazzar applies the very lesson that he now hands down to his students at Yeditepe University in Istanbul, Turkey, where he is a professor of anatomy. "I never planned on doing 'humanitarian' work," Elgazzar said, "I found the chance to do it, saw people in need, and decided to do it. I believe I will be rewarded from Allah [for] that. I have need of nothing else."

Without hesitation, he said, he would do it all again. "Even sometimes my wife asks me, 'If it is repeated, would you accept it all again?'" he said, "and I always answer, 'Yes, I would accept it.' At the end of the story, I am still alive. And so are many others."

2

Cultural Empowerment

I realized that the marginalized have a voice and the only way to make them heard would be to include them within the social fabric.

BADR BAABOU (MUSLIM)

Faith doesn't give us answers. It gives us courage.

MARY SCULLION (ROMAN CATHOLIC)

The Buddha's teachings are not just sayings, but a raft to cross the river and reach the other side.

ASHIN ISSARIYA (BUDDHIST)

Introduction

Cultural empowerment can be a slippery subject to cover. In a world of increasing and compounding diversity and difference, a range of ethnic communities, people groups, and racial constituencies—or intersectional coalitions thereof—have rallied around identity politics or formed identitarian movements to press their claims and position themselves at the center of public discourse and policymaking.

On the one hand, the goal of identity-based political formations is to challenge dominant (mis)characterizations of a people group or culture, secure freedom for that marginalized community or constituency, and, as a result, win a greater degree of self-determination. The Black Civil Rights movement, efforts aimed at LGBTQ+ liberation, or Indigenous rights coalitions have all based their claims on injustices against them by dominant social groups (whether it be white, heteronormative, or colonial powers). Each of these has been undergirded and advanced by academic literature, nuanced reportage, and engaging public fora around the origin, characteristics, and futures of the identifications being claimed and defended.

On the other hand, identitarian movements can be interpreted as a counter-reaction to the increasing power and persuasion of identity politics writ large. In navigating the shift from privilege to plurality, identitarians in Western contexts reassert claims to whiteness and what they believe to be its associated elements (e.g., culturally dominant Christianity). That assertion becomes not only their attempt to retain or grasp at power, but the basis for identification. Examples include the Bloc Identitaire in France, the American Identity Movement (AIM)/Identity Evropa in the United States, certain Christian nationalist groups in the United States, or Patriotic Europeans Against the Islamisation of the West (Pegida), which originated in Germany. Identitarian groups such as these are opposed to multiculturalism or cultural mixing and promote the preservation of supposedly homogeneous ethno-cultural entities (despite their own history of cultural hybridity and miscegenation). Thus, while the concept of "identity" is central to both identity politics and identitarian movements, the key to understanding how to report, comment on, and analyze each lies in interpreting the pernicious effects of power and privilege.

As journalists and cultural commentators, it is important to cover and critically examine the identitarian politics of those populations navigating the shift from privilege to plurality via a return to supremacist rhetoric and re-entrenched nationalisms through the prisms of power and privilege. This chapter, however, focuses on exemplars who champion what might be called "subaltern" cultures and communities—populations who are socially, politically, and geographically excluded from the hierarchy of power and have been historically sidelined, silenced, or slaughtered by the thousands and millions through processes and infrastructures of colonization, nationalist politics, and/or fascism.

Behind these movements for cultural empowerment included in this chapter are the crimes of race and empire that sought to erase them: genocide, forced removal, missionary zeal. As is evident in both history and in the telling of the exemplars' contemporary narratives, religious actors and communities are often complicit in such crimes. This chapter prompts us to remember they can also be part of resistance to marginalization and embody potential solutions in the fight to overcome the legacies and lingering impacts of colonialism and destructive nationalisms. Speaking from various corners of the globe, motivated by multiple beliefs and practices, and embracing a range of religious identifications and political postures, the exemplars in this chapter advocate and act on behalf of marginalized constituencies so that they may reclaim the necessary tools, resources, and knowledge to assert their cultural identifications; gain recognition and validation for their cause; overcome barriers to active participation in society; and otherwise undermine hierarchical social divisions and classifications that prevent their people from full expressions of being and co-becoming.

In the first story, Nick Street profiles Cirilo "Sapi" Bawer. An environmental activist, Bawer is a "culture-bearer" for the Kalinga, an indigenous group that inhabits the mountainous Cordillera region of the northern Philippines. As a culture-bearer, Street details "how Bawer has devoted his life to preserving Kalinga rituals, cosmology and folkways to ensure their transmission to future generations." This not only includes a stinging critique of the Spanish conquistadors, Catholic missionaries, and American imperialists of the past, but a concomitant censure of the machinations of global capitalism and how they continue to threaten Indigenous ways of life in the Philippines and beyond. Street's profile shows how Bawer's sense of "spiritual rootedness" empowers him and other Kalinga to resist global capitalism and neo-colonialism, offering potential lessons to other Indigenous communities and their allies across the world.

Then, I profile Alan Bern, the father of "Yiddish music's renaissance" in Germany. Bern, the founding, artistic director of Yiddish Summer Weimar (YSW) and the Other Music Academy (OMA), is viewed as a central figure in the wider revival of *klezmer* music—an instrumental musical tradition of the Ashkenazi Jews of Central and Eastern Europe. Dancing, playing the style's ritual melodies, and leading virtuosic improvisations for listening audiences on a central German square once frequented by Adolf Hitler himself, Bern and others are reclaiming sonic and embodied space for contemporary Yiddish culture that allows for participants to recognize the painful past without reference to either Zionism or religious practice. The festival is about more than showcasing Yiddish music; it is about exploring Yiddish culture as a complex, and continually evolving, convergence of European and non-European customs. It is also about empowering people for creativity and connection on a continent evermore marked by diversity and difference.

In the third story, Nick Street and Richard Flory profile Hinaleimoana Kwai Kong Wong-Kalu. A Kumu—or "cultural teacher"—Wong-Kalu is also an activist, filmmaker and cultural liaison between Hawai'i's Indigenous community, which numbers about 150,000, and non-Native entities such as the state's Office of Hawaiian Affairs. In that capacity, Wong-Kalu administers spiritual rituals and serves as a touchstone for the revival of Hawaiian language and Native Hawaiians' relationship with the land. Her dream, however, is to de-colonize and re-Indigenize the state of Hawaii. Though that may be an impossible goal in the present political context, Street and Flory highlight how "inklings of what a more Hawaiian Hawai'i might look like" emerge in Wong-Kalu's life and in the resistance she embodies. Wong-Kalu believes "that the assertiveness of a new generation of Native Hawaiian activists will beget broader discussions around governance and the political status of the state's Indigenous people," write Street and Flory, offering an example of how other colonized peoples and minoritized communities might carve out a greater level of respect and dignity for their cultures and customs that goes beyond being relics of the past, but a very present voice in contemporary politics and policy.

Finally, in his profile of Makvala Margoshvili in Georgia's Pankisi Valley, Clément Girardot shows how one woman can leave a legacy for her people, even if her dreams and designs were frustrated during her own lifetime. A Kist woman, Margoshvili endeavored to open her community up to the world while at the same time maintain, respect, and pass on their time-honored traditions, carved out in the mountainous terrains of the Caucasus and informed by the spiritual legacies of Sufism. Arguing that "not all exemplars are created equal," Girardot shows how Margoshvili's efforts at honoring her people and fostering peace were constrained—by limitations of geography, politics, and gender—but that her legacy might yet prove long. Her story is an encouragement to those engaged in the daily fight for cultural empowerment, a narrative of sustenance on the long and hard road to recognition and respect.

Altogether, these entries could also be considered profiles in cultural resilience or resistance, rather than simply "empowerment." These exemplars are pioneers of cultural renaissance for their people. But that rebirth involves an implicit unwillingness to accept the terms and limits set by majoritarian cultures on the marginalized. Furthermore, while their efforts often involve a deconstruction of some sort—decolonizing discourse, popular opinion, economics, politics, or practices; challenging and revising historical narratives; reclaiming spaces and places—they also prompt us to "future think," and imagine a transformed world reality where being and belonging go beyond identity politics to embrace more intersectional identifications of who "We" are and how we might live together in a world of emergent co-becoming.

"Sapi's Struggle: Indigenous Resistance to Cultural Assimilation in the Philippines"

Cirilo "Sapi" Bawer (Indigenous/Philippines)

By Nick Street

The buoyant chatter of children drifted down from a wooded ridge as we pulled up to the teaching farm. A well-maintained trail led us from the parking area past a few rustic buildings, then above rows of farming terraces that descended to the base of the ridge. Cirilo "Sapi" Bawer offers instruction on blending sustainability into traditional agricultural practices at the farm, one of the sites of Bawer's work as a culture-bearer for the Kalinga, an indigenous group that inhabits the mountainous Cordillera region of the northern Philippines.

Children filed past us as we ascended the trail to the ridge overlooking the farm and the broad Chico River valley. Bawer told me that it was not traditional farming they had come to learn. Teachers from the village elementary school bring their students to the farm because the ridge above it provides an unobstructed view of a new cellular tower on the far side of the valley. "This is the only place near the village where the kids can get the Internet," Bawer said. When we reached the top of the ridge, Bawer—a tall, lean man in his mid-seventies—took a seat at a picnic table shaded by pine trees. A few minutes later, one of his grandsons brought up a typical Kalinga lunch of rice, beans, boiled pork, and chayote (a squash-like vegetable).

As we settled into our meal, Bawer gazed across the lush valley and remarked, "Why would you think you have to open a book to find God?" Bawer explained that God, called Kabunyan by the people of the Cordillera, is everywhere. "I know the body of Christ in rice and chayote," he said.

As a culture-bearer, Bawer has devoted his life to preserving Kalinga rituals, cosmology, and folkways to ensure their transmission to future generations. He scoffs at the notion that the Spanish conquistadors, Catholic missionaries, or American imperialists were bringing "civilization" when they ventured into a region known both for the ruggedness of its terrain and the fierce independence of its inhabitants. "We were already civilized," he said. "You say you are preaching the word of God? It is written in the hearts of men." He added, "That's why my God should not be white! Easier for my God to be brown. We want to join the God who struggles with us."

Bawer said that, like the colonizers of the past, the consumers whose appetites drive the machinery of global capitalism are "robotized" by behaviors and beliefs that they never stop to question. These unthinking "robots" never reflect on the divine truth written in the human heart and reflexively oppress those who resist assimilation. "The systems that hold us captive do not make us more human," he said as he gestured toward the distant cellular tower. "This is my struggle now."

It is tempting to see indigenous people like the Kalinga as fellow travelers in wider, non-Indigenous movements of resistance to global capitalism. That would be a mistake. A closer look at the Kalingas' struggle shows that spiritual rootedness in a particular place, rather than advocacy for universal anti-capitalist values, is the animating force behind their opposition to colonization. For non-Indigenous groups seeking allies in the fight against global capitalism, the history of the Kalinga offers a useful lesson: Not needing to see the zeal for your own movement mirrored in the eyes of your ally is the mark of a liberated mind.

The sword, the cross, and the ethnographer's notebook

Forty years ago, the Kalingas' struggle was against Ferdinand Marcos, the right-wing dictator who ruled the Philippines from 1965 to 1986. The Marcos regime wanted to build four dams along the Chico River in Kalinga and Mountain provinces—an area roughly the size of Delaware. Opposition to the dam project—which would have displaced about a third of the region's 300,000 people—created an unprecedented alliance among the Indigenous groups of the Cordillera, including the Kalinga. That united front formed the Cordillera People's Liberation Army. The Indigenous militia then joined forces with a communist guerrilla movement that flourished in the Cordillera for the duration of Marcos's right-wing government, which lasted from 1965 until his ouster in 1986. "There were many bloody skirmishes here," Bawer recalled about that time.

The alliance between a pan-Igorot ("mountain people") Indigenous rights movement in the Cordillera and communist partisans hiding out in the Cordillera's densely forested mountains was a central focus of research for Nestor Castro, a professor of anthropology at the University of the Philippines, who became a deeply embedded participant–observer in the world of the Kalinga and their communist allies. "Especially in upland and interior areas," Castro said, "the government there is just symbolic." As a college student, Castro traveled to the Kalinga homeland to observe the peace pact ritual that united the tribes of the Cordillera against proponents of the Chico River dam project. Castro explained that the peace pact, or bodong, is a distinctive element of Kalinga culture—a way of managing conflict among warrior clans that can exact deadly vengeance against transgressors. "Of course, the Americans established roads and built schools," Castro said. "But the key thing that they adapted in the Cordillera is the use of the peace pact. Their pacification campaigns would include the broad use of the peace pact system."

Though Spain ruled the rest of the Philippines from 1565 to 1898, the Kalinga and other Indigenous groups in the Cordillera were never successfully colonized. Following Spain's defeat in the Spanish–American War of 1898, the president of the short-lived First Philippine Republic ruled for ten weeks from the Lubuagan municipality—a cluster of eight Kalinga villages, including Sapi Bawer's home village—before he was captured by the Americans. The United States occupied the Philippines from 1898 to 1946. "The Americans were ultimately more successful in colonizing the Kalinga and other Igorots because they adapted their cultural practices," Castro said. "Unlike the Spanish, who came with the cross and the sword." That process of adaptation was facilitated by the research and advice of American social scientists, who began to venture into the Cordillera to study the cultures of its inhabitants within the first few years of American rule.

During this time, the Congregation of the Immaculate Heart of Mary (CICM), a Belgian Catholic missionary society, established churches and parochial schools in the Cordillera, succeeding where Spanish missionaries had failed by adapting their strategies to accommodate—and partly absorb—the indigenous cultures of the Cordillera. "In terms of religion there would be this interface—in anthropology, we will call it syncretism—of Catholic and indigenous beliefs," Castro said. "Like, the traditional skirt is worn [by women] in church, and the traditional chant is used in masses."

The Japanese briefly ousted the Americans and occupied the Philippines during the Second World War, eschewing adaptation and syncretism in favor of the sword. The Kalinga, in turn, dealt with the Japanese garrison that occupied the American-built school and CICM mission in Lubuagan as they had dealt with Spanish incursions during the previous three centuries. The villagers retreated to hidden redoubts in the forests above the Chico Valley, and Kalinga warriors began to test the defenses of the garrison and kill Japanese scouts. Soon the sound of Kalinga war gongs, ornamented with the jawbones of slain Japanese soldiers, echoed through the valley—reminding the Cordillera's latest would-be colonizers that they were attempting to hold complex terrain, defended by Indigenous headhunters, for whom the land itself is sacred.

On May 12, 1945, fighter planes of the United States Army Forces in the Far East (USAFFE) bombed the Japanese garrison at Lubuagan. Then the villagers descended from the forest en masse and hacked the survivors to death with machetes. Cirilo "Sapi" Bawer's mother was not part of the melee on May 12. She remained in the forest to give birth to Sapi, whose nickname is a Kalinga rendering of USAFFE.

Innocence and education

Sapi Bawer is a morning person. On the second day of my visit, we agreed to meet at the big, round Bawer family dining table before dawn, which would give us about an hour and a half to talk before the kitchen filled with the bustle and clatter of breakfast. We drank mild, lightly sweetened coffee from one of the large thermos bottles that had been prepared the night before. Every home we visited in Mabilong—the oldest settlement in the Lubuagan municipality—had similar thermoses at the ready for anyone who might stop by for a visit. As we began our conversation, roosters crowed nearby, and village dogs offered their commentary on the new day. In the washroom next to the kitchen, water from a spring-fed pipe steadily gurgled into a large sink. When I remarked on the peaceful vibe, Bawer said that the simple rhythms of village life reflect divinity for him. He described his childhood in Mabilong as "the innocence of paradise."

Bawer and his family lived for the first years of his life in a traditional A-frame timbered house, with livestock penned beneath an elevated communal living space, where soot from the cooking fire blackened the interior planks and timbers. When he started grade school at the CICM mission in Lubuagan, Bawer learned to write his clan's name using the Roman alphabet. "The Kalinga people cannot write their language or dialect," Bawer explained. "My grandfather was a hunter, and 'Bawer' means a stick that's attached to a trap to catch birds and wild four-legged animals. So, in memory of this practice, they said Bawer is my name."

After attending public middle school and Protestant high school, Bawer earned a degree in education at St. Theresita's, a local CICM college. Concurrent with his Catholic, Protestant, and secular instruction, Bawer was learning Kalinga religion and folkways from elders in his clan. By the time he reached college, he had gained local renown as a powerful performer of Kalinga ritual dance. In 1967, Sister Aurora Zambrano, the major superior of the CICM congregation that administered the school, tapped Bawer to represent the Kalinga at the national Indigenous theater company, which would stage a televised performance in Manila. "Sister Aurora was very progressive," Bawer said. "She understood the plight of indigenous people."

The year 1967 was full of high points in Bawer's life: He married Maria, with whom he would have eight children and twenty-two grandchildren. He also graduated from college and took the first steps on his path as a bearer of the torch for his culture. It was also the year that his innocence was shattered. He and Maria—a descendant in a lineage of Kalinga shamans—were married by a shaman in a traditional Kalinga ceremony. That was a step too far in the eyes of the local Catholic hierarchy. Bawer was expelled from St. Theresita's, and only when he and Maria agreed to have their marriage sanctified by a Catholic priest was he allowed to return. Then, during his trip to Manila, as Bawer was waiting in the wings at a television studio along with other performers in the Indigenous theater company, dressed in the traditional woven loincloth of a Kalinga dancer, he overheard one member of the production crew say to another, in English, "I thought mountain people were supposed to have tails." "We are only half-naked people to them," Bawer said as he recalled the exchange. "They were laughing at us because they think we are too simple; we are not organized enough as a people to be able to understand them."

In that moment—not long after his and Maria's humiliation by the Catholic hierarchy in Lubuagan—Bawer saw the dangerous effects of colonizing forces on the minds of those without the capacity for self-reflection. "They have robot minds," Bawer said. "Once you have that prejudice where your mind is already closed when you encounter me, that is harmful for me. Why? Because you don't have the basic element of looking at people through the eyes." Seeing others "through the eyes"—not just as objects in one's field of vision, but as beings like oneself, with minds and emotions akin to one's own—is the first of three laws that govern the Kalinga way of life. Bawer described "having the eye-image" of another person as a way of connecting to Kabunyan—the divine creator-being in Kalinga cosmology. "The next law means respect for one who has the same eye-image of a person," Bawer said. "Third is the rule to discipline yourself, for your health and the environment. These are the three laws that regulate us—this is a moral anchor of our behavior." He added, "This was the law that governs the moral conduct and behavior of the people here, before the missionaries came or before Christianity was established. We cannot cut it from my world and daily life because it is our celebration of our life. This is the thing that is written in the heart."

How does this square with the brutality of Kalinga warfare, not just against outsiders like the Spanish and Japanese, but even between warring Kalinga clans? Bawer called out the hypocrisy behind the question—noting that the superpower that had instigated the Vietnam and Iraq wars, for example, was responsible for far greater carnage than the Kalinga. Brutality, Bawer concluded, is in the eye of the beholder. "This is the way we see justice," he said. "We don't just indiscriminately kill because the heads are free, or the necks are free. That's insensible!" Violence is constrained within ritual, just as the comity sealed by the peace pact is ritualized. The shaman acts as the intercessor between the community and Kabunyan, ensuring that the circumstances of war and peace reflect the moral conduct idealized by the three laws. For those enacting the rituals, the point is to experience the living presence of the divine and to see their experience as a connection to the deep spiritual past. Bawer said that the costumes and rituals of the Kalinga are meant to symbolize "the indwelling of my ancestors."

As sunlight chased away the last shadows in the kitchen, one of Bawer's daughters and one of his daughters-in-law greeted us and began to prepare rice, eggs, and plantains for breakfast. Yana and Czarina—two of Bawer's young grandchildren—joined us at the table. They practiced their English a bit and talked about their upcoming day at school. Their commute would be short: The elementary school in Mabilong adjoins the compound where the Bawer clan lives. Wrapping up our conversation as the kitchen filled with life, Bawer said, "Many are trying to find something, but they cannot find it, because they're going outside themselves. The whole answer is you. The whole answer is what Kabunyan has given you. Don't go and look for the answer outside your own God. Divine eternity is in the stories of the ancestors."

Over and out

The Bawer family home is a testament to Bawer's role as a bearer of Kalinga culture, not just metaphorically but in a literal sense too. A room set aside for social gatherings contains display cases stocked with archival photographs, along with samples of Kalinga textiles and pottery. From the social hall, a short staircase leads into an even larger space—a former evangelical church—where traditional weapons, looms and musical instruments are stored.

Late one afternoon, after showing me pictures from one of his dance performances in Manila during the 1980s ("Imelda Marcos was enchanted with us"), Bawer suggested that we go for a walk. On our ramble through Mabilong, it was apparent that Bawer is almost universally known and respected. His notoriety isn't solely a function of his prowess as a dancer. Chances are, anyone who attended the CICM mission school before 1996 knew Bawer as the elementary school's principal or as a classroom teacher.

Bawer became a teacher at the school in 1968, the year after his college graduation. He served as principal from 1978 to 1996, ensuring that Kalinga history and culture were woven into the school's curriculum.

For Bawer, being a culture-bearer entails not only preserving artifacts and traditional knowledge but also ensuring the welfare of the Kalinga themselves. Bawer's retirement pension allowed him to purchase the land for the teaching farm that we had visited—with the ridge that offered a view of the new cellular tower. The nonprofit organization that he cofounded—called SCODA, an acronym for Salidummay ("festive song") Community Development Association—sponsors the farm's education projects. Bawer and SCODA's other cofounder, his daughter Ophelia—Czarina's mother, who lives with her husband and three children in a smaller house on the family compound—manage SCODA. Ophelia, a social worker, serves as president of the organization, which has collaborated with a German foundation to build a small water pumping station and a Swiss NGO to construct a maternal health clinic in Mabilong. SCODA has also partnered with the local municipal government to improve the village's drainage system and provide public toilets to improve sanitation.

It's the toilets that Bawer wants to show me on our walk. By most standards of human development, Mabilong and the other villages of the Lubuagan municipality are quite humble. Houses lack running water; communal water sources are fed by springs or small uphill reservoirs. Chickens and semi-wild dogs roam the "village highways"—narrow concrete paths that wind through the steeply terraced housing plots and along open sewage channels. Every family has at least one pig. In a rocky ravine traversed by a footbridge, a concrete structure next to a creek served as the communal toilet facility for some of the poorest homes in the village. Bawer said that such simple improvements reduce the prevalence of waterborne disease and offer a measure of dignity to people whose lives are already very austere.

We descended through the village to the patchily paved two-lane road that connects the 8,000 residents of Lubuagan to the outside world. Heading south, the road climbed a small hill that offered a sweeping view of Bawer's history and the heart of Kalinga culture—Mabilong, the oldest village of Lubuagan, where Bawer grew up and where three of his children now live with their families; the mission school where he was educated and subsequently taught; the deep gorge of the Chico River; and the steep mountain ridge separating the upland tribal areas of the Cordillera from the flatlands to the east. I wondered who would succeed Bawer as a bearer of the torch for his culture. There is much love in his family, and the portion of the Bawer clan that has remained in Mabilong seems to share Bawer's deep appreciation for the Kalinga way of life. But I did not sense a passionate intensity from any of his children or grandchildren that might match Bawer's and ensure his legacy as a culture-bearer.

Bawer shrugged off questions about who might follow in his footsteps. He preferred to keep his eyes on the bigger picture. "We are Nazareth compared to the Roman Empire," he said. "That's why it's continuously a struggle to represent yourself and your values as indigenous people." Non-Indigenous progressives might interpret that as a declaration of common cause with those who oppose a global capitalist empire. It's really a plea to respect the specialness of Nazareth.

Nestor Castro, the anthropology professor at the University of the Philippines, remarked that, when the Chico River dam project was cancelled after the ouster of Ferdinand Marcos, the communist guerrillas in the Cordillera expected their Indigenous allies to continue to fight against the more benign but still capitalist regime of Corazon Aquino. "The communists believed their own propaganda," Castro said. "So they were surprised when Marcos was overthrown, and the mountain people said, 'Thank you for your support. You can leave us now. We had the common enemy that was Marcos and his machinery. But now we have to continue our own struggle.'" If you insist on assimilating your ally, you're just another colonizing robot.

At the overlook that was the last outbound stop on our evening walk, Bawer gestured toward the terraced villages of Lubuagan and told me that the people who live there maintain the forests and the river because the land and their identity are one and the same.

"They're good people who just live one day at a time," Bawer said. "Our needs are simple: just to eat together and be connected with the soil. Plant rice, plant vegetables—we are satisfied. Over and out."

"Yiddish Music's German Renaissance"

Alan Bern
(Jewish/Germany and the United States)
By Ken Chitwood

In a clear homage to the album cover for the Beatles' 1967 "Sgt. Pepper's Lonely Hearts Club Band" and its wonderful whirl of colorful visuals, the poster for 2021's Yiddish Summer Weimar (YSW) festival features a menagerie of cut-out visages: from famous Germans Johann Sebastian Bach and Johann Wolfgang von Goethe, to wandering cattle and a bedecked bass drum reading, "Makonovetsky's Wandering Stars Club Band." Together, the collage symbolizes the transcultural and time-spanning story of Yiddish culture and music—its progenitors and critics, its historical influences and contemporary performative interpreters.

At the center of it all stands Alan Bern. The Bloomington, Indiana-born composer, musician, educator, and cultural activist first made his way to

Berlin, Germany in the 1980s, where he helped found Brave Old World, a band described by *The Washington Post* as the first "supergroup" of klezmer music's contemporary revival movement.

Klezmer music is an instrumental tradition of Ashkenazi Jews of Europe. Simply meaning "musician," the word "klezmer" reflects, and conveys, its broader Yiddish roots. The spoken language of a considerable portion of Ashkenazi Jews for centuries, Yiddish emerged in ninth-century Europe as a mix of German vernacular, written Hebrew, and Aramaic, Slavic, and Romantic linguistic influences and vocabulary. Meaning "Jewish" in the language itself, Yiddish is also the vehicle for a rich culture heritage of everyday Jewish life and celebration: proverbs, humor, idioms, and music.

Over the last thirty-odd years, klezmer—and Yiddish language and culture in general—has been enjoying quite a comeback. In the midst of this rejuvenation, Bern and Brave Old World were invited to conduct a workshop on Yiddish music in the central German city of Weimar as part of the European Summer Academy in 1999. The workshop was a wild success, and Bern became the founding artistic director of what is now known as YSW—a five-week summer institute and festival for the study, creation, and performance of Yiddish culture and music in the heart of Germany.

Today, it is one of the most widely recognized programs for the renewal of Yiddish culture in the world, receiving awards from the European Union and the German Music Council, among others. In 2016 Bern was awarded the Weimar Prize in recognition of his significant cultural contributions to the city. For Bern, YSW is about more than showcasing Yiddish music; it's about exploring Yiddish culture as a complex, and continually evolving, convergence of European and non-European customs. It's also about empowering people for creativity and connection on a continent evermore marked by diversity and difference.

"A long odyssey into different kinds of music"

The Beatles cover tribute is more than just a clever promo. It's also a throwback to when Bern's musical journey began. As a child in the 1950s, Bern started off as a classical pianist. "But then the '60s arrived," he told me, and people were listening to The Rolling Stones and the Beatles, not Beethoven. "There were composers in the '60s," said Bern, "but compositional music had become divorced from people's everyday lives and experiences. I didn't go into music to play something in a corner in front of ten other people who had exactly the same training as me, I wanted to be in contact with other people." And so began what Bern called "a long odyssey into different kinds of music."

But it wouldn't be until the 1970s that Bern would really discover klezmer. Yiddish culture, though it was a part of his family's history, hadn't featured much in Bern's life growing up. Bessarabian Jews, Bern's grandparents came to the United States from Moldova alongside scores of other Jewish immigrants in the late-nineteenth and early-twentieth centuries. Bern's parents, as second-generation Jews in the United States, "were thoroughly 'American,' you could say. They raised me on hot dogs and baseball," said Bern. "They could speak Yiddish, but they weren't looking backwards, only forward."

When 23-year-old Bern made his way to Boston, he arrived at the beginning of what would later come to be known as klezmer's contemporary revival. Across the United States and Europe, jazz musicians, bluegrass players, and others were finding their way to klezmer and capitalizing on a social climate that encouraged the remixing of old styles as part of the multicultural mix of the 1970s. Bern connected with the scene in Boston—including the world-renowned Klezmer Conservatory Band—and became part of a new generation of klezmer musicians. Together, they began to delve deep into Yiddish culture's past, resurrecting music lost for generations.

That journey, back and forth between then and now, there and here, was both personal and professional for Bern, who struggled to build a bridge between the world of Jewish immigrants in 1915 and his 1970s milieu. The struggle reflected the historical decimation of Yiddish culture and language. While before the Second World War there were some 13 million native Yiddish speakers, only around half a million remain today. Of the estimated 6 million Jewish victims of the Holocaust, 85 percent spoke Yiddish as a native tongue. "When I began to look backwards and think about the world that was lost and what could still be recovered and used to grow a new culture, I wasn't aware that my family had this whole history," said Bern.

Weimar: The capital of contemporary Yiddishland?

To help rediscover that personal history, Bern moved to Berlin in 1987. He not only reconnected with his European roots but started to discover different aspects of Yiddish culture "and its relationship to all these other cultures of the world," he said. At that time, the goal shifted from reviving and performing Yiddish music, to inviting others into the process of learning, exploring, and recreating the music and culture alongside him.

Ethnomusicologist Phil Alexander, who wrote the book *Sounding Jewish in Berlin: Klezmer Music and the Contemporary City,* wrote how there, Bern became part of "a rapid increase in bands, performance spaces, and workshops—helped along by enthusiastic headlines proclaiming things like 'In Berlin, it's hip to be klezmer.'"[1] Alexander describes in vivid detail how klezmer wove itself into the city's musical fabric, with klezmer bands busking "on street corners or at the unofficial weekly mini festival on the former death strip of Mauerpark" and performing unapologetically Jewish music "in the city's scruffy bars, urban festivals, and funky clubs."[2]

In this way, klezmer noisily manifests its contemporary identity "alongside the official discourse of Jewish culture days and 'Open Synagogue' nights, Holocaust commemoration and centrally organized tours to smaller Jewish communities,"[3] wrote Alexander. Recognizing that Germany has a long, if ambivalent, relationship with Yiddish culture, Alexander suggests that klezmer not only carries the "imagination and memories of a part of Jewish life all but wiped out by the Holocaust" but is also "reinvented music" that "points to a discourse of Jewishness unafraid to confront the dark history of the long twentieth century, but also a refusal to be defined by it."[4]

It is exactly that sensibility that Bern brings to Weimar through YSW. The festival invites students, artists and audiences into experiential workshops, concerts, lectures, and jam sessions each summer in a city not often associated with things "Yiddish." In fact, to many, Weimar has a much darker—and anti-Semitic—legacy. Weimar was important to Adolf Hitler not only because it represented the Weimar Republic, which the Nazis reviled, but also—as the adopted home of revered heroes of German literature, Goethe and Friedrich Schiller—a historic center of German high culture. Hitler visited Weimar numerous times, often staying at Hotel Elephant in the city center. Just 10 kilometers from that hotel lay the Buchenwald Concentration Camp, where some 56,545 people were exterminated during the Holocaust.

Bern does not shy away from the power of hosting YSW in such a city. "When we're playing a jam session on the public square in front of the Hotel Elephant; when people are dancing to Yiddish music where thousands of Weimarers used to shout 'Sieg Heil' up to the balcony where Hitler used to stand, there's something meaningful in that," he said. "In one of the crucibles of early National Socialism, the integration of sound, remembrance, and mobile togetherness [at YSW] addresses itself directly—sonically and in real time—to German Jewish history," wrote Alexander.

At the same time, Bern says YSW draws inspiration from Weimar's cultural legacy, which is a key reason for hosting the festival in the city year after year. "Yiddish culture was not historically at home in Weimar, but the inspiration for secular Yiddish culture comes from there," he said. That's why famous Weimarers like Franz Liszt and Friedrich Schiller are featured on the YSW 2021 poster right alongside contemporary klezmer stars. "It's a poignant irony that secular Jewish culture was directly inspired by German culture in the nineteenth century," said Bern. "Schiller. Liszt. Bach. Wagner, they were all influences on Jewish people and Yiddish culture." And although Weimar's most famous son, Goethe, had a mixed relationship with German Jewry, his notebooks feature his struggles learning the Hebrew alphabet and scribblings of the Judeo-German dialect (*Judendeutsch*). Goethe even planned to write a book that would feature *Judendeutsch* alongside other languages found in Germany. Not only did non-Jewish German culture influence Jewish German culture, it worked both ways, said Bern—in fact, YSW celebrated with its 2019 theme: "The Weimar Republic of Yiddishland."

For all these reasons, Bern feels YSW is right at home in Weimar. "It is that more complex story of the relationship between non-Jewish German and Jewish German culture we are trying to tell at YSW," said Bern. "It's not an apology for Nazi Germany. On the contrary, it's an attempt to regain a culture and a narrative."

Empowering creativity and connection

Not only is YSW an effort in regaining the past, but it's also meant to help create new music through the connections that occur through the festival events. Alexander says that how YSW deals with these "paradoxes of heritage" makes it a particularly powerful learning experience, creating musical and emotional connections between Yiddish legacies and contemporary Jewish German and non-Jewish German lives. Incorporating multiple—and sometimes conflicting—voices into a creative dialogue, Alexander believes YSW, "creates a feeling of ownership and inclusivity through easygoing lectures, panel discussion, and participatory involvement."

Those connections, and that creativity, are multivalent, said Bern. Far from monocultural, Yiddish music is a window into Europe's long and ongoing intercultural story. "The festival is not about diving into some obscure culture but using the lens of Yiddish culture to find out more about European history and culture in general," he said.

Through YSW—and as artistic director of the Other Music Academy (OMA) and other projects in Weimar and Berlin—Bern hopes to inspire an open, collaborative, transcultural atmosphere beyond the festival.

Although this was a priority since the festival's humble origins in the 1990s, it continues to be a prime purpose of Bern's wider efforts. That's even more so the case as a wide swathe of right-wing populists have sought to pushback on Europe's once-hoped-for *Multikulti* future. In contrast to such reveries, xenophobia and racism are re-emerging as issues of critical concern across the European continent. From rising waves of Islamophobia to the radical success of the political far-right in Germany and Europe, Bern understands that YSW's work is about much more than reclaiming Yiddish culture or confronting Germany's past and present anti-Antisemitism. "For any minority group, xenophobia is a problem, you never know when your group is going to become the object of aggression—whether it's anti-Black racism or anti-Asian, antisemitism or Islamophobia, it's all one big constellation of xenophobic impulse," said Bern.

To counter the concurrence of populist xenophobia, YSW invites participants into a learning community that challenges them to grow in ways that go far beyond the topics of the festival. "The people who take part," said Bern, "come from all over the world. With folks from so many countries, it's even hard to communicate sometimes and so we integrate various forms of kinetic and non-verbal learning: jam sessions and dances in Weimar's cafés."

In 2021, the YSW community danced and sang their way through the collection of The Kiselgof-Makonovetsky Digital Manuscript Project (KMDMP), a digital humanities project making major collections of klezmer music materials available for researchers and musicians around the world. Beyond more than tripling the klezmer music available to musicians in the twenty-first century, the project encourages an even deeper dive into the scene's extensive, global history.

Indeed, in one more artistic nod to klezmer's many influences and expressions over the years, the ethnographers and composers who helped unearth this treasure trove of music are featured alongside the historical personages and contemporary artists framing Bern on the Beatles-inspired YSW 2021 poster. In the poster and the festival, Bern hopes that looking forward by looking back will help move participants—and society at large—in a more meaningful and multicultural direction. "Taking the long view, society is always changing. We just get to decide a bit about how we want to guide it," said Bern, "YSW—and Yiddish culture and music—is all about long-term strategies of change." "Many people have told me that the experience continues to change them long after they've returned home," he said. "It's a journey that pushes you to challenge your boundaries, explore connections, and grow through encounters with others and with ourselves."

"A Very Hawaiian Place: Native Activists Fight for Land, Language, and Identity"

Hinaleimoana Kwai Kong Wong-Kalu (Indigenous/Hawaii)

By Richard Flory and Nick Street

It's a weekday evening rush-hour in Honolulu, and Hina Wong-Kalu is driving us to a practice session of a Tongan choir she belongs to—her way of unwinding after a long day of meetings. Kumu ("cultural teacher") Hina, as she is most widely known, is an activist, filmmaker, and cultural liaison between Hawai'i's Indigenous community—which numbers about 150,000—and non-Native entities such as the state's Office of Hawaiian Affairs, where we met her. As *māhū*, or a third-gender person, she is also called upon to administer spiritual rituals and serve as a touchstone for the revival of Hawaiian language and Native Hawaiians' relationship with the land.

Looking out at suburban sprawl encroaching on tropical hillsides and eight lanes of congested freeway traffic, she says, "Hawaiians are the most colonized of everyone." Wong-Kalu, who is Native Hawaiian, explains that Native people from Tonga—a Polynesian monarchy that retained its sovereignty during the era of European and American colonization—never lost their Indigenous languages and folkways, largely because they have been able to preserve their relationship to the landscapes where those cultural traditions arose. Experiencing that unbroken spiritual through-line to Indigenous ancestors is what appeals to Wong-Kalu about singing with the Tongan choir. Among Indigenous Hawaiians, only a handful of families living on the protected island of Niihau—the smallest and westernmost of Hawai'i's inhabited islands—have managed to preserve a similar relationship to ancestral lineages. "Whereas most other Hawaiians are dispossessed in their identity through the land and culture, language," Wong-Kalu says, Niihau Hawaiians stand apart because "they haven't been dispossessed of their identity."

In 1893, American businessmen staged a coup against the Hawaiian monarchy and installed a provisional government with the backing of the U.S. military. A few years later, the teaching of the Hawaiian language was banned in public schools. By the time the ban was lifted in the 1980s, only a few dozen young adults were fluent in Hawaiian.[5]

"We know that we were colonized," Wong-Kalu said. "We know that they took over our schools. We know they took away our language. We know all of this, so we're just trying to bring all those things back."

She describes the uptick in activism among a younger generation of Native Hawaiians, particularly around resistance to the construction of another large observatory on Mauna Kea, as a process of de-occupation. "Us going to the legislature, becoming elected officials—we could use those terms, de-occupy," she says. "But when I go there, I don't want to just de-occupy the building. I want to de-occupy the whole state."

That's a quixotic ambition. Yet the very steepness of the odds against them also seems to galvanize Hawai'i's Indigenous activists across generations—from young firebrands like Lanakila Mangauil to mid-lifers like Wong-Kalu and elders such as Walter Ritte, who made headlines in the 1970s for evading arrest on an uninhabited island that the U.S. military was using for target practice. For all of them, a deep spiritual connection to the land—confronted with a colonizer culture that is both implacable and oblivious to any sense of place—has become the driver for a movement that envisions a much more Hawaiian Hawai'i. Even if de-occupying the entire state of Hawaii is a nearly impossible dream, inklings of what a more Hawaiian Hawai'i might look like help to keep the dream alive. Wong-Kalu smiles when we tell her we are going to Molokai to interview Ritte, whom she calls Uncle Walter. "When you go to Molokai," she says, "it's a very Hawaiian place."

A visit with Uncle Walter

Ritte—a lean, bearded, gray-haired man in his mid-seventies—met us at Molokai's modest airport in a well-used pickup truck. Molokai is about half the size of Oahu but has less than 1 percent of Oahu's population.

Though it boasts forested coves and spectacular sea cliffs, there's little tourism infrastructure—a consequence of local resistance to the kind of development that has altered the landscape of other populated Hawaiian islands. "We see Honolulu as something we don't want to aspire to," Ritte told us when we remarked on the absence of resorts, name-brand hotels and golf courses as he drove us to a local diner for lunch. He explained that the tropical coves that resort developers covet were used as fisheries by Molokai's traditional inhabitants.

The relatively flat land on the west end of the island, once used for cattle ranching and pineapple plantations, is slowly returning to its precolonial ecology. Ritte, who is also Native Hawaiian, grimaces as we pass vast gated fields across the road from the local high school. The land is controlled by the seed development division of a global chemical conglomerate—the island's sparse population and year-round growing season make it an ideal location for developing new strains of corn and other non-Indigenous crops.

Though the agribusiness outpost is the island's single largest employer, Ritte still sees it as a blight on sacred land. "I know what all my ancestors did on the land," he said. "That also gives me the obligation for future generations—those are important to our ancestors. This is kind of like what we're trying to protect. It's really, really difficult."

Ritte's struggle against colonizing outsiders began when he was a young man hunting deer on Molokai. His initial encounters with newly erected fences and "No Trespassing" signs didn't faze him. "The deer weren't paying any attention to those signs," he said. "So I ignored them, too."

That casual rebelliousness changed in 1976, when the U.S. Navy refused to stop using Kaho'olawe, an uninhabited island near Maui, as a training ground for military exercises. After a lawsuit to stop the bombing of Kaho'olawe failed in federal court, Ritte and several dozen other Indigenous rights activists attempted to occupy the island in a flotilla of small watercraft. Two activists were lost at sea when their boat capsized in rough weather. Ritte and eight others made it to Kaho'olawe, evading capture for a few days, until hunger and thirst compelled them to surrender to military police. Ritte recounted his time on Kaho'olawe and eventual evacuation from the island on a military helicopter as we sat at a shaded table outside the diner where we stopped for lunch. "When we went to Kaho'olawe, that changed my life," he said. "It had nothing to do with politics. Nothing to do with anything except the land."

That drive to protect and reclaim ancestral lands galvanized Ritte's generation of Native Hawaiian activists in the 1970s. Recalling the animating spirit of that era, Ritte said, "We were trying to figure out how to explain it to people, what we're doing. So, we came up with this term called *Aloha 'āina*—love of the land."

Aloha 'āina is the antithesis of the colonizing impulse, which obscures the life-giving function of the land by commodifying it and conjuring rules of ownership that privilege those who wield power and control wealth. It also connects Ritte and other Native Hawaiians to their ancestors, whose language, religion, and folkways were intimately tied to the landscapes where those cultural traditions developed. "So today, it's not bombs that are killing the land," Ritte said. "It's the greed, and the uncontrolled commercialism, the need to make money by extracting from the environment to the point where you're killing the environment."

Ritte nodded as we remarked that pushback against the rapacious commercialization of land seems to thread through Indigenous activism in the continental United States, Brazil, the Philippines, and elsewhere. "People are now seeing this is a problem for the whole world," he said. "There's still this cancerous growth, that's how I see it. I have to stop that."

After lunch, we climbed back into Ritte's truck and got a brief tour of the homestead plots—land set aside for Native Hawaiians by the federal government in the 1920s—that Ritte and his extended family have cleared and developed over the past quarter-century. Ritte relished the fact that the hilliness of the area set aside for Native homesteads on the island's flatter, more arable west side made the homestead plots undesirable for growing pineapple during the plantation era. We then headed east toward the lusher, mountainous side of the island, where Ritte wanted to show us one of the roughly seventy tidal fishponds that his ancestors had built in coves around Molokai before the American takeover of Hawai'i in the late 1800s.

Restoring the island's fishponds is a focal point of Ritte's current activism through 'Āina Momona ("fertile land"), a non-governmental organization he founded to promote social justice and sustainability through Native Hawaiian sovereignty over the land. "We're needing some kind of way of living that's not dependent on extraction," he said, as he led us along a muddy path cut through reeds and mangroves to the edge of a lagoon. "A lot of people don't believe we can do it, but I believe we can. Because our ancestors did it for thousands of years."

Ritte noted that the availability of homestead plots, coupled with local activism that has curtailed the development of tourism and other industries that would despoil the land, has kept Molokai's population stable at about 7,000 inhabitants even as other islands have seen explosive growth. "They managed to feed the same amount of people that we have today," he said, as he surveyed the low stone barrier at the mouth of the cove that allows the high tide to bring fish into the cove, then traps them in an artificial lagoon as the tide recedes. "They didn't have barges or airplanes or oil," he said. "So, we need to go back to our ancestors to get some of those answers."

Ritte said many Indigenous people who want to reclaim ancestral folkways must undertake a process of inward-looking, spiritual liberation, if their political activism is to have any chance of success. For a colonized people struggling to reclaim their identity, an individual's learning to venerate their precolonial history—particularly their ancestors' language and ritualized relationship to the land—can be a radical and deeply spiritual act of personal decolonization. "We were brought up seeing that our ancestors, the Hawaiians, were lazy," Ritte said as we walked away from the fishpond to inspect a small field of taro—a starchy root vegetable that is a staple in the Native Hawaiian diet. "We were taught not to be proud of our past or anything like that. Total opposite of what I believe to be right. I'm pretty much convinced that the past is going to tell us how we survive."

Ritte said that the long-term survival of Native Hawaiians hinges on their relationship to the land, not just as a way of reclaiming their language and spiritual identity, but in preparation for the collapse of the unsustainable colonial systems that currently control most of the planet and its resources. Future generations, he believes, will have no choice but to reclaim the farming and fishing practices of their forebears.

That sense of urgency is motivating Ritte and other Native Hawaiian activists to run for political office—a Trojan Horse strategy to dismantle systems of oppression that they have previously struggled against as outsiders. Ritte recently ran to represent Hawai'i's District 13 in the state house, and lost by just a slim margin, despite making no effort to soften the rough edges of his reputation as an activist. "One of the first questions I got asked by the news media was, 'Do you believe that the state of Hawai'i is legal?' And I said, 'Of course not. Any fool knows that without a treaty you cannot just go take some country.'"

That ability to enter the fray of the colonizers' politics without compromising his devotion to his forebears is rooted in Ritte's experiential relationship with his ancestors—something he hopes to transmit to younger activists who seek his counsel. "Hawaiians think that when you're born, there's a soft spot on your head," he explained. "That's called the *piko*, and then the umbilical cord is the other *piko*. When the elders want to talk to you, they'll talk to your gut. That's what I tell all the young ones: Listen to your gut. That's your Hawaiian elders talking to you."

Ritte sees Native activists' two-pronged strategy—thwarting projects like the Thirty Meter Telescope on Mauna Kea while they attempt to win local political contests—as a sign that, after more than a century of dispossession, Hawaiians are finding ways to reclaim their power. "That tells me that there's an awakening of people that understand that they can do something against a seemingly huge foe," he said.

Kumu Hina listens to her gut

Back in Honolulu, after the practice session with the Tongan choir, we head back toward downtown. The rush-hour traffic has abated, and Wong-Kalu is more relaxed. "When I'm around Tongans," she said, "all the understandings of our culture—everything that I know from being around my Niihau Island family, who are still Hawaiian language as first-language speakers—it's all the same kind of aesthetic, it's the same kind of heart, it's the same kind of mind."

As a young person growing up in Honolulu, Wong-Kalu attended the original Kamehameha School, which was established in 1887 and funded through the estate of Bernice Pauahi Bishop—a great-granddaughter of King Kamehameha—to educate native Hawaiian children about their history, language, and culture. Since the 1990s, the school has expanded to three K-12 campuses and thirty preschool sites statewide. In addition to the Kamehameha Schools, where the language of instruction is English, Indigenous children can learn Native Hawaiian language and culture at a *Punana Leo* ("language nest")—family-run, nonprofit language-immersion preschools that initially operated illegally when they were started in 1984.

Wong-Kalu's early attraction to her Native Hawaiian heritage also brought her face-to-face with a challenge that Ritte and other Indigenous activists have had to confront: an antipathy toward their own culture that often pervades later generations of colonized peoples. "There was a time much earlier in my life where some of my own family questioned why I was taking all the Hawaiian classes," Wong-Kalu recalled. "They said, 'What are you going to do with that? It's not going to give you anything. It's not going to help you. It's not going to get you ahead.' I knew I could not agree with that. It's not something that you can tell me is right."

Wong-Kalu said that the omission of Native Hawaiian instruction in the public education system was partly to blame for this cultural ignorance and self-loathing. The bigger problem is the fundamentally anti-Indigenous values of the religious and economic systems that have been imposed on Native people by Hawai'i's colonizers. "Once you get sprung," she said, "once you have gone through the decolonization process and your sense of awareness continues to grow, it becomes very challenging to look at capitalism and Christianity in the same way."

Wong-Kalu felt the need to "get sprung" from an anti-Indigenous ethos as part of her coming out process as *māhū*—a third-gender person. The word is sometimes used as an epithet for LGBTQ+ people among Christianized Native Hawaiians, though Wong-Kalu described the presence of *māhū* people as "extraordinarily ordinary" in traditional Hawaiian culture, where they were often seen as healers and spiritual leaders. For Wong-Kalu, reorienting Indigenous communities toward a more expansive view of gender identity and expression goes hand in hand with helping Native people find their voices and assert their authority in the public sphere—a sense of empowerment that was transmitted by Wong-Kalu's mother and her Niihau Island lineage. "Speak in Hawaiian!" Wong-Kalu recalled her mother telling her when she began to appear before state officials as a young community activist. "This is our land." "The people in political and economic power in our islands feel that we are an inconvenient nuisance," Wong-Kalu said. "Why is it that you feel that we have to speak English to you in our home? Because we can all speak English, you think we should just speak English? That's not right."

Wong-Kalu said that many "foreigners"—meaning any non-Native people in Hawai'i, including non-Native citizens of the United States—failed to appreciate the importance of their land and language to Native people, even as they traded on the allure of the Aloha spirit. "Some of the foreigners in this state are really just despicable," Wong-Kalu said. "You think that Hawai'i should be promoted to the rest of the world—all the elements of Aloha and making Hawai'i so 'perfect vacation'-looking." She continued, "You pimp us out, you prostitute our culture. Yet, when we actually stand up for who we are and the things that are a part of us, how do you justify treating us in the way that you do?"

The fight over who gets to determine whether the Thirty Meter Telescope will be built atop Mauna Kea has become a catalyst for activism around language as well as land rights. Following the lead of Wong-Kalu and others, many young activists have insisted on speaking in Hawaiian when they appear before judges, legislators and other officials. Like Ritte, Wong-Kalu believes that the assertiveness of a new generation of Native Hawaiian activists will beget broader discussions around governance and the political status of the state's Indigenous people.

As we returned to the parking lot at the Office of Hawaiian Affairs, Wong-Kalu wrapped up our conversation on a note of cautious hopefulness. "It will probably never return to its rightful place as a very Hawaiian Hawai'i," she said. "But we can restore a greater level of respect and dignity. We can decide whose voice can start to prevail more."

"*Миру мир* (Peace to the World)"

Makvala Margoshvili (Muslim/Georgia)

By Clément Girardot

When Makvala Margoshvili passed away on May 26, 2021, at the age of 83, she left several, unfulfilled dreams behind. The most niggling, perhaps, was to organize an international peace festival in the amphitheater overlooking her village—Duisi, Georgia. A rather large village with maze-like streets set on the bank of the Alazani River in the heart of the Caucusus, Duisi boasts two mosques, a café, several shops, a museum, a cultural center, and a judo training facility. Economic activities and opportunities for youth are limited but the locality does better than most rural settlements in Georgia, according to residents. The pace of life is slow, largely centered on agricultural activities and the rhythms of the seasons. Most families, even if farming is not their prime economic activity, still own a few cattle, grow maize, and cultivate vegetables in their own gardens.

I first came to Duisi and met Margoshvili on a sweltering day in August 2019. Nicknamed "Badi," she invited me to her large family house. Her home, like many houses in Georgia, possesses an expansive balcony, providing shade for family and friends to rest in the terrace during the summer months. The kitchen, by far the house's busiest room, is on the ground floor. There are countless bedrooms accommodating members of the extended family on both floors. A few steps from the terrace lies a well-maintained garden with various types of flowers. On one side are kiwi trees and on the other Badi had planted bushy, green boxwoods in the shape of the Russian words *Миру мир*, "Peace to the World."

The garden's lush character reflected Margoshvili's interior exuberance. And good thing, for she had not been able to leave her home as much as she might like in recent years. "She had to stop being socially active a few years ago, not because she has leg problems and cannot walk but because of short-term memory issues. Otherwise, she would still be active," said her daughter-in-law, Nata Borchashvili, who shared the same house,[6] serving as her constant caregiver.

Despite being confined within the walls of her lush property, Margoshvili remained inquisitive, energetic, and optimistic. As we sat on the shaded terrace and she plied me with snacks and drinks for over three hours, Badi recalled[7] the main chapters of her life in her characteristically soft voice: a childhood marked by the tragedy of families mourning their lost sons during the Second World War, her marriage to a Soviet judo champion and collective farm director, her nursing studies and professional life during the Cold War period. She closed off the retelling of her life chapters with tales from the Chechen wars in the 1990s, which brought thousands of refugees to her quiet valley, and how, in the end, this event summoned her into humanitarian service.

Every guest a gift from God

Badi was a Kist woman. The Kist are a Sunni Muslim community closely related to the Chechens, who live on the other side of the Greater Caucasus range. In the eighteenth century, the Kist came to settle in the Pankisi Gorge—a remote valley in northeastern Georgia—and some adjoining provinces such as Tusheti and other parts of Kakheti. At the time, they were refugees. But today, the estimated 7,000 to 10,000 Kist in the region are Georgian citizens, bear Georgian surnames and speak Georgian, Russian, varying levels of English, and despite their forced relocation and adaptation to Georgian society and language, the Kist managed to preserve their own Chechen dialect along with a range of culture and traditions.

At the foot of the snowy Caucasian peaks, the Pankisi Valley boasts some breathtaking landscapes. The valley is narrow, with little agricultural land, surrounded on both sides by mountains where farmers bring their cattle in the summer. The main road crossing the Pankisi is a dead end that continues after the last houses and an impressive police station as a bumpy

FIGURE 2.1 Makvala Margoshvili sitting in her bedroom and wearing the green robe she used for religious ceremonies and for performing with her musical ensemble. Courtesy of Julien Prebel.

and rocky path sinking into the forest. The small region is also the starting point for adventurous treks to the high mountains, such as the dream-like and secluded region of Tusheti, with its ancient stone villages.

Although listed since 2020 in the Lonely Planet guidebook, the narrow valley is far from being a mainstream tourist destination. Along with several other Western governments, the U.S. State Department cautions visitors against traveling there due to the "current security environment and the potential for civil unrest."[8] For years, Georgian and international media alike depicted the small territory as a dark place full of criminals, militants, religious extremists, and terrorists.[9] In other words: In the newly independent Christian-majority country of Georgia, Kists were the "Other."[10]

While words like terrorism, jihad, warlords, and blood feuds have long been associated with the region—being bantered around by the likes of the BBC[11] and Reuters[12]—the Kist insist they are simply a proud people, honest and fair, with an almost stoic character, forged in the mountains and ravines they call home. They value friendship, they say, to the point of being willing to give their life for the other if necessary. But above all, the Kist are known for their hospitality.

Intrepid travelers still made their way there, however. And when they arrived, Badi was ready to welcome them. There is a popular Georgian saying that a guest is a gift from God. Among the Kist, this means more than accommodation. It is about preparing lavish feasts with countless regional dishes like *zhizhig galnash*, liberally stuffed beef Chechen dumplings and *khachapuri*, Georgia's national pie, typically filled with cheese. And so, like her Orthodox neighbors, Badi cherished hospitality. "We spent our life hosting people," her daughter-in-law, Nata, said as she was busy preparing food for a relative's birthday. "20 years ago, all tourists would be directed to her family and she received them without money,"[13] said Eter Tsikhesashvili, a neighbor who is also a member of the local women's elder council, an institution that amplifies women's voices and interests in a context that remains predominantly patriarchal. "She had so many guests that close relatives and neighbors were helping."

Badi was on a mission to present Kist people and their culture in a positive light to the outside world, to foster mutual understanding and build peace through relationships. And food. Lots and lots of food. She steadfastly believed the people she received—and fed like the kings of old—in her home would become ambassadors for her community and help counter bias in the wider world.

Seeking solace in the shadow of the Soviet Union

Part of this involved introducing guests to the peculiarities of local traditions. One Czech geographer Vincenc Kopeček, recalling his first encounter with Badi when he first arrived and opened the door of her house, said, "I was completely shocked: 'It's great, our neighbor died, we can take you to the funeral,' said this woman sitting in the yard."[14]

More than host, Badi was a community champion after the fall of the Soviet Union, at a time when she was already in her fifties. During Georgia's Soviet period from 1921 to 1991, civil activism was limited, and personal initiatives were deterred. The fall of the USSR meant more freedom in a sense, but also economic recession, corruption, and instability. Even though citizens could participate more freely in political, business, and humanitarian activities, they remained limited in other ways. Further north, Chechnya also declared its independence. But unlike Soviet republics, Russia found it hard to accept the secession of one of its own provinces. Two bloody wars ensued (from 1994 to 1996 and again from 1999 to 2009) and Chechnya remained in Russian hands. During the second conflict, newly elected Russian president Vladimir Putin not only shattered Chechen hopes for self-governance but tightened his grip on the Russian state and post-Soviet society.

At the time, Georgia tried to exit Moscow's orbit and endear itself to Western powers. Following a rigged election, citizens took to the streets of Tbilisi in November 2003 and forced President Eduard Shevernadze—a former communist leader—to resign. New elections brought to power the leader of a peaceful revolution. Educated in Ukraine and the United States, Mikheil Saakashvili,[15] 36, wanted to rid Georgia of corruption, crime, and its lingering Soviet legacy. There was no easy escape for those looking to flee the landlocked territory, like the Kists in the eighteenth century before them. One of the few options available to them was to take a long and perilous journey across the Caucasus to the Pankisi Valley. As they arrived in their thousands, local infrastructures were quickly overwhelmed. Badi remembers gathering with a group of women at Duisi's old mosque, with its sinuous minaret made of black and red bricks. "With tears and with all our hearts, we prayed for peace in the Caucasus and all over the Earth," Badi said. "I was hosting one Chechen refugee at my place and, in general, I helped them as much as I could."

Performing Peace in the Caucasus

After our interview, Badi posed for a portrait, sitting in her bedroom. She was wearing the white veil and green robe that she put on when she was leading a singing ensemble, gathering women from the local Sufi community. A member of the Qadiriyya Sufi order—a widespread order with *tekke* in India, Bangladesh, China, Turkey, Indonesia, Afghanistan, Pakistan, the Balkans, Russia, Palestine, as well as in East and West Africa—Badi created a women's musical ensemble called Aznash in 1995, with the aim of making Kist and Sufi Islamic cultures better known in Georgia and abroad.

But she had even more in mind. Looking to formalize her vision, she founded an NGO in 1999: Marshua Kavkaz (meaning "Peace in the Caucasus" in Chechen). The organization's main objective was to promote the development of rural tourism in Duisi and the surrounding villages. Badi was convinced that if more families were hosting visitors, it would not only foster economic development but put an end to the negative stereotypes plaguing the Pankisi Valley.

For all her enthusiasm, Badi lacked the know-how. After decades of single-party rule, neither she nor anyone around her had the experience of setting up and managing a nonprofit. Following its creation, the NGO mostly remained an empty shell and only organized a few workshops on rural tourism in the late 2000s with some token support from the Polish state. At one point during our conversation, Badi went to one of her rooms to find a small, printed directory with names of big NGOs and foreign organizations that provide funding for grassroot activities. The pages were dog-eared, and some names had blue marks next to them, singling them out for potential financial aid. She would write letters advocating for supporting the Kist community and culture, travel to the capital Tbilisi to have them translated into English and then send them by post or fax to Europe using the addresses and phone numbers listed in the repertory.

All her efforts were in vain. "Georgia is a poor country, I never really relied on the state," Badi said, "I was hoping more for more attention from foreign philanthropists." Badi remembers one tourist from London who gave her 200 Lari (around US $75). "I was so happy as though it was 2 million," she said with a laughter.

Not all Badi's initiatives were unsuccessful. The musical ensemble she founded quickly gained attention and started to tour abroad, performing folk songs and Sufi rituals at music festivals in Türkiye and across Europe. To reach that achievement, she first had to battle with her own community's recalcitrance. "The resistance I met back then was huge," she said, "I went through a lot of hardship, constantly looking for an appropriate place for rehearsals. Sometimes we were even gathering in an abandoned building over the river and cleaning it took us a week or so," she said.

According to Nata, people in Duisi would not give their support for several reasons. Margoshvili was already too old when she started to be socially active. She wanted to initiate projects in fields where she was not trained. She was not fitting into the traditional framework for what Kist women were meant to be. Meant to do. Even if they were accomplished professionals, women were expected to not be so outspoken and active in the public sphere. When talking with villagers, most confirmed that Makvala was alone in her struggle. "But social pressure didn't work on her," Nata said with a sense of pride.

Not all exemplars are born equal

After enjoying Badi's hospitality, I spent a few more days in the Pankisi Valley, wandering along the river. Kids were bathing, youth were playing volleyball, and horses were galloping. As I left on the only road exiting the valley, I thought I'd come at the right time. Margoshvili's memory was fading and to record her life was, in a way, to share the message she so badly wanted to deliver to the wider world.

At the same time, I could not help but wonder what Margoshvili could have achieved had she lived in another environment, another context, another valley. What if she was born in a country with a long-standing civil society and volunteering culture? What if she could get the support of a well-organized religious denomination? What if the Georgian state had a more proactive stance toward minorities like the Kist? Not all societies and religious communities support cultural and humanitarian action in the same way. Not all exemplars are born equal. Resources needed to succeed in such a situation, things like organizational skills, social and political capital, support for entrepreneurship, and the culture of giving are not only personal, but embedded in the collective, cemented—or not—in society.

It can be easy, when compared to other exemplars, to discount Badi Margoshvili. To assume she had not accomplished all that much. No foreign investment. No major impact. No awards or accolades. Just a bunch of boxwoods appealing for peace and a table always ready to serve. Her story is one that may not inspire as much as it confronts us to rethink what accomplishment means. Maybe it is not just about maximizing the number of beneficiaries and bringing in big numbers. Instead, maybe it is deeply connected to the ability of one individual—with the help of allies—to break through social, economic, and cultural boundaries.

Badi's story can also teach us another lesson: Not to be shortsighted when it comes to assessing someone's work. In many respects, Badi failed. But the seeds she planted have radically changed the Pankisi Valley. Despite the pushbacks, Badi gradually became a role model for a younger generation of Kist women—a generation of women less constrained by the past and more open to the future and the world around them. Her musical ensemble has lived on and developed into a more professional outfit, as well.

But above all, her idea of developing rural tourism in the Pankisi has finally come true. There are now eight guesthouses run by women in the valley. There may be no gift shop with plastic snow globes—and perhaps that is for the best—but there are guided walking tours, horseback adventures in the hills, and cooking workshops on offer for visitors to enjoy.

And, since 2018, an NGO called the Pankisi Valley Tourism and Development Association (PVTDA) brings together a collective of guesthouse owners, guides, and local cheese and honey producers. Their aim is to "elevate Pankisi Valley and the Kist community onto the global stage, through promoting Kist culture and sustainable ecotourism." Led by women, the organization provides English language training for guides and youth, supports local heritage rehabilitation, and collaborates with book and exhibition projects promoting Kist culture. On their website's homepage is a picture of Makvala, who they call a "visionary pioneer."

PVTDA's director is 36-year-old Nazy Dakishvili, a former public servant who worked in Tbilisi before moving back to Jokolo, a village a few kilometers from Duisi, to open her own guesthouse in 2012. Meticulously renovating her family dwelling, Nazy's accommodations are a far cry from Badi's. If staying at Badi's is about informality and serendipity, being invited to local funerals, and folding in with the locals, Nazy's attention to detail is up to a modern cosmopolitan's highest travel standards. Prices and eating hours are clearly marked on a board, there is a small corner with books about the Caucasus and print versions of a few travel articles hand-selected by Nazy. There is a parking lot for cars and a huge vine trellis covering the garden in front of the house, providing shelter from the heat during the summer months.

"Tourism is the only viable industry because we don't have huge lands for agriculture," said Nazy, who was wearing a thin blue veil around her shoulders and belongs to the local Sufi community. "I see more and more people involved in the tourism industry, but I want to avoid mass tourism. I don't want our traditions to change because of tourism," she added. An assertion Badi Margoshvili would have full-heartedly endorsed.

3

Health Care

You are not much of an example ... of the love of Christ if you take off when things get tough.

TOM CATENA (EVANGELICAL CATHOLIC)

If there is one thing that my relationship with God teaches me, it is compassion. It makes me ready to serve in such a difficult time as Ebola.

NOÉ KASALI (PROTESTANT)

The Quran is not coming from Allah just to be read. Religion is your behavior. It's not just theory, not just for reading. It's your life.

MUHAMMAD ELGAZZAR (MUSLIM)

Simply by becoming aware, we plant the seeds of transformation.

BART WEETJENS (BUDDHIST)

Introduction

Tom Catena is the only doctor for a population of nearly a million people in Sudan's Nuba Mountains. He fashions himself an "evangelical Catholic," whose first stop every morning at 6:30 a.m. is Mass before he heads to rounds and surgery. The area he works in, wrote Don Miller, is "a desolate, rebel-held area that was bombed repeatedly from 2011 until 2018 by the Khartoum government when Omar al-Bashir was president."[1] Catena is often asked why he gave up a potentially lucrative career in his native

United States to instead become a medical missionary with the Catholic Medical Mission Board, beginning in 2008.

Likening himself to bank robber Willie Sutton, who responded when asked why he robbed banks with the pithy line, "because that's where the money is," Catena felt called to go where there was the greatest medical need. When Catena arrived in Nuba in 2008, there were no hospitals and no clinics in an area roughly the size of the U.S. state of Georgia. Now, there are numerous trained nurses and midwives, qualified medical officers and doctors, along with Catena himself, who still performs weekly surgeries.

Both Catena's story and the Nuba region's needs underscore how health-care access remains one of humanity's greatest and most pressing disparities. According to the World Health Organization's (WHO) 2024 report on world health, not only has the average global life expectancy decreased (thanks in part to the impact of the Covid-19 pandemic), but the world is far behind its goal of expanding access to health coverage to 1 billion more people by 2025. Though 585 million more people have health care as of 2024 than in 2018, there are 4.5 billion—more than half the global population—without access to "essential health services without incurring catastrophic health spending." Particularly vulnerable are migrants, refugees, and other displaced or asylum-seeking populations. Though they are not "inherently less healthy" according to the WHO, they often face suboptimal health conditions and often limited access to health care, creating a massive disparity in comparison to host populations and higher rates of illness, suffering, and mortality.[2]

Even though many of our worst fears were not realized during the Covid-19 pandemic, it was an "apocalypse" nonetheless. The pandemic was an apocalypse in the sense of its original, Greek meaning: A revealing. The pandemic further exposed the various, overlapping levels of inequality and discrepancies in access to resources of care. At a time when we might have come together despite our differences to confront a common challenge, the Covid-19 pandemic seemed to only deepen divisions and curdle existing inequalities. In the future, as the world faces the calamitous effects of climate change, quickly aging populations in numerous nation-states and rapid-spreading global pandemics and non-communicable diseases, weak and limited health-care infrastructures will only exacerbate the damage.

Enter this chapter's exemplars. Each of their narratives illustrates how religious actors play a significant role in health-care delivery, influencing various aspects of patient care, health-care practices, and an individual's or community's overall well-being. Furthermore, their stories illustrate that religion's impact on health care is multifaceted, encompassing spiritual, ethical, and cultural dimensions. At the same time, their stories are further testimony to how religious actors of various traditions advocate for change, providing new systems of care, or challenge existing health-care infrastructures they feel do not meet the needs of vulnerable populations. Their impacts are shown in various subfields of health care as well, including psychological care, reproductive medicine, care for older adults, and vaccine distribution.

At the same time, their stories are not clean cut. Nor do they always sit comfortably with one another. Their narratives challenge some notions of health-care delivery and do not always fit accepted norms within the global health-care community. This chapter does not seek to cast judgment on their practices or positions, but simply to present them as they are. These exemplars are not angels. They are not innocent. Their hands are dirty and some of their decisions questionable. They are human beings, with all the variety and character; muck, mess, and magnificence; faults, foibles, and failures that implies. Each journalist endeavored to share the whole person, rather than a caricature to fit our prefixed notions of who an exemplar should be or what opinions they should hold. In this way, their accounts are examples of "ethnographic journalism," which helps make the strange, familiar and the familiar, strange.[3] It also helps make their stories all that much more interesting and important. What happens to them, and what they think, say, and do, is crucial to our shared life on Earth.

As profiled by Shaina Sealy, Noé Kasali—the father, mental health counselor, and evangelical pastor—provides counseling, believing it is critical for personal and community transformation in the Democratic Republic of Congo, where his people have suffered political violence and resulting trauma for decades. Moreover, his counseling practice, focused on providing care, love, and compassion, is grounded in his Christian faith. In 2018, Noé and his team at the Bethesda Counseling Center responded to an Ebola outbreak in the Beni region. Noé developed alternative burial rituals for people who could not safely inter their loved ones during the epidemic. At the same time, Noé and his colleagues provided psychological support for health-care workers on the frontlines and grief counseling for family members of Ebola victims. Together, Noé and his team learned valuable lessons they were able to apply to the next great pandemic.

Meanwhile, Catalan physician, Benedictine nun, and social activist Teresa Forcades i Vila is routinely called, "Europe's most radical nun." A one-time politician who left the Benedictine order from 2015 to 2018 to campaign for Catalan independence from Spain, Forcades i Vila is known for her public disagreements with the Catholic Church's position on reproductive rights, contraception, same-sex marriage, and women's ordination. She is also a vocal critic of pharmaceutical companies. The latter position helps explain, at least in part, her notoriety as a vaccine skeptic during the heights of the Covid-19 pandemic. Profiled by Linda Freund, Forcades i Vila's story highlights the various vicissitudes and fraught politics of health care, along with the nun's radical desire to protect and defend the rights of the vulnerable, marginalized, and oppressed, even when facing intense criticism from those in positions of authority.

Masue Katayama of Yokohama, Japan, is a devout Catholic who has spent four decades of her life creating nursing homes and childcare facilities in the most aged society in the world. Born into a Buddhist family during the Second World War, Katayama converted to Catholicism and credits the church as the source of many of her entrepreneurial ideas to help and serve Japan's aging population. As founder of the Social Welfare Corporation Shinko Fukushikai, Katayama is more than a business leader—an idea-maker according to Magdaléna Rojo, who profiled her. In Rojo's telling, she has set trends in social service, such as meeting international standards for quality management in nursing home care; improving the quality of public housing; employing immigrants, the unhoused, and other marginalized groups; and making nursing homes places where the wider community—and multiple generations—gather and connect.

Finally, Kezevino Aram's story illustrates the holistic approach many faith actors take to providing health care and addressing issues related to medical policy in the context of their calling. Aram, who is both a medical doctor and leader of a religious organization, engages in work that is multifaceted (including childhood immunization programs, food distribution, preventive pediatric interventions, interreligious peacemaking, addressing the root causes of childhood poverty and violence, etc.), involves multiple stakeholders (policymakers, religious leaders, local youth, academics, medical professionals, civil society organizations), and is multivalent, operating at both the grassroots level and prioritizing policy engagement at the local, regional, national, and intergovernmental levels. Her work, alongside that of Noé Kasali, Teresa Forcades i Villa, and Masue Katayama, illustrates again how these are not contrasting, but complementary approaches to religiously informed health care—or, for that matter, spiritually engaged humanitarianism.

"More than a Hundred Trees"

Noé Kasali (Protestant/Democratic Republic of the Congo)

By Shaina Sealy

The car was covered in orange dust when Noé Kasali and two of his colleagues pulled into the small town of Mangina, in the far east of the Democratic Republic of Congo, near the border with Uganda. They had driven about an hour down winding and bumpy roads from their clinic in the city of Beni, only some 20 miles away. While it was a warm day in late summer, Noé and his colleagues all wore long sleeve shirts. And long pants. "We did not have any PPE [personal protective equipment] with us. We came just wearing simple, simple clothes," he said. It was August 2018, during one of the largest Ebola outbreaks the region had ever known.

Noé and his colleagues got out of the car, walking toward a brick church with a rusted metal roof. Dozens of people were sitting outside, waiting on him and his colleagues. Noé approached them but tried to not get too close. The same public health guidelines that restricted funeral attendance stopped him from making physical contact with patients. Instead of shaking hands, he looked each person in the eye, saying in Kiswahili, "Poli poli. We are together. And we are sorry for what happened." With compassion, he repeated to each person he saw that day, "Poli poli poli poli … We are just so sorry," he said, over and over again.

Noé introduced himself and his colleagues as mental health counselors. Slowly, the people gathered around in a circle, raising their hands to speak. Noé called on a short woman, sitting by herself, Katoomba Kenyatole. Within three months, Ebola had killed her mother, grandmother, five siblings, four aunts, and two cousins. Kenyatole told Noé that her remaining family had warned her not to trust him and demanded that she stay away from this very kind of gathering. Kenyatole's family said people like Noé were bringing the sickness to the town, Noé recalled. He knew what it was to blame others for a loved one's death. Understanding, empathizing, he listened on. "The Ebola people," Kenyatole told him, "They are the ones who are responsible for death." The Ebola people: Otherwise known as doctors, nurses, Red Cross workers, and burial team volunteers who disposed of infected bodies. And counselors like Noé, who could not heal bodies, but sought to soothe the spirits of those who survived.

Fighting Ebola, fighting fear

Months earlier, Noé could not have imagined he would be working on the front lines of the epidemic. In his mid-thirties, he was pursuing his dream of operating a mental health clinic in his hometown, Beni—the site of fierce political violence in recent decades. After working long days in his clinic, helping heal people from ailments like PTSD and depression, he spent his evenings laughing with his wife, singing with his daughters. "My first and ultimate role," he said, "is to be a good husband to my wife and a good father to my children." When television and radio stations started broadcasting warnings about Ebola, Noé worried about his family first.

When the outbreak began, he was terrified by the degree to which he saw people breaking public health rules. When Red Cross workers tried to help, Noé said, people would attack them in the streets out of confusion and fear. Noé heard stories of youth throwing stones at burial team volunteers when they tried to remove deceased bodies from their homes. "A lot of them would get injured while they are doing this precious work of going to bury people safely," he said.

Some locals believed burial volunteers had actually arrived to kidnap them. Noé started becoming afraid that more people than necessary would die from Ebola in the DRC because people did not trust public health messages. That made the first six months of the Ebola outbreak feel more like a war, he said, a phenomenon he knew all too well.

"A broken boy"

Before Ebola, the DRC had already endured a lot: harsh Belgian colonial rule, abductions that forced people into slavery across the Atlantic, political corruption and violence, forced labor in gold mines and on rubber plantations. The disruption continued after 1960 when Congo became independent. "The country was already very shaky, very fragile," Noé said.

In 1996, when Noé was just sixteen years old, news broke that armed militias—fighting to overthrow the president, leaving hundreds of thousands dead and widespread destruction in their wake—were heading for Beni. He immediately left school. Everywhere, people were running. Once he was home, his siblings told him to pack quickly. "One shoes, one pants, whatever you have put in your small bag, be ready," Noé recalled them saying. "We are leaving right now." Noé and his family were already in mourning. It had only been a few months since their father Ye-Ye Kasali, a well-known evangelical pastor, collapsed and died while gardening. "I was angry at the doctors," Noé said, "because they may have made him die somehow. And I was angry against the world."

With the civil war, Noé only became more incensed. After he, his mother, and siblings fled town on foot, they hid in a shelter built from found materials. Noé didn't know how long they would have to keep hiding, or whether they would make it out alive. His sister didn't. She died of an otherwise preventable illness when she could not access health care on Christmas Day, 1996. She was only in her thirties. "During that time, nobody was even available to come and comfort us as we were burying our sister," Noé said. "That was terrible." Finally, his family got word that their hometown was safe again. A year later, he was back in school. "My grades were very poor," Noé said. "I was a broken boy."

Noé studied just enough to finish high school and enroll in a university near his home. When it came time to choose an area of study, he thought about his scattered family—the people he loved. What they had endured. He wanted to work in a profession that could help people like his family. He also felt inspired by his father's work as a pastor, helping people heal from pain and suffering. So, he chose psychology.

Noé did well in university and, a few years after earning his undergraduate degree, married the love of his life, who had their first daughter in 2012. Around the same time, Noé learned about Wheaton College, a private evangelical university in the United States. There, he could continue studying psychology. But now, through a Christian lens. He applied and won a full scholarship to a graduate program.

In August 2013, he got on a plane to Chicago with his wife and their toddler. Slowly, Noé settled in, starting graduate classes in counseling and psychology. One of the requirements was for students in the program to be enrolled in therapy. When his therapist realized that Noé hadn't grieved his dad, he asked if he would like to. What followed was "a powerful grief journey" in his office, using a model called "the empty chair technique." Noe's therapist sat Noé in a chair facing an empty chair in the middle of the room. Noé was told to envision his father sitting in the empty chair. "I went back to being a young boy," Noé said. "I said, 'Dad, How am I going to go through this life without you?' There was something that was kind of moved out of me, like a weight that has been taken off my shoulders."

Helping others heal

After two years, Noé had earned his advanced degree. Then, he started packing yet again. When his friends and family back home heard he was planning to return, they were incredulous. "You are coming back here?" they exclaimed. "You are coming to this place that is on fire? Don't come. You stay there."

At that time, in 2015, the United Nations called his home province, North Kivu, one of the most volatile regions in the world. Armed groups had a history of sporadic but serious outbreaks of violence and terror, but Noé did think twice about moving back to the DRC. "It's unsafe," he remembered saying. "And how can we go as a family? Now I'm a father." But he resolved to act upon the lyrics of a Gospel song by singer Rob Kenoly: "If you can use anything, well, you can use me ... Take my hands, Lord and my feet. That's my heart. Lord. Speak through me. If you can use anything, Lord, you can use me."

Noé and his family packed their bags and flew home. His goal: Starting a mental health clinic back in Beni, the place of so much pain, but also his home. He was inspired by his father's ministry, which Noé describes as a ministry of love. As a bridge-builder, Noé remembers his father providing aid to all kinds of people, even those who didn't share his faith. "He was really that person who brings people together from different tribes," Noé said.

One year after Noé moved back to the DRC, he opened the Bethesda Counseling Center with four staff members. People of many backgrounds, beliefs, and religions walked, drove, and rode their bikes to the clinic from towns nearby. They would stand in line for hours to get treatment from Noé and his team of mental health professionals. In part, it was because Noé didn't charge his patients. "As soon as people discovered our approach, our work, our services. Whoa," Noé recalled, "the office was packed." Mostly, the team saw people who had experienced domestic violence, depression, and nightmares.

Sometimes, Noé felt helpless. But he continued with the work, sometimes recalling the lyrics, "If you can use anything, Lord, you can use me."

Reinventing ritual

Then, two years after his clinic opened, Ebola reared its ugly head in town. With symptoms including vomiting, diarrhea, and bleeding, Ebola is a rare and deadly disease. Among infected people, the fatality rate ranged from 60 to 90 percent. By all accounts, Ebola is a horrible way to die.

Still, Noé heard rumors that some were saying Ebola was a hoax. The symptoms not real. The town of Mangina reported the most deaths. The survivors there, Noé said, were portrayed as aggressive people, resisting treatment and shirking public health advice. Based on what he had learned through his many years of study, he identified that aggression as a trauma response. These people were not conspiracy theorists. They were not ignorant or unjustifiably angry. Instead, he said, "These people need to grieve."

To help them, he planned to go to Mangina, the epicenter of the virus. At this point, he had three daughters; the eldest was five years old. His wife asked him why he had to keep making dangerous decisions. Noé reminded her that God called him to do this work. "If there is one thing that my relationship with God teaches me, it is compassion," he said. "It makes me ready to serve in difficult times." Still cognizant of his role as a father and husband, Noé evacuated his family to Uganda while he worked with Ebola victims in Mangina.

When he first got to the town, Noé found that, indeed, many people were very angry. A big element of their anger, he said, was that people could not attend their loved ones' burials. "You cannot even come close to the body because of how infectious it is," he said. In normal times, one of the major ethnic groups in North Kivu, the Nande, would wash the dead and clothe them with new clothes. People would come to touch and smell the body, to sing and dance around it, to cry. "The sense of showing up is very important. Without any invitation, people come and come and come and come and come," Noé said. "And all of a sudden you see a huge community of people gathering around the grieving family." During Ebola, trained burial volunteers wearing protective gear picked up bodies to bury them safely—often, in unmarked plots. The absence of ritual, Noé said, detached people from their loss and left them "kind of questioning—if it happened or not." He knew what that was like. He had felt that way when he fled from his hometown during war, losing many members of his own community. "I remembered my sister," Noé said, "and then I knew exactly what we lacked here."

What he and his staff could do for the living was to somehow recreate the rituals they had lost—to help them grieve. That, Noé thought, might help them work through their denial and, by extension, their anger, ultimately changing their responses to the disease itself. Noé remembered an email a colleague had sent over a Wheaton alumni list-serve. It contained a link to a technique called "a goodbye letter," which grieving people could write to the people they'd lost. Noé sensed it was similar to the empty chair exercise his therapist had walked him through in graduate school. The letter would help people say goodbye. Noé translated and printed the letter. On it was a space to write the name of the person who died. "It was a breakthrough when I found that tool," he said.

With public health a top priority, the letter exercise became part of a grieving program Noé developed with his team in Mangina. During group sessions, survivors shared stories about their deceased relatives. They brought photos, prayers, music. All of it helped fill in for what they'd traditionally done at burials. "They'll say, 'My loved one was a carpenter.' Another will say 'He was a farmer,'" Noé said. One woman wrote a letter to her mother. When she read it out loud in front of a dozen people, she held a flower she had picked outside. "[She] started to say her words while she was touching that flower and it was so much tears, but the flower fell from her hand," Noé recalled. "She went down on the floor and put her hands on the flower. That's the part that really, really touched me."

The last step in Noe's program replicated a Nande graveside ritual called *Mahima Mojarro*. In it, people cover the grave with seeds. Three or four months later when they return to visit the gravesite, flowers had bloomed. Many Ebola survivors couldn't identify where their relatives were buried. So, Noe's team told families to choose a tree and a special place to plant it. Some requested fruit trees, he said, because one day they could eat the fruit from that tree. Others decided on trees that provided a lot of shade to sit under. Katoomba Kenyatole—the woman who had challenged Noe's presence in her town—used to sell fresh fruit with her mother. To honor her mom, she chose a tree that produces bright red fruit, something like avocados. People have planted more than a hundred trees around the Beni area in memory of loved ones who died. "The last time I was in Mangina, looking at all the trees that were planted," Noé said, "I really felt the sense of like, 'Yes, there's hope, but also this sense of … then what?'"

Whomever, whenever, wherever

After his experiences with Ebola, and then Covid-19, Noé is convinced pandemics will impact more and more people around the globe, not just in villages like Mangina or cities like Bani. "We're going to face another crisis even larger than what we have already seen," he said.

Beyond these diseases, Noé knows his country has plenty else to heal from. As soon as the Ebola crisis wound down, Noé asked God how he could allow this country to suffer so much. "I told God," Noe said, "This is too much." But Noé's father's ministry and his own faith, he says, grounded him so he could continue to serve. He holds a certain conviction that his role is giving hope to whomever, wherever, and whenever he senses despair. He doesn't want to reflect and regret that he did not do what he was supposed to do when he had the energy to do it. Despite the open questions, the lingering fear of what comes next, Noé says this sense of certainty drives him to serve more and more—whomever, wherever, whenever. Rather than a burden, he counts it an immense blessing.

"The Nun Who Refuses to Be Cancelled"

Teresa Forcades i Vila (Roman Catholic/Spain)

By Linda Freund

When Teresa Forcades i Vila took her first vows to become a Catholic nun at Spain's Monastery of Sant Benet de Montserrat, she planted a ceremonial olive tree. Fifteen years later, in 2015, she convened an exclaustration assembly with her Benedictine sisters. The topic: Would Sister Forcades take a break from the nunnery for three years to help revolutionize Catalan politics? That same day her olive tree split right down the middle, damaged by a fallen pine tree. "The sign was there, and I prayed, and I thought, 'Okay, I'll do it,'" Forcades shared with me during an interview at her monastery tucked between the jagged mountains of Montserrat, Spain. The Catalan nun applied a cast to help heal the tree, traded in her habit for a T-shirt, and entered Catalonia's political trenches. Forcades didn't plan to simply enter government, she strove to transform the political system. This move, as radical as it may seem, is in keeping with a life dedicated to disrupting complacency, provoking questions, and bracing for the vilification that often follows.

Principles, politics, and a public referendum

When Forcades entered politics in 2015, momentum was behind her. In 2013, Forcades and economist Arcadi Oliveres co-wrote a manifesto calling for Catalonia's independence from Spain, a nationalized bank and energy sector, a withdrawal from NATO, and fair wages for workers.[4] We will build "the Catalan Republic of the 99%" and the movement will spread "like an oil spill," Forcades said to some 5,000 followers at a 2013 kick-off event in Barcelona.[5] The Procés Constituent party was born, drawing more than 45,000 members overall.

At the time, there was a growing regional push for a referendum to vote on Catalonia's separation from Spain. From 2015 to 2018, Forcades, now independent from the church, worked to spark debates within communities about what the constitution of an independent Catalonia might look like—even floating the idea of running for political office herself. "It was a very clear and explicit attempt to build something socially, a movement that could effect change," she said.

Even during her sabbatical from the church, her reputation as a nun preceded her. Typically, "exclaustration" isn't a complete separation from the church; rather, it's a period for one to contemplate whether she will permanently leave the order or not. For Forcades, this transitory status drew both ire and praise in political circles. Some criticized her for blurring the line between church and state, for espousing an ideology that exacerbated divisions between Catalonia and the central Spanish government. Others praised her role as a contemporary Christian in politics, a refreshing counter to the Catholic Church's decades-long support of the repressive Franco regime, which ruled Spain from 1939 to 1975.

Whatever the opinions, transforming an entire system of government proved no easy feat. Catalonia's regional parliament is composed of several parties with a mix of divergent, overlapping ideologies. Collaboration and coalition-building across these parties is how regional politicians achieve a working majority and elect heads of government. Though the intention is to promote the inclusion of multiple perspectives, Forcades believes this can ironically silence radical ideas—including her own. "As I spoke to different political parties, I could very clearly see that people were all attuned to the fact that you speak one thing inside and a different thing outside," Forcades said. "Even people that seemed to believe what they were saying were not doing the thing that was needed for that change to happen."

In the 2015 Catalan regional election, all 135 parliament seats were up for grabs. Forcades, eager to retain her party's original, decidedly socialist agenda, proposed that Procés Constituent would campaign independently rather than within a coalition. "What is the risk? The risk is that nobody votes for us?" she told an assembly of party members. "That's fine. We can have one seat. Two seats. We'll have complete freedom." Her dissenters argued that building coalitions with other left-leaning parties was an essential part of the democratic process. A vote was cast. Only 10 percent of party members sided with Forcades. "It was like a dream failed," she said. "I was ready to run, to be in parliament. But not if the price to pay was to betray [the ideas]."

In October 2017, Catalonia's regional parliament held a public referendum in which citizens voted on whether Catalonia would become independent from Spain. Madrid declared the process unconstitutional. Police cracked down on voting stations and fourteen senior Catalan officials were arrested for alleged sedition and misuse of public funds. Forcades didn't directly organize the vote, but she was one of several independence supporters to speak at events and across the media. In the end, she re-entered the nunhood a year later. While her efforts didn't result in immediate change, they did prompt an "open debate about the rules of the game."[6]

And the olive tree? When Forcades returned to the monastery and removed its cast, the tree split again, permanently forming two separate trunks. In 2019, a gardener added some nails to reinforce each side. "I thought of the crucifixion," Forcades laughed. "So, it's nailed now, but it's beautiful to me. It's grown very tall, and it gives olives."

Radical roots

Crucifixion: an apt, albeit controversial, metaphor for the reaction to radicals in society. As disruptors of complacency, they rattle the frameworks that people rely on to discuss urgent questions. Their opinions fall outside of mainstream narratives, provoking fiery reactions and debate. Radicals are vilified, censored, canceled. And while their ideas may be unsettling, sometimes even dangerous, they serve a critical function: to force people to confront their biases, debate and sharpen their opinions, and let go of false binaries.

Routinely dubbed "Europe's most radical nun," no third-rail topic is off limits for Forcades. She has publicly challenged the Catholic Church's position on same-sex unions, women's ordination, and abortion, risking censure from the Vatican. A trained medical doctor, she is also known for her criticism of Big Pharma,[7] vaccine skepticism, and promotion of alternative

FIGURE 3.1 Sister Teresa Forcades in the Monastery of Saint Benedict of Montserrat, Spain. Courtesy of Linda Freund.

medicines like sodium chlorite for treating ailments—the latter of which led to the suspension of her medical license in 2023 for 18 months by the College of Doctors of Barcelona (COMB).[8]

For Forcades, the roots of her radicalism can be traced back to childhood. When she was 11 years old, her parents divorced. Being the eldest child, she swallowed her pain to shield her two sisters. She reflected, however, "It remains inside, and it doesn't remain in a positive way." As an adult, she vowed never to closet her thoughts again—never to hold back for the sake of others' feelings. Now, the self-described "radical" aims to point out incongruences, no matter how controversial. "[Radicalism is] something that points to this wanting to be congruent, and not accommodating it," Forcades said. "That's how you sometimes come out with a better solution for all, or how you acknowledge difference, by confronting it." Many of the things society takes for granted today, she said, were made possible by the pursuit of radical ideas, including a woman's right to vote.

The word *radical* originates from the Latin word "radix" which means "root." Radicals, like Sister Forcades, approach societal problems much like a doctor, aiming to expose their root causes rather than just their symptoms. This effort differs from reactionaries like white supremacists or other so-called "radical" extremists who extol hate and promote violence. The reactionary wants to go back in time, to effectively collapse history, while working within the present political-economic framework to achieve their goals. Radicals reveal that the promises society makes are impossible to fulfill within the current structure. Only by changing the entire framework, they profess, can we create a different future.

The news media sets "permissible parameters of debate around acceptable topics and discussion," wrote media scholar and journalist Diane Winston.[9] Through repetition, this sets the cultural and political agenda, "creating and sustaining consensus on everyday reality." When ideas fall outside of these parameters, they are either misinterpreted or deformed to squeeze them into a pre-existing paradigm. Alternatively, they are rejected, sidelined, or left out of the narrative entirely.[10]

Radicals occupy the liminal space outside of standard discourse. Neither here nor there, *ni de aquí, ni de allá*, they occupy the space betwixt and between. Though a more liberal-leaning person may support Forcades's opinions on reproductive rights and feminist theory, for example, they may disagree with her concerns about vaccines for the flu, HPV, and Covid-19. While a practicing Catholic may agree with her call to honor the dignity of laborers by giving them fair wages, he or she may disagree with her support for abortion rights.

This tension presents a challenge for the press and the public when working with Forcades: Can you only engage with a radical if you agree with their ideas? If you disagree with one perspective they hold, do you silence or discredit them entirely? And how does your reaction limit the conversations we have and the stories we tell?

"I want to be a nun"

Teresa Forcades was born in Catalonia, Spain, in 1966, during the authoritarian rule of Francisco Franco, a Spanish military general who led Nationalist forces in overthrowing the Second Spanish Republic, ruling Spain as a dictator until his death in 1975. From an early age, she harbored a deep distrust of the Catholic Church, who supported the regime. "Without the support of the church, Franco's practices could not have gone on," she said. Then, as a teenager, her mother enrolled her in a Catholic secondary school where she became captivated by quotations from the gospel. "I felt a deep connection, as if they were addressing me personally," she recalled. For many years, she grappled with this tension between her strengthening faith and the church's sordid history.

At first, Forcades chose to pursue a career in internal medicine. But then, when the time came to take her medical boards in 1995, she sought out a tranquil place to study: The Monastery of Sant Benet de Montserrat in her native Catalonia. This month-long encounter would dramatically alter the course of her life. "I saw the nuns exiting the chapel and I became conscious of a desire in me." Roaming the grounds, she asked herself: "Can you imagine how good it would be to live like this?"

Coincidentally, the Abbess asked Forcades if she would like to give a presentation to the nuns about the HIV/AIDS epidemic. Forcades, who specialized in infectious diseases, relished the opportunity. This would mark her first radical engagement with the church. "There was no way I was going to talk about AIDS and not mention homosexuality," she said. She decided to "set a trap" to ascertain whether the Benedictine community aligned with her beliefs. While Catholics maintain and promote a variety of perspectives on homosexual orientation, the Catechism of the Catholic Church deems the inclination "unnatural" and homosexual acts contrary to God's will. So, Forcades planned to share the story of her friends—a group of Catholic homosexual priests who clandestinely met to take the Eucharist together so they could feel "that God loved them exactly as they were." She anticipated that the nuns would respond in one of three ways: supportively, dogmatically (reiterating the church's stance on homosexuality), or diplomatically (sidestepping her remarks altogether).

Forcades stood before forty Benedictine nuns and made her case: "My experience as a medical doctor is that people with AIDS have of course physical pain," she said, "but there is also an emotional pain in most of the patients from being rejected by their families." Then Forcades mentioned the third type of pain: spiritual. "Your faith community tells you that God rejects you as you are. Not only as you are passively, but as you want to be actively. You want to love, and you want to love with your whole body." The nuns' responses surprised her. They didn't shy away from, dismiss, or uncritically applaud her account. Instead, they directly engaged with the controversy. They sought additional details about the priests to better empathize with their struggles. In this interaction, Forcades witnessed the distinctive and intriguing promise of nunhood. Nuns are married to Christ but maintain intellectual and spiritual independence. They have the capacity to embrace contradictions, existing simultaneously within and outside the framework of their faith, being both devout and critical. Forcades's mind was set. "I want to be a nun," she said.

Calling the Vatican's bluff

From the early days of Christianity, radical nuns have pushed boundaries and advocated for justice, equality, and social change. Saint Clare of Assisi and Saint Catherine of Siena challenged norms by helping the poor and actively participating in theological and political discussions. In the latter part of the twentieth century, feminist nuns like Sister Elizabeth Johnson and Sister Joan Chittister questioned traditional gender roles in the church and challenged theological frameworks that excluded or marginalized women's voices. Today, a significant number of nuns are advocating for greater leadership roles in the 1.3-billion-member worldwide church, partly in response to abuse scandals, financial improprieties, and a shortage of men pursuing the priesthood. It's due time, they say, for women to be ordained as deacons, and, eventually, priests.[11]

These efforts inspired Forcades, who penned the book *Feminist Theology in History*,[12] in which she reimagined theological arguments and religious practices that subjugate women, finding an opening for radical reinterpretation of Catholic Christian beliefs.[13] "I don't like the sexist aspects [of the church], and I fight for them to be changed," Forcades told me. "But it's not only discrimination that I find in the church. I find much more nourishment. And that's why I'm not an idiot by staying in the church."

For someone as outspoken as Sister Forcades, she doesn't just choose to stay in the church—she must often fight to stay there. In 2009, during an appearance on the Catalan interview-news program "Singulars," Forcades said all women should have the "morning-after" pill in their purses.[14] Appearing in her nun's habit, she clarified, "The medicine makes it highly improbable for conception to occur." This led to backlash from conservative Christian news outlets, branding her as "The Abortion Nun" and "The Nun of the Devil." "I could not breathe normally when I read this," Forcades said. The Vatican urged Forcades to retract her views and face discipline. She refused. Then she raised the stakes, sending the Vatican a full theological case for abortion rights that she argued was both "compatible with the Gospel" and "defendable within the church."

According to Catholic belief, in the words of Pope Francis: "Abortion is murder. Those who carry out abortions kill."[15] Sister Forcades's take: "The fetus or the embryo, it's a very particular form of life because it's within another. It's within a mother who must be able to make decisions in her life as a full human being." Drawing on Immanuel Kant's philosophy, she asserted that all individuals, regardless of their status, possess equal intrinsic worth and dignity. "You have two fundamental principles at play: the dignity of a human being (the pregnant person) that cannot be instrumentalized, and the sanctity of life," she said. "What happens when those two conflict? You better let God, and the woman sort it out." The Vatican did not reply to her dispatch, nor was she punished.

Blowing up binaries

Forcades is quick to clarify she's not a "pro-choice" nun. Calling her "pro-choice" limits the possibility that she can simultaneously believe in the sanctity of life *and* the right to an abortion. Her radical proposal: To escape the tyranny of the anti/pro binary by reimagining the abortion debate entirely.[16]

Indeed, when tackling controversial topics, Forcades straddles the intersection between theology and the sciences. She holds both a medical degree from the University at Buffalo School of Medicine and a Master of Divinity from Harvard Divinity School. These fields may seem distinct, one based on empirical evidence, the other rooted in faith, but they share the common pursuit of a foundational truth, Forcades says, which is what drives her—no matter the discipline. It's just one more binary Forcades's work calls into question.

In the church, Forcades is both critical, and representative, of the institution. The same goes for the medical field, where she questions established scientific beliefs about vaccine safety yet still identifies as a woman of science. Within the disciplines of science, as within theology, she resists the public's compulsion to force her into one category or the other. "In science, you are not *anti*, and you are not *pro*," Forcades told me. "I absolutely do not have the 'vaccines are bad' dogma. I'm just saying if the evidence is not there, let's get it," she said, "but you cannot express something like this without being labeled anti-vax or pushed by polemics that are completely out of place."

Necessary accountability or dangerous conspiracy?

In 2009, during the H1N1 "swine flu" pandemic, Forcades condemned a proposal for a mass vaccination campaign. Why force vaccination if "this new virus has a lower mortality rate than the common flu," she asked in an online video that garnered more than one million views. For Forcades, the video—presented with evidence from medical journals and established press—was an opportunity to provoke urgent questions: Is it possible for for-profit incentives to align with public health objectives? Can we trust profit driven corporations to provide safe vaccines? She took particular aim at Baxter, one of the health-care companies responsible for distributing the annual flu vaccine. In February 2009, Baxter sent flu vaccines to Europe that were contaminated with a mixture of H3N2 seasonal flu viruses and unmarked H5N1 viruses, resulting in the death of lab ferrets. If their contents had been administered to the public, the results could have been mass contagion and death. Though the specific cause of the incident is unclear, Baxter chalked it up to human and technical error.[17]

Forcades was skeptical, however, suggesting that there is a low probability for error in secure medical environments that require high-level clearance. She went on to insinuate something controversial, if not conspiratorial: What if the mix-up had been intentional? What if Baxter were creating the viruses they planned to vaccinate against? The 2009 pandemic was declared just a few months after the detection of the contaminated lab materials, a fact Forcades found suspicious. After that, Baxter was tasked with administering a new vaccine to protect the public. How could the public trust Baxter's vaccine, she asked. "I won't wish it on me, on my child, nor anyone close to me."

While many viewers praised her candor, others called her proposal unsubstantiated, marred in half-truths, and outright dangerous. Forcades herself felt conflicted about her proclamations. "The spectacular nature of talking about international plots, global mass murder, shadows of the other side … I think it's self-defeating," she admitted in the video's conclusion. "I mean, now I would have liked not to have said it." Still, she asked that people use her research and provocations to make their own informed decisions.

Her distrust of the medical industry is informed by experiences during a three-year medical residency in the United States at Buffalo General Hospital, Erie County Medical Center, and the Roswell Park Cancer Institute. These institutions had significantly different protocols compared to her home country of Spain, where residents enjoy universal health-care coverage. In the United States, Forcades said, hospitals prioritized profit over patients, turning doctors into "eyes with dollar signs, like Scrooge McDuck."

Forcades pointed to the diagnostic billing categories she was required to use. "These are categories we use to bill the patient, but, as a physician, why do I need to be trained in billing categories?" she asked. Consider *hyperkalemia*, the presence of high potassium in the blood. "If the limit is five and my patient has five-point-one that means nothing," she explained. Typically, a doctor would disregard such minor variations, as potassium levels can naturally fluctuate from day to day. "But of course the hospital can bill for hyperkalemia, so then I had to make sure hyperkalemia was written." This practice could lead to frivolous tests and risk burdening the patient with an incorrect diagnosis (a.k.a., a pre-existing condition), which might, in turn, jeopardize their future insurance coverage.

During the Covid-19 pandemic, the now nun made news for questioning the safety and efficacy of the vaccines. Forcades pointed to documented side effects of the mRNA-based technology, from menstrual irregularities to blood clots. "There is a lot of uncertainty about the long-term effects," she told Vilaweb, a Catalan news site in 2021.[18] She argued that pharmaceutical companies lacked incentives to rigorously monitor and prevent these side effects and attributed this situation to a precedent initiated by U.S. President Reagan to grant "immunity for companies" and designate pharmaceuticals as an essential public service, leading these companies to prioritize profit over public health.

She faced criticism for allegedly leveraging her position as a nun to mislead the public during a time when the global economy was reliant on reducing transmission rates through vaccination. The public consensus: Even questioning vaccines during a pandemic contained the embers of a public health disaster. Vaccine hesitancy could lead to unnecessary deaths, critics argued. Forcades rebutted in a 2021 interview with *The New York Times*: "The answer cannot be that in the time of a crisis, society cannot allow criticism—it's precisely then that we need it."[19]

Thinking in a radical age

"Western democracies," wrote British journalist Jamie Bartlett, "are entering an age of radicalism." From the rise of extreme weather events and the threat of artificial intelligence to Brexit and Trumpism, assumptions about what is either possible or acceptable are changing fast. The digital age has brought on a rapid flood of memes, articles, and information. What should spark more critical engagement has, instead, created polarized echo chambers.

Instead of blindly accepting received wisdom, radicals like Forcades invite us to critically examine difficult or contradictory views. "It's so easy to be immature," Immanuel Kant wrote. "If I have a book to serve as my understanding, a pastor to serve as my conscience, a physician to determine my diet for me, and so on, I need not exert myself at all. I need not think."[20]

Forcades aims to break people from exactly this: "self-imposed immaturity." Whether the public is engaged or enraged by her ideas, the key is to use those reactions as an opening to ask, what do I really think? Or, even more radically, what do I really know? According to her, this political engagement is not only our prerogative but our *duty*. "I don't want to be ethical only. I want to be political because I think that's what we are called to, from the Gospel," she said. "To not limit ideas to yourself or your immediate community, but to be open to creation."

"If I See There Is a Problem"

Masue Katayama (Roman Catholic/Japan)

By Magdaléna Rojo

Upon entering Crossheart Saiwai Kawasaki nursing home's lobby in Kawasaki, a significant city in the Greater Tokyo area, one is welcomed by a space that bears a striking resemblance to a modern, well-equipped coffee shop. At the heart of the spacious first floor lies a wooden bar boasting a collection of coffee makers for anybody who visits to craft their own cup of coffee. Armchairs and low tables create a cozy setting to savor the warm beverage, while marveling at a beautifully maintained traditional Japanese stroll garden. Less serene, perhaps, there is a kids' playground as well, for the children from the neighborhood or family members of those staying in the nursing home to play in.

Masue Katayama, an 85-year-old Japanese social entrepreneur, decorated the space this way after being inspired by coffee shops in the United States she visited. "A place where everybody can meet and share moments," said Katayama, "where things start happening when people gather, that is what I consider a sense of community." Large windows provide plentiful light in the airy building, well suited for people on wheelchairs or in need of special machines to exercise. In another part of the first floor, a group of older adults can be seen sharing lunch together. They all laugh at some unheard joke. Professional staff is there to attend to any need with respect and empathy. The atmosphere is home-like indeed, just like Katayama intended when she founded her first senior home about four decades ago. She said, "I wanted to create places where people can naturally be who they are."

Setting up standards

The building where Crossheart Saiwai Kawasaki is today, was an elementary school until there were not enough children in the area. The symbolism of such a transition is telling in a country where the proportion of older people is the highest in the world.

Indeed, Japan's population is aging at a rapid rate. By 2024, the elderly population—those 65 and older—constituted about one third of its population. In the past forty years, the number of children in Japan has been declining.[21] In 2022, Japan's population decreased by 800,000 people, with deaths outpacing births at record rates.[22] As a result, schools are closing across the country, just like the one in Kawasaki did. Traditionally, children used to take care of their parents as they aged and needed special attention. Because of this, not many nursing homes existed in Japan before the 1980s.

There were public homes, but they were perceived to be of poor quality and generally avoided. There were also luxurious private homes, but they were only available for more affluent families. Up until the 1980s, there were very few viable options for the middle class to spend their later years in the care of professionals. But due to Japan's rapidly changing demographics, the caretaking of parents by their children became more difficult and, in some instances, unattainable. The demand for affordable homes with high standard services and professional care grew.

Katayama decided to act. By 1986, she was already running a few childcare facilities when she decided to rent a company dormitory, remodeling it into her first private nursing home with a loan from a bank. The facility was filled almost immediately. Knowing the stigma attached to nursing homes, Katayama ensured her nursing homes were held to standards that had never been set before. She guaranteed that all of her nursing homes simulated actual homes in terms of level of comfort, décor, service, and food.

In doing so, Katayama was challenging existing Japanese laws: "In terms of the laws, it always had to be wide enough for at least two wheelchairs. You had to feed people three meals a day," she said. "But maybe some people do not need to eat three times a day," she continued. "You had to take records about everything. The services I was providing challenged these laws," said Katayama, as they transformed care homes from hospital-like to home-like. But Katayama knew these changes needed some kind of standard. And for that, she turned to an unexpected source: The world of manufacturing. By introducing ISO-9001 standards, which until then were criteria used to certify and ensure high standards in manufactured products. Setting up these standards not only helped address the stigma nursing homes faced in Japan but the social standing of their caregivers, who were often undervalued. The changes, she said, proved quite popular.

Over the intervening 15 years, Katayama renovated fifteen abandoned bachelor dorms into private nursing homes. This model of occupying unused buildings was soon copied by other businesses and became a popular practice, gaining its own turn of phrase: *Shinkou-kai*—a model that is affordable while retaining a quality in the nursing care environment.[23]

Inspiration from church

In 1999, however, Katayama's life trajectory, and business outlook, changed dramatically. "It was January and one person with severe dementia went missing," she told me. "She just went outside of the facility alone." Katayama's staff went searching for her but could not find her. It was cold and the patient passed away. Her passing hit Katayama hard. "I was thinking of quitting everything I created," Katayama said.

In the end, the Benesse Corporation, a company active in nursing care and childcare as well as education, bought her business. But after some time, she decided to continue changing the nursing home industry by bettering the quality and thus, nursing homes' public image, which still struggled despite the reforms she introduced. For these purposes, she started Social Welfare Corporation, Shinko Fukushikai,[24] which runs a few dozen public nursing homes, as opposed to the private homes she ran in the 1980s. These group homes not only serve elderly populations, but children and people living with disabilities in the Kanagawa Prefecture, just outside Tokyo.

In contrast to the coffee shop feel in the Crossheart Saiwai Kawasaki nursing home, the entrance to the very first nursing home established under Shinko Fukushikai featured exercise machines. When I arrived, a few people were exercising with them. Apart from the residents of this nursing home, older adults that come for daily care services can also utilize the exercise machines for their workout. Beyond the machines, the home is equipped with only the newest technology. But true to Katayama's style, the human touch is not forgotten. The dayroom has a beautiful view on the surrounding neighborhood. A few residents are playing board games here. Here is where the family members can gather with residents. They are welcome to come at any time of the day. On the other side of the dayroom is a restaurant. Lunch is about to be served. It must be said: Katayama is a big fan of food. So, she makes sure her nursing home residents enjoy high quality, balanced meals. The decorations are also bespoke, decorated with paintings, vases with flowers, and cups with variety of patterns, just like one would have their own home adorned.

FIGURE 3.2 Masue Katayama prepares sushi for her employees. Photo courtesy of Noel Rojo.

Below the first floor is a room where people are brought after they pass away. In Japan, nearly all funeral ceremonies follow the Buddhist tradition.[25] However, in this space, a cross is hanging on one of the walls. Catholics accounted for only 0.34 percent of the overall population of Japan in 2021.[26] Katayama is amongst them. While she does not participate in church activities actively anymore and only goes to masses, she stresses that her Catholic faith has inspired her in her business. "Actually, everything I have learned was inside the church, and that's not an overstatement." For example, Katayama had created space for foreign caregivers long before the Japanese government put in place conditions for their regularization and her Catholic faith inspired her to do so. "I was always moved by things that were happening in the church," she said. For example, when Vietnamese refugees arrived in the 1960s and 1970s, they were in desperate need of help. "I just saw how people in the church were helping each other. I learned so many things," she said.

A Venezuelan nurse greets us in the corridor and is happy he can speak his native Spanish for a moment. Ashoka, an international organization supporting social entrepreneurs across the world, that made Katayama their fellow in 2012, writes that immigrant caregivers back then made up 3.3 percent of the 800 employees, which was considered a significant percentage in a Japanese workplace setting.[27] During those times, it was rare to see foreign caregivers in nursing homes in Japan. The country was still not that open to immigration, despite its changing demographics. The situation started changing after 2017 when the government introduced the nursing care residence qualification, allowing certified foreign caregivers to stay as long as they wanted. The pandemic later on accelerated the growth in the numbers of foreign caregivers even more.[28]

A strange child

Katayama is aware that maybe, if she had grown up in a Catholic home, the actions she observed with Vietnamese newcomers at the church would not have been so surprising. That was not the case, however. Her parents, like many people in Japan, mixed beliefs and practices from Buddhist and Shinto tradition[29] and thus did not have much understanding for her faith. They also did not agree with some of the actions she took for those in need.

Katayama's family were well-off. Her father was a merchant, her mother was from a very respected family of *Ikebana*, or flower arrangers. They escaped the horrors of the Second World War, moving to the countryside. Katayama remembers her father as being very religious. She described what she saw of his devotion: "He would honor his ancestors, especially his father after he passed away. Every morning, he would go to the grave, leave flowers there and pray." But she remembers having a somewhat cold relationship with her mother. "I don't remember her saying anything warm ever," she said. "She did listen to me when I had something to say but she didn't really make food for us," she shared, with a bit of bitterness. When Katayama decided to volunteer at the age of 15 after being moved by a movie about people with disabilities, her parents called her a "strange child." She walked her own path anyways. "In terms of common sense, there is a common sense from my family and a common sense from my church. And the common sense that I learned from the Bible resonates with me much more, especially now that I'm nearing the end of my life," she said. She was challenging her parents the same way she would later challenge Japanese laws.

While Katayama did not find common ground with her family, she found it at church, first becoming Protestant and later converting to Catholicism since she felt that the Catholic Church was not as strict. There was also a U.S. priest who had a particular influence on Katayama. "He taught me that we as human beings are very small and there is a greater power," Katayama remembered. For example, she said, "our church is very small, there's nothing there. But everybody can save ¥5 every day and then they come together to make something out of what they collected. I thought this was something I could apply to my company." And thus, she puts a lot of emphasis on teamwork in her facilities. She also places a high priority on servant leadership. Because her mother never cooked for her, she cooks for her team on a weekly basis on the days when her team meets; a practice she also picked up at church. "In the church kitchen, I loved to make food for everyone almost every day to eat together," she said. Every piece of sushi she wraps is done with evident love and care. While she said she is not a fan of whole day meetings, she can at least lighten the mood with a well-prepared meal.

A greater power

If it seems Katayama is a source of boundless energy and inspiration, she does not attribute it to any innate sense of purpose or calling. Instead, she said, it is the result of a greater power at work in her life. "There is always this unimaginable power that is creating so many miracles," she said, "I am actually just an old lady and there is always this greater power that is surrounding our team and everything what we do." She fashions herself as a woman who simply seeks solutions to the problems she encounters in her life. For example, Katayama said she had to balance her work with her calling as a mother, a path with very few exemplars to follow as she is one of only a handful of female CEOs in Japan. "When I was blessed to have children, I was working and so I had to make a choice," she said. "If I choose work, then I'm neglecting my children and vice versa. This was the issue that led me to establishing childcare facilities first. I just wanted to sort out my own situation," she said. Later, she met a woman at church she was close to. "I went to see her in the hospital once and she was very sad there because of the sad environment. I just wanted to make that sister happy. If I see there is a problem, I turn it into work for myself," Katayama comments on why she started expanding her work to older adults as well.

This has helped her find solutions to multiple problems. After establishing a few dozen childcare and elderly care facilities where she provides support in the most individualized way, and yet with an overall dedication to community, one could say Katayama succeeded in finding solutions for many more people than herself or a single sister. But the scale of her impact has come at a cost. "Normally, when you're this age, you have photos of your grandchildren on your phone screen," she said, "I don't have that on my phone." In order to build what she built, the one thing Katayama said she sacrificed were her children and grandchildren. "I probably inherited this from my mother," she admitted. "I was always working so I wasn't a very good mother to Seiko. She is probably going to just put me in one of my homes that I have created," Katayama said about her daughter who is an executive director at Shinko Fukushikai. "I'm kind of nervous about it. I only have a few hours, a few days. I do not know how much time I have left, but I feel like I want to make the homes better, and I want my staff to be trying harder."

"Joy in Serving the Most Vulnerable"

Kezevino Aram (Hindu/India)

By Ken Chitwood

The township of Kovaipudur has a reputation. Located in the foothills of the Sahyadri Mountain range and part of the city of Coimbatore, in Tamil Nadu, India, the township enjoys gentle mountain breezes and monsoon rains that create a generally serene setting amidst lush vegetation. Cooler than the rest of the city, locals look to Kovaipudur as a respite from the urban heat bubble. Kovaipudur is also known as the home of Shanti Ashram, an international center for development, learning, and collaboration founded by Dr. M. Aram and Mrs. Minoti Aram in 1986 on the Gandhian principle of *Sarvodaya* (progress for all). According to Shanti Ashram's records, its community work impacts more than 250,000 people in Coimbatore and its environs, providing a different kind of respite for those in need of access to various forms of care.

Dr. Kezevino Aram has been leading the ashram as its president since 2014. Through her hands-on, collaborative approach, Aram has responded to numerous challenges and crises in her community—most recently the Covid-19 pandemic. She has developed a pattern for dialogue and policy development based on convening multiple voices from various communities. With a particular focus on involving women and children, Aram has helped further establish Shanti Ashram as a center for learning, development, and collaborative action that addresses inequalities, provides care during catastrophe, and produces leaders for future development.

"Our faith does not permit us to talk alone"

Aram first attended medical school in Coimbatore before serving as a doctor at Shanti Ashram for several years. She then pursued a master's degree in public health at Harvard University, with a double major in children's and international health. Returning to Shanti Ashram, she has been key to the process of developing its capacities to address poverty alleviation, provide health services and leadership training, as well as support and convene interreligious dialogue.

For Aram, Shanti Ashram's founding principles and 36-year legacy continue to inspire their work today. "We were founded on Gandhian principles and Gandhi said that our faith does not permit us to talk alone. It's not enough to just speak a good word, we have to take the next step: useful action in the community," she said, "we must find a link between what we think, what we see, and what we do together." Aram's father began with the idea that the ashram could address global issues *and* meet the needs of vulnerable communities in Coimbatore and its surroundings. Working in conjunction with community stakeholders, Shanti Ashram has programs that focus on literacy, food insecurity, education, vocational training, psychological well-being, interreligious dialogue, and health care. Aram said, "the scale of these problems requires convening."

Convening means they must be addressed as shared challenges requiring collaboration at the global, regional, and local levels, she said. The emphasis on convening is based on Shanti Ashram's commitment to human interconnectedness, their belief that every human being has something to offer, and the awareness that democratic institutions have shown that working together is a proven way of making progress. "Shanti Ashram is a place to come together for social action," said Aram, "we can write the best policies, but we have to learn from people on the frontline—mostly women—who work at the interface between evidence and experience. We are asked not only to think together but challenged to build upon each other's comparative advantages. Strengths have to be multiplied, and challenges responded to together," she said.

Covid-19: A once-in-a-century situation

That emphasis on working together has come into sharp focus for Aram when confronting the Covid-19 pandemic. "We are in the midst of a once-in-a-century situation," Aram told me at the time, "convening is helping us cope with the crisis and come out of it stronger, more resilient, but also more trusting." Dr. Aram and Shanti Ashram have been particularly active during the pandemic. The state government even invited Aram to be part of the expert committee formed to tackle the Covid-19 pandemic at the national level. At the local level, Aram and the ashram's women's health team helped organize a "Marathon for Solidarity" fundraiser, which received a 20,000 EUR donation from Pope Francis. Through their food bank, medical facilities, and training centers for female entrepreneurs, Shanti Ashram came to the aide of 50,000 children and their families in the villages around Coimbatore during the pandemic. Along the way, they vaccinated over 3,000 people.

Beyond vaccinations, Shanti Ashram also provides holistic help for vulnerable communities. To that point, Aram shared that the ashram is inspired by one of the final notes left behind by Mahatma Gandhi in 1948, in which he wrote:

> I will give you a talisman ... Recall the face of the poorest and the weakest man or women whom you may have seen, and ask yourself, if the step you contemplate is going to be of any use to him or her ... Then you will find your doubts and yourself melt away.

For Dr. S.R. Subramanian, Program Coordinator at the Shanti Ashram, this quote stays with him when he is facing the sheer immensity of needs in his community. The confluence of challenges that Covid-19 forced upon the poor and vulnerable weighed heavily on Subramanian in particular. But as he contemplates Gandhi's wisdom, he considers the ashram's approach to addressing overlapping issues, saying, "Shanti Ashram is a creative laboratory where we come *together* to address the problems faced by our community," he said. "We work with the people we serve to find common solutions."

Chief among those solutions? Vaccination. At Shanti Ashram, vaccination is more than a means to fight a particular disease. It is a kind of talisman that provides the opportunity to address a range of issues, Subramanian said. "Vaccines are a way for us to address the holistic health of the communities we work with," he said, "and it's proving the first step in helping individuals, families, and religious communities integrate multiple aspects of health into their everyday life."

Health "not merely the absence of disease or infirmity"

Aram said their focus on vaccination comes from two sources: science and the scriptures she and others turn to at the ashram. Both speak to the multivalent nature of challenges like the Covid-19 pandemic. "Science and scripture tell us things do not develop in isolation," said Aram. "They are connected to other societal dynamics like physical and mental well-being. This pandemic has highlighted the importance of health in all its dimensions: mental, physical, social, and spiritual," she said. Aram said this definition of health is in keeping with the World Health Organization's own definition. Affirming that health is "not merely the absence of disease or infirmity," Shanti Ashram delivers life-saving vaccines "without distinction of race, religion, political belief, economic or social situation," but also works toward helping those in their care "flourish in all dimensions of life and health."

A medical doctor by training, Aram appreciates the advances science has brought to addressing public health crises like Covid-19 or, for that matter, the HIV/AIDS pandemic. And yet, in her training, she found that the social and spiritual dimensions to health were largely ignored. Aram believes the Covid-19 pandemic has helped remind government agencies and intergovernmental organizations that when using science as a means for societal progress, "dialogue with religious communities is not only extremely important, it's absolutely necessary," she said.

A more holistic framework for addressing vaccine inequity

That's particularly the case when it comes to the ongoing problem of vaccine equity. As some developed nations were rolling out their third and fourth rounds of Covid vaccination, many low and lower-middle income countries are still struggling to vaccinate their populations at all. According to the United Nations (UN), vaccine inequity not only left millions or billions vulnerable to the virus, but exacerbated inequality, deepened the gap between rich and poor, and reversed decades of hard-won progress on human development.

Aram said that the global moral framework inherent in the UN's and WHO's approaches was not challenging enough to prevent hoarding, wasting, and other issues contributing to vaccine inequity. In the future, Aram stressed, religious communities can help provide an ethical foundation that stresses the intersectional nature of the pandemic, the necessity of addressing holistic health and interdependent issues, and the need to consider how vaccine equity is imperative for all. In this way, vaccination programs may serve as a reminder and a template to show how "when science society and spirituality are in dialogue, we are able to give to common people a much more integrated answer to life's issues, rather than a fragmented response," she said.

Addressing the gender gap

Monica Cristina, a member of Shanti Ashram's staff, said one facet of this inequity that they are trying to address is the gender gap. Cristina said that for every 1,000 vaccinated men in India, there are only 954 women. "This is a major gap," she said. There are multiple reasons for this, Cristina said, from men having more access to vaccines through the institutions they work with to the fact that many women feel they cannot afford to take a day off from taking care of their families to receive the vaccine.

Through their "Vaccination for All" program, the ashram employs a combination of community mobilization, public and private partnerships, and interreligious cooperation to address vaccination hesitancy and reach the most vulnerable communities—like the poor, people with co-morbidities, and women. By going directly to the people around Combiatore and addressing their biggest concerns and questions through dialogue, Shanti Ashram is reaching those unreached by institutional vaccine programs, said Cristina. Putting that model to practice during the Covid-19 pandemic, Shanti Ashram was able to vaccinate thousands through numerous vaccination sessions at hospitals, at their facilities, and through a mobile service, without wasting a single dose of the vaccine.

Dialogue key to success

Dialogue with other religious partners has been key to the program's success. Working with local Hindu, Muslim, and Christian communities, Subramanian said they are, "together addressing vaccine hesitancy among vulnerable populations." That willingness to convene multiple stakeholders to address the most pressing issues facing humanity today—whether that be a pandemic or climate change, hate speech or violent conflict—reminds Subramanian and his colleagues at Shanti Ashram of another Gandhi quote. "Gandhi said, 'the future depends on what we do today,'" said Subramanian. "And what we are doing today is bringing people together to share information, build alignment, and solve problems. This is our standard policy and strategy, for vaccinations and any other issue we face," he said.

For Aram, this shows how vital it is to involve religious communities in every step of the policy and implementation process when responding to crises and endemic issues. "We have to go beyond looking at religious communities as the last step," she said. "During the pandemic, the global community recognized the religious community's assets, its moral voice, and its contribution to composite solutions," Aram said, "the question is if we will learn our lesson and do it more frequently and openly in the future."

Children: A lifetime's commitment

From the outset, Aram vowed to apply her training as a doctor to address children's foundational needs and women's fundamental rights. "My core expertise is not only health," she said, "it's children; they are my life's commitment." And the pandemic highlighted just how important it is to work together to uphold and protect children's rights and provide for their basic needs. "When the pandemic happened, it allowed me to connect various parts of my expertise, linking broader leadership needs and particular aspects of public health," she said. "They say 'It takes a village to raise a child,' but in the twenty-first century, we've relegated the responsibility to parents alone," she said, "in the pandemic, we are revisiting this code."

In India, pandemic-related lockdowns adversely impacted children, preventing them from attending school or accessing basic services. "School is not just a center for education here," said Aram. "It's a societal institution nurturing skill sets and knowledge to transition to adult life. If school gets disrupted, everything gets disrupted," she said. With 43 percent of the Indian population consisting of children, this meant that almost half of the country's population was at risk of missing critical development interventions and opportunities for growth.

Undaunted, Aram used the opportunity to provide expertise in consultation with local and national governments, drawing on her shared experiences with women and children on the ground in Coimbatore. "At the Ashram, we have integrated children and children's voices in everything we do," she said.

For her legacy of service over the last two decades, and her critical work during the pandemic, Aram was recently awarded an Alumni Award from Harvard University's Harvard T. Chan School of Public Health. But for Aram, her joy doesn't come from awards and recognition. It comes from serving the most vulnerable. "As schools closed, services were disrupted, the collective community had to step up. Shanti Ashram found the time to address these issues together with women and children, with governments, with different religious communities," said Aram. "I could not have asked for a better template to put my expertise and experience to work."

4

Education

The goal is companionship, community, and connection—and healing through those things. Not healing through fixing; healing through this very experience of love and community.

JULIE COYNE (HUMANIST)

The Jain faith gives me identity. It gives me a sense of purpose, a sense of being, but also a sense of who I am, because it largely defines my vision of right and wrong.

MEHOOL H. SANGHRAJKA (JAIN)

If there's one prayer, I always ask is that God's grace upon my life be multiplied so that I'll keep doing the things I do.

HELINE BABIENE EWENI (PROTESTANT)

Introduction

At the turn of the nineteenth century, it is estimated that fewer than one in five adults had even a basic education. Education remained a luxury; reserved for the elite. Over the last 200 years, however, there has been a revolution in educational access, inputs, and outcomes. Enrollment is widespread, attendance is strong, and literacy rates have greatly improved. In the first quarter of the twenty-first century, education is no longer seen as an elite luxury, but a fundamental human right.

Even so, due to poverty, social stigma, digital divides, inadequate infrastructure, lack of materials, or marginalization based on gender, language, religion, or race, access to education remains unequal. According to UNICEF, the United Nations Children's Fund, over 600 million children worldwide are unable to attain minimum proficiency levels in reading and mathematics, even though two-thirds of them are in school.[1] For the more than 72 million children still not in school around the world—with particularly high concentrations in sub-Saharan Africa, Central and Eastern Asia, and the Pacific—foundational skills in literacy and numeracy remain even further from grasp. And without a foundational education, children face considerable barriers to employment later in life. They are also more likely to suffer adverse health outcomes, be more susceptible to crime and violence, and less likely to participate in politics and public debates about issues that impact them.

The stories in this chapter feature individuals working to expand access to education and improve the quality of what is learned. Their contexts are different, their religious motivations distinct, and their specific objectives not the same. But their end goal is held in common: to expand and improve educational access, so that children grow into adults who can contribute to better futures for their societies and the world as a whole. Muslim, Jain, and Catholic, each of the exemplars believes a good education offers individuals the opportunity to lead richer, more fulfilling lives—and, at a societal level, it creates opportunities for humanity to solve its most pressing problems.[2]

First, from northeastern Nigeria, readers meet Zannah Bukar Mustapha. Mustapha, known to some as "Boko Haram's lawyer," can seem a contradiction. As journalist Innocent Eteng points out, the Boko Haram movement, which literally means "Western education is forbidden," believes foreign-styled education in Nigeria is an affront to Islamic society and culture. Mustapha has caused concern and controversy in Nigeria, as he has represented of the government at top-level negotiations with Boko Haram, educates children of Boko Haram members, and provides support to widows Boko Haram combatants killed in the conflict. All of this, as Eteng shares, is motivated by a desire to not allow *anything* to get in the way of an individual's education. The negotiations were about freeing schoolgirls from captivity, including Boko Haram's children in his educational programs as a means of keeping them from choosing a path of "radicalization," and providing support for Boko Haram widows, an intentional decision to radically include, so that cycles of internecine violence do not continue to tear northeastern Nigeria apart.

Then, in Athar Ahmed's profile of Mehool H. Sanghrajka, readers get to know how the Jain "tech mogul" expanded access to education for millions through his global social enterprise, Learning Possibilities Ltd. Motivated by principles of his faith and a strong commitment to community, Sanghrajka founded Learning Possibilities in 2007 to provide learning management software for schools, including customizable virtual learning environments, curriculum delivery tools (e.g., blogs, wikis, discussions, surveys, picture libraries), and homework drop boxes. They now operate in countries such as India, Cambodia, and Wales and are estimated to have benefited 25 million users globally.

Finally, returning to sub-Saharan Africa, Eteng profiles Edmund Kaszibuloh Koroma, a Catholic in Sierra Leone who sacrifices his own well-being to provide tuition-free education to students in one of the continent's weakest economies. That sacrifice was so great, and Koroma's commitment so impactful, that it moved Eteng himself to endeavor to better use his journalism for good—not only to inform others about what is happening, but to educate them about how they might make the world a better place.

Together, these stories testify to the ongoing need for educational justice. They also show how faith actors are part of efforts to expand education access, improve delivery, and provide better outcomes through inclusion, innovation, and personal sacrifice. They also point to how, in the words of social entrepreneur Ken Wytsma, education justice does not have a finish line.[3] Though statistics show that education has vastly improved and expanded over the last two centuries, we cannot know when—or if—the pursuit of educational justice will end. But as these stories make clear, the pursuit itself can make for a better story. And perhaps, a more just and verdant world.

"Radical Inclusion in a Terror-torn Society"

Zannah Bukar Mustapha (Muslim/Nigeria)

By Innocent Eteng

Zannah Bukar Mustapha is something of a local hero in Maiduguri. The capital of Nigeria's simmering, northeastern Borno State has been under heavy, consistent assault by Islamic jihadists since 2009. All the while, Mustapha has been championing child safety and education amidst—and despite—the violence. At the same time, the 64-year-old father of ten has also earned an unpleasant moniker—"Boko Haram's lawyer." The two-sided reputation as a local hero and lawyer for terrorists ironically stems from the same source—a desire to *radically* include.

On May 12, 2022, inside what he calls his "relaxation point," a small, shaded area just outside his home in Maiduguri, I joined Mustapha, a smiling man with a generous round face, to continue a series of interviews we started the day before. Between the exchanges, we pressed pause to play a little chess. Pillared with Indian bamboo, capped with a thatched, raffia roof, and rounded with a net that keeps malaria-infecting mosquitoes away, the shelter provided not only shade but privacy. I tried to keep the conversation less formal, allowing Mustapha to share his story calmly. But calm is not the first word that comes to mind for a man who towers over others at well above six feet tall. He stewards that physical presence well, with the ability to vividly, engrossingly recollect events from early childhood to adulthood, easily recalling the moments that molded him into a bold and life-saving humanitarian—and a subject of intense criticism.

Our father, our husband

Among his many nicknames good, bad, and in-between—over 2,000 orphans and other vulnerable and forcefully displaced kids in this city call him "Baba" (father). In one of Nigeria's most educationally challenged states, they see him as the sole shepherd for their futures, eternally grateful for educating them at no cost through his four nonprofit schools.

Boko Haram believes foreign-styled education in Nigeria is an affront. They are fighting to carve out an Islamic state in Nigeria, one where only an education based on their ideology will be permitted. Thousands of teachers and students in the northeast region are among the more than 35,000 people its members have killed, directly and indirectly through hunger and disease in the wake of conflict, since 2009.

Beyond "his children," hundreds of widows also call Mustapha "our husband." Not because he has married them all, but because his nonprofit—the Future Prowess Islamic Foundation—has provided for their livelihoods since 2014. Its Future Prowess Cooperative Society trains widows and displaced women with the necessary skills to provide for themselves, furnishing small seed grants to get their new enterprises started.

While the foundation retains the word "Islamic" in its name, most subjects are decidedly secular, with a focus on math, English, civic education, social studies, and biology. However, at the same time, Muslim students have one hour each day for Islamic studies and additional hours of religious training on Saturdays. But in the eyes of his critics, Mustapha is hiding behind humanitarianism to support the terrorists in their cause. That is partly because Mustapha, who almost always wears *jalabiya*—a flowing, loosely fitting traditional garment worn by Muslims in the region—uses a radically inclusive approach to education and humanitarianism. That means educating children of Boko Haram and supporting their widows if their husbands are killed in the conflict.

That approach is not only magnanimous, but strategic. Mustapha said it is his way of building an inclusive institution and showing his neutrality, especially on behalf of the safety of his schools and students. It is also part of his personal plan to equip Boko Haram's children with knowledge that he hopes can prevent their future radicalization. "It's not only about being neutral but playing an inclusive institution where the home and the school are brought on one page. In the African society, if the husband dies, the widow becomes as vulnerable as the orphans," he said. "Otherwise, they don't have any livelihood as housewives."

None of these reasons make sense to his critics. People across Borno State cannot abide the thought of providing for the families of those who have harmed their own. But Mustapha does not allow such criticism to discourage his determination to spark social change. Instead, he is spurred on by his firm belief that, by helping orphans and widows from all sides, he is following in the footsteps of the Prophet Muhammad.

His persistence on his own path has paid off. Not only have insurgents never attacked his schools, but between 2015 and 2017, they trusted him enough to accept him as a stand-in for the government, negotiating the release of schoolgirls kidnapped by Boko Haram in 2014. The negotiation led to the successful release of 103 out of 270 girls. Without Mustapha, many feel those girls might still be in the hands of Boko Haram. Mustapha's efforts have also caught global attention, with him receiving the highly prized United Nations Nansen Refugee Award (2017), the Aurora Prize (2017), the CNN Heroes of the Year Honoree (2021) designation, and the Global Citizen Award (2023).

The seeds of a radical idea

Under the shade of his raffia-roofed "relaxation point," I asked Mustapha how he came around to this "radical" idea of inclusion. "I count myself lucky to have had a father who allowed his children to gain Western and Islamic education," he said. That combination, when Mustapha was a child, was quite rare. So rare, in fact, Mustapha said that in northern Nigeria in the 1960s, access to Western-style education was a near miracle. Despite the destruction it has had to endure over the last decade and a half, Maiduguri is a significant place of pilgrimage for Muslims visiting the area from other parts of Nigeria—as well as neighboring countries like Niger, Benin, and Chad.

Their attachment to it dates to before the sixteenth century when the Borno area of Nigeria was a key and respected part of Kanem-Bornu, an African trading empire that spanned wide swathes of western Africa for nearly six centuries. With agriculture as its mainstay, the Islamic empire sprawled from modern-day Nigeria to Chad, Libya to Cameroon. In the seventeenth and eighteenth centuries, Bornu was a vibrant center for Islamic learning and religious charisma in the Sahel region, as Borno sultans rooted their political legitimacy in the generative soil of Sufi spirituality.

East of Maiduguri sits Mafoni, a small district that, until recent decades, was inhabited mainly by Islamic clerics, scholars, and teachers. It was in this district that Mustapha was born in 1959 because, as he said with pride, "My father was one [of the clerics in Mafoni]." The second of seven children born to Alkali Mustapha, Mustapha's paternal lineage boasts generations of clerics and imams.

Nigeria is almost evenly divided into a predominately Muslim north and a Christian south. A shortage of trained Sharia court lawyers in the north following Nigeria's independence in October 1960 warranted the selection of experienced Islamic clerics with no background in legal studies to be hurriedly taken through basic judicial courses to become *alkalis* (or *qadis*,

Sharia court lawyers) in the Islamic justice system granted by the Nigerian constitution for northern states. Alkali, Mustapha's father, was one of them.

While Western-style education was gradually integrated into the social construct of present-day Borno and the larger northern region in Nigeria's pre-independence and early independence eras (1960s–1970s), most northern parents viewed it as a slow-seeping poison, eroding their commitment to an Islamic educational system. As a result, many parents forbade their kids from partaking in it, even when it was readily available.

That Mustapha came from a family of respected Islamic clerics meant that, from childhood, his extended family sought to limit his interaction with people of other religions, training him only in Arabic and Islamic studies. They hoped to see him rise to become a respected Islamic scholar or cleric like his father and grandfathers before him.

Learning diversity and inclusion first-hand

Working his way up the legal ladder, Alkali soon became an area court judge. This position involved many interactions with the broader world than what northern Nigeria might normally offer. As part of his work, Alkali met highly educated Muslims who attained Western-style education without, he noted, compromising their faith.

Convinced that one could attain secular education and still be a dedicated Muslim, Alkali started allowing his children to attend secular classes during the day, provided they continue their Islamic studies courses in the evenings. For the first time, he even let them travel to other parts of the country, including the largely Christian south, for educational purposes. "My father was seen as somebody who left his way to accept Western-style education before the [northern] society started accepting it, which allows for diversity, the acceptance of an inclusive institution," Mustapha said.

Taking advantage of this newfound freedom, Mustapha took a 700-mile journey from Maiduguri to the southeast to attend a government-funded boarding school before returning to the north to enroll at a teachers' training college, where he was certified as a primary school teacher. That time in the east gave him a firsthand experience of diversity and inclusion as he shared things, activities, and thoughts with students and friends from different tribes and religions.

After three years of classroom teaching, Mustapha proceeded to the University of Maiduguri, where he studied Sharia and Customary Law before moving to Lagos for law school in the southwest, believed to be Nigeria's most liberal region, where interaction and inter-marriage between people of multiple faiths is *de rigueur*. "I met a lot of Yorubas (southwestern people). I met a lot of other tribes and religions. It shaped my thinking of what Nigeria is," he said. And, possibly, of what it could become. That experience of inclusion, diversity, and tolerance made Mustapha resolve to see and relate with people first with an eye toward their humanity—and to place mutual love above religion and tribe. It also helped him appreciate the value of a well-rounded education—of not having to sacrifice one's religious commitments in the pursuit of knowledge.

Tradition meets ambition

This is a journey Mustapha himself knows personally. When he started planning to have a family of his own in the 1990s, he decided that he would build one around the pillars of freedom, education, tolerance, and love. At the same time, he also wanted to continue the tradition of plural marriage. So, he married two wives. Luckily, each wife had a strong passion for education with a determination for personal career progression, making it easy for Mustapha to support their dreams. In fact, Fatima, his 49-year-old wife is a journalist and deputy director of information at the Borno State Ministry of Information. Fatima agreed to marry Mustapha in 1996 when she was just 22 years old, during her first year at the university, because "he respected my dreams," she said. "He encouraged me to get to where I am today. He gives you the opportunity to develop and grow," the mother of his ten children said. Mustapha's second wife, Maryam, was in medical school when Mustapha indicated his interest in her. At first, she paid no attention to him. But later, the 44-year-old said, "I felt that since he endures and is interested in what I am doing too [my studies], he was the person I should spend the rest of my life with."

In their household, the blend of time-honored tradition and contemporary opportunities is par for the course. "My daughters are the eldest; two studied software engineering, one studied mass communication, and the youngest is still in secondary school," Fatima said. "He gives them opportunities and encourages them, both males and females, to go out and be the best. I always tell my younger sons they should be like their sisters because we give them the wings to fly."

Risks and sacrifice

After nearly twenty years as a lawyer, Mustapha started the Future Prowess Islamic Foundation in 2007 to offer free education to orphans he saw roaming the streets of Maiduguri, begging for food and handouts during school hours. "We started with four classrooms with two teachers and thirty-six orphans," he said. With the Boko Haram insurgency throwing more children out of school, international donor dollars helped him expand his original four classrooms to build three separate primary schools and one secondary school comprising forty classrooms with over 100 paid and volunteer teachers overseeing more than 2,000 students.

But the risks and sacrifices Mustapha has taken to build such institutions have been enormous. During the negotiations for the release of the schoolgirls, a government helicopter picked Mustapha up as early as 1:00 a.m. in the morning, dropping him in the forest to meet Boko Haram members in the middle of the night. To save his family from worrying too much about his safety, he sometimes hid his appointments from them. "During the negotiation, we didn't even know it was on. Sometimes, you don't feel comfortable when he does these things, but you just pray and wish that he succeeds," Fatima said.

At 64, Mustapha considers himself not energetic enough to pilot the foundation's affairs for too much longer. He is setting up a succession plan: "Training the younger ones to take over from me and take it to a higher level, even to the university level," he said. In the meantime, when he is not moving around supervising activities in the schools, he is gardening, feeding his herd of sheep and goats, or playing table tennis or chess to ease stress. He plays both games, I came to find out, very well.

"Ancient Faith, Modern Ed-Tech"

Mehool H. Sanghrajka (Jain/United Kingdom)

By Athar Ahmed

"Education, Education, Education." That was how former Prime Minister Tony Blair famously spelled out what he saw as being the United Kingdom's singular priority back in 1996. Around the same time, Mehool Sanghrajka, then in his early thirties, was also reflecting on the power of education. At the same time, he was considering the existential question of his purpose on earth.

The son of Indian migrants, Mehool recognized the vast potential teaching and learning had in dramatically changing lives—not only of the individuals around him in Britain, but of the millions of people living in developing countries, where access to education remained a dream beyond reach. How Mehool himself fit into that picture, however, was something he was still figuring out. He knew his desire to socially uplift those most in need had firm roots, fueled by his beliefs as a Jain, a worldview grounded in ancient Indian philosophy. Yet it was his passion for state-of-the-art technology (at a time when the internet was still in its infancy) that appeared to Mehool as being the most likely vehicle by which to further his ambitions of bringing about meaningful and impactful change. Fast forward almost thirty years and Mehool is now a globetrotting tech mogul, Member of the British Empire (a prestigious honor awarded by the UK government and monarchy) and a prominent figure in Britain's Jain community.

A Jain spin on the traditional English

I first met Mehool in the Summer of 2019. Like me, he lived in northwest London, a part of the capital known for housing an eclectic mix of diverse communities and immigrants who had made the UK their home. Unlike me, however, Mehool is a committed vegan. So, I met his invitation for me to join him for a Jain spin on the traditional full English breakfast with intrigue. Beyond questions about meatless sausage, I wanted to find out more about what drove him as a person.

Sitting down to eat, I noticed the usual greasy meats had been replaced by their grilled vegetarian counterparts, fried eggs substituted with scrambled tofu, with oat milk lightly coloring our cups of Earl Grey. *Ahimsa*, the café we were dining at, means non-violence in Sanskrit. As well as rustling up a great breakfast, I learned it was also the philosophical approach to life responsible for shaping Mehool's worldview.

It doesn't take long being in Mehool's presence to realize he's as British as the breakfast (with of course, the Jain spin)—despite his background in distant regions of the Commonwealth. "I'm Gujrati Indian but in terms of heritage by birth, I'm an African. I was born in Kenya, and I've lived almost fifty years in the UK," he said. "So, I understand and recognize all of those identities," Mehool said.

With so many distinct influences in his life, it is perhaps no surprise that Mehool has quite the cosmopolitan community of friends. From Jain nuns at his local temple, to Members of Parliament, all speak of Mehool's desire to empower others in an ongoing quest for both equity and equality. One MP praises Mehool's "ability to reach out and talk to all sorts of people, from those within the Jain community to those beyond it," describing him as an "impressive operator."

At the root of his motivation is his Jain faith and a desire to help people rise above their circumstances. "It gives me identity. It gives me a sense of purpose, a sense of being but also a sense of who I am, because it largely defines my vision of right and wrong. What I see the purpose of this life as being," Mehool said. "I mean, it doesn't matter what profession I'm in, it doesn't matter where I live. Those things will change. But this identity, you know, it's something I've grown up with and it's never going to change."

High tech, deep faith

Technology expands humans' reach. And that's exactly why Mehool decided to study tech as a youngster. For him, technology and education went hand in hand. That was true even at a time when it wasn't immediately clear how tech would be utilized in the classroom. Mehool, though, has always believed education is the best way to get people out of poverty. And though a well-rounded education and economic opportunity may be the ends he pursues for others, the means are tied deeply to his faith.

Mehool's spiritual practice as a Jain is underpinned by the principle of *karma*. Like Hindus and Buddhists, Jains believe in reincarnation. The goal is to attain ultimate liberation, which means escaping the continuous cycle of birth, death, and rebirth, allowing the immortal soul to live forever in a state of bliss. Jains achieve this by eliminating all *karma* from the soul. With that, Mehool tells me, comes the responsibility of serving others. "Ignorance is the cause of most misery and so the opposite of that is education," he said. "For me, it's something you do once for a child but will have a lifelong impact. Providing knowledge to kids is what I'm very comfortable doing as a Jain, because it has a strong basis in my belief."

Mehool's desire to give children around the world the opportunity to receive an education led to him reaching out to other tech leaders within his network toward the end of the 1990s. With those who bought into his excitement and vision, he began brainstorming the possibilities of expanding learning beyond the traditional classroom. In a world where Zoom meetings are banal and the idea of being taught by someone halfway across the other side of the world is the norm, it's easy to forget that until recently, virtual education wasn't always *a thing*—or even readily accepted. Mehool, however, spotted remote learning's potential early on, setting up a social enterprise, Learning Possibilities, with the aim of serving the needs of children across the world. They now operate in countries from India and Cambodia to Wales. It's estimated that 25 million users globally have benefited from the company's services.

"Being a social enterprise means that we focus massively on the impact we create—not just the financial results we generate," he said. "To go out into areas where the internet isn't always there, where children don't have basic desks and books and the kind of things you take for granted ... sometimes they don't have teachers. So, we're heavily focused on this idea of impact and of improving lives."

For such a time as this

During our first meeting, back in June 2019, neither Mehool nor I could imagine how timely his story—and work—would become. As the Covid-19 pandemic took hold in 2020, businesses, educational institutes and workplaces all had to rapidly adapt, adjusting to a new way of working almost overnight. Having spent years trying to convince skeptics that remote learning technology was a viable way of educating students, it felt like a justification of Mehool's lifetime of work. "It's really sad that it takes a pandemic for people to open their eyes and see this, because we've been talking about this since the late '90s. I think there comes a time which gives you a golden opportunity," he said. "Whether it's the universe, whether it's karma, whether it's God," Mehool said, "this is the point at which everything we've said up to now is starting to come through. From a faith perspective it's a huge reward and that keeps you engaged, keeps you fighting the hurdles and overcoming them," he said.

With the pandemic unexpectedly putting his work front and center, Mehool's outlook on remote education was fast tracked almost without choice. It also provided him the chance to connect with organizations and governments who were keen to tap into his expertise, with Mehool offering free access to the resources and technology he already developed. The irony of the shift in how Mehool and I communicated with one another wasn't lost on me either. After initially discussing the merits of virtual communication over a coffee, we were soon required to conduct our interviews online, practically implementing the very essence of Mehool's vision for remote knowledge exchange. But it also provided the opportunity to see how Mehool worked toward ensuring Jains in the UK maintained the ability to practice their faith during the pandemic, both at home and as a community.

Though the overwhelming task of helping meet the need for remote learning globally occupied much of his time, making sure his close-knit religious circle wasn't left isolated also occupied Mehool's time. When the community couldn't perform religious rites and rituals in person like they usually would, Mehool and his wife Arshana helped focus minds on what was within their control. The couple worked to foster a sense of togetherness by organizing lectures, prayer sessions, and even yoga classes over Zoom, ensuring their small community—many of whom are elderly—weren't without spiritual, mental, and emotional support. "Mehool helped practices become much more accessible for the community at a very difficult time," Arshana said. "People began to actually invite a whole community into their home over Zoom while they were in prayer or anointing a statue, which was so important to their well-being."

God sent us to our rooms to learn our lesson

Hearing how Mehool served his immediate religious circle and those far beyond during the pandemic offers insight into what defines him: Faith, education, technology, and community. During the pandemic and its response, they all came together, complementing one another, speaking to one another, interwoven into Mehool's every waking moment.

Before Covid-19, Mehool spent less time in his home office than in far-flung parts of the world. Yet it was the pandemic that brought the essence of both his work and faith to the forefront, leaving what he hopes will be a lasting legacy for his family, the Jain community, and society at large. "This drive to eradicate poverty, to do better, all of these things I think are an awakening," Mehool said. "Because what we have seen with the pandemic ... it's almost as if God kind of, you know, sent us to our rooms, to learn our lesson before we could come out again."

"Learning from the Exemplars' Examples"

Edmund Kaszibuloh Koroma (Roman Catholic/Sierra Leone)

By Innocent Eteng

As I dropped hundreds of thousands of devalued Sierra Leonean *leons* into a donation box inside Edmund Kaszibuloh Koroma's office in July 2019, I wondered about the teacher, psychosocial counselor, and father of three sons. "How does he cope with obvious personal and family poverty," I asked myself as the money slid through a thin slot, "yet still manage to cheerfully invest in educating over 200 students in his community every year?"

Twice, I met Edmund Kaszibuloh Koroma eating raw cassava roots—the last resort for sustenance among those with little income in Sierra Leone. One of our interview sessions was under a leaky roof—an extension of his home in Makeni town in the West African country's northern province. As rain descended, water dripped, poured, and otherwise made its way through six spots in the ceiling, puddling in various parts of the approximately 28x32 foot room. The overall impression told me the then 65-year-old and once-savior-of-Sierra-Leone's child soldiers struggled to afford basic needs for himself, his wife, and boys.

Yet, Koroma showed me a small structure under construction, which he intended to be a free library and bookshop for students, explaining how he was saving money to complete the building in the coming years. He also explained how he gathered proceeds from his small farm and used it to purchase a 1.4-acre parcel of land to expand his tuition-free school, which sat on a 27x21 meter space. The expansion was planned to accommodate more kids without access to education in one of Africa's weakest economies, where the inflation rate sits around 50 percent, a troubling currency devaluation continues to cause consternation, and general economic mismanagement combines to keep Sierra Leone's economy vulnerable, leading to widespread poverty and inadequate educational infrastructure across the country.

Koroma, who was then chairman of the Catholic community in Makeni, told me he was making those sacrifices with limited support, with his only hope for reward being in heaven. "My whole life, I believe we are here [on Earth], but temporarily. This is the thing that rules my life," he said.

My donation came after spending four days interviewing him, getting to know his teachers and students, and observing his everyday life and work.

Perhaps poor in means, he was rich in relationships. He bonded effortlessly with people around him and his community, creating connections with young and old alike. No matter who they were, he called them "my own," and they, in return, shouted back "Okame" (my own). On July 22, I waved goodbye to Koroma. On the flight back to Nigeria, I started to question my everyday actions and relationships. Were they selfless or selfish? Were my friends "my own" and I, in turn, theirs? Who did I belong to? What kind of community was I building, and how was I giving myself to others? Koroma had triggered something within me. It would stay with me for years.

I'm pregnant

Koroma was a psychosocial counselor who led eighty-seven former child soldiers and sex slaves to safety during the country's 11-year civil war (1991–2002), saving them from capture by combatants. During the crisis, he managed an interim care center (ICC) set up in Makeni by Caritas, a global charity of the Roman Catholic Church, to rehabilitate children affected by the conflict. Caritas cared for about 400 former child fighters, helping rehabilitate them at the ICC after the insurgents struck a peace deal with the government in 1999. The children were under Koroma's direct care.

But when rebels reneged on the deal and resumed fighting in 2000, they came to the ICC, forcefully taking away about forty kids, promising to return for more. Desperate, Koroma started hiding the children, sending them to Freetown, the government-controlled capital, on trucks. But when the war became fierce and vehicular movement ceased, he dashed into the jungle with the remaining eighty-seven kids, trekking and hiding with them for five days until they arrived in the capital. Tired. Hungry. Haggard-looking. But safe.

When the war ended in 2002, and Koroma disengaged from Caritas, he started a nonprofit secondary school to educate polio victims and former child soldiers in Makeni, children who were returning to their communities without rehabilitation. Today, Alagendra Secondary School provides free education to about 200 students every year. It is this school that Koroma fought so hard to sustain until his death in August 2022. Thankfully, I managed to stay in touch with him via phone calls, WhatsApp, and Facebook messages years after I first met him in Sierra Leone's northern district. Each time, he prayed for my safety and my healthy return.

Now, Koroma is dead, but I feel full. Of ideas and thoughts, melding into a solid impulse to act. I am still unsure of how it will coalesce, how the abstract elements will form into something tangible, touchable, relatable; but I know that after my time with Koroma, I feel called, both professionally and personally, to be more "others" oriented, using my journalism for public service. I am pregnant with the possibilities that encountering Koroma provoked within me.

Journalism for good

I have been telling social impact stories since 2018. As a reporter, I use a solutions journalism approach to highlight how people are responding to social problems. However, my encounter with Koroma in 2019 was my first time spending days with someone deeply motivated by his spiritual convictions. More than profile his life and responses to problems in his community, his story moved me to change my own. Now, that "called" feeling is pushing me toward founding a religion-centered nonprofit media company. The aim? To discover more Koromas. To tell their stories. To inspire others.

My resolve has been further strengthened since my encounter with another faith-inspired humanitarian. Though the two seem set apart in terms of space and approach, they are similar in spirit, sacrifice, and commitment to child safety and education. His name is Zannah Bukar Mustapha, who you read about earlier in this chapter. I grew up in the predominately Christian-majority southern regions of Nigeria. There, a common story suggests, "every Muslim in Islam-dominated northern Nigeria is intolerant, blood-thirsty, and unbearable." For this reason, I long avoided traveling to the north. My first ever trip to spend a night in a northern Nigerian state was in May 2017, when the National Youth Service Corps deployed me to Zamfara State in the northwest for my compulsory one-year national youth service. I was almost 30 at the time. Even then, I had to redeploy back to the south after three weeks because, in reaction to hate directed at northerners by separatists from southeast Nigeria, northern youths had given southeasterners residing in the north until October 1, 2017, to vacate or be attacked. I am no southeasterner, but I had to leave because, during such conflicts, it is usually a no-questions-asked attack on non-Muslims and non-Hausa language speakers (the north's language).

Fast forward to 2023, and I found myself traveling more frequently to the north to tell humanitarian stories, relating more comfortably with Muslims, including multiple sheikhs and imams. Thanks to Mustapha, who helped me disabuse my mind of stereotypes passed on to me during my childhood, I was able to tell a different kind of story about Muslims and northern Nigeria. Mustapha showed me what it is to radically include. Like Koroma, Mustapha carries in his heart a seeming unconditional love he distributes to all kinds of people. The Future Prowess Islamic Foundation, his nonprofit, caters to the educational needs of children affected by the Boko Haram insurgency in northeast Nigeria and the livelihood needs of widows. This includes children and widows of Boko Haram members and those of soldiers. Despite the crimes members of the group have committed since 2009, Mustapha teaches that their innocent children and widows cannot be excluded from the institutions (schools) designed to build a wholesome person. This non-discriminatory posture has inspired love, healing, and forgiveness in families and communities throughout Borno.

From Koroma and Mustapha, I learned never to rope an entire region into one prejudiced narrative, especially before getting to know the people you hear such stories about. Traveling to the north, getting to know Muslims who inspire, and spending time with them, I also understand that there is no limit to how much trust and cooperation one can enjoy from anybody, if you first bring respect for their religion and culture. This understanding has helped me build professional and personal relations, including with some controversial imams, sheikhs, and traditionalists in Nigeria.

Good journalism can save lives

I once asked Koroma why he spent most parts of his life educating children despite his personal financial struggles. He explained that besides his faith-based beliefs compelling him to help the poor, he believed in the saying that education is not preparation for life but life itself. So, he saw his education of children as birthing lives, for there could be no meaningful life for a child without access to education.

Months and years have passed, but I often ruminate on that lesson. Each time, they birth within me a strong desire to not just be a journalist but an educator. Someone who uses his journalism to share not only facts, but knowledge and insight.

That is why my proposed center for religion reporting will not just discover more Koromas but train other Nigerian and African journalists to do the same. It is also to use workshops and conferences to lead compelling discussions on constructive and balanced religious reporting. The emphasis on "constructive" and "balanced" is so important because, while Koroma birthed lives with his provision of education, I will attempt to save them with balanced, accurate, and insightful reporting. Religious riots since 1987 across several Nigerian states have taken the lives of thousands of my people. For example, in Kaduna state alone, according to government data, about 20,000 have died in such conflicts over the last three and a half decades. The failure of the Nigerian media to report religious issues in a constructive and balanced manner has been identified as one contributor to the escalation of such conflicts. Despite the competitive nature of the media ecosystem in a highly religious country, there is no single religion-focused media house in Nigeria. To establish a nonprofit media with a focus on constructive reporting, investigation of religious crimes, and the promotion of the use of religion for social good is, as I hope, to save lives. But more emphasis would need to be given to training other journalists in ethical religion reporting and leading compelling conversations toward innovations within the realm of religion journalism.

The registration process at Nigeria's Corporate Affairs Commission is already ongoing, and a constitution has been adopted by the board of trustees, comprising a state chairman of the Christian Association of Nigeria, a university lecturer (Muslim), and a financial and security expert (Christian). Hopefully, as the initiative discovers many more Koromas and Mustaphas and younger writers share other stories, it will become a long-lasting contribution to prolonging peace and understanding in a country so often torn apart by conflict and a narrow vision of who counts as "our own."

5

Gender and Sexual Equity

Meditation helps me cultivate stillness that makes my heart grow. But when I see ugliness in the world, it's more important to take action.

CHAO-HWEI SHIH (BUDDHIST)

Religion ... is the heartbeat of anything that we think we can do to heal the world's problems.

AZZA KARAM (MUSLIM)

If you are not feeling challenged, there is something very artificial about you and your spirituality.

SWAMI AGNIVESH (HINDU)

Introduction

Connor is looking for a role model. A college student at a small, liberal arts college in the United States Midwest, Connor grew up in a conservative, Lutheran family. After beginning to identify his gender differently from the sex he was assigned at birth, Connor knows he was lucky to find a supportive network within his religious community. Inspired by the experience, he wants to deepen and expand his spiritual practice. He is even considering going into ministry. But he is not sure where to look for a guide. "There just aren't many trans people leading religious groups—on campus or off," he said. "There are plenty of gay leaders, queer leaders, even drag leaders," Connor said. "Ironically, if I still identified as a woman, I'd have plenty of examples to follow, but I feel there are no trans leaders like me." For now, Connor plans to remain a part of his local congregation's leadership, even while looking for role models that have gone before him. "If I have to be the first within my community, I'll be the first. Then, maybe, I can encourage others to follow in my footsteps," he said.

Gender and sexuality remain key symbolic boundaries for religious actors and communities in societies around the globe.[1] While a range of research shows how religion, gender, and sexuality are embedded in patriarchal norms and prejudices that have shaped the repression of the female gender and the criminalization of certain kinds of sexuality across time and place, this chapter provides examples of individuals doing something different. Inspired by religious values and spiritual practices, they endeavor to create intentionally inclusive communities or reach beyond the conservative norms of their communities to establish better relationships with lesbian, gay, bisexual, transgender, and queer (LGBTQ+) persons. Doing work on the frontlines of the intersection between gender, sexuality, and religion in India, the United States, and at the intergovernmental level, the stories in this chapter underscore not only how gender and religion are sites of power assertion and control, but the implications of such intersections on human rights, public health, and issues of social justice. They also feature exemplars advocating for new directions, improved networks of care, and making space for fresh leadership—perhaps even leaders like Connor.

More than anything else, this chapter is about visibility. That women, transgender persons, and male sex workers be seen and recognized—that their stories be told. In making these individuals visible—both the exemplars and those they serve or represent—it underscores how religious actors from various traditions (and of varying identifications) believe that whatever gender, whatever sexual orientation, and whatever walk of life individuals are in, they are all human, all deserving of rights and recognition. And, if readers are not there yet, the exemplars in this chapter compel us to at least listen to their stories.

Take, for example, Ranjita Sinha in Kolkata, India. A vocal and visible activist, Sinha is at the forefront of the movement for the rights of transgender people in India. She was one of the leading voices behind India's 2014 Supreme Court ruling granting the right of self-determination for trans people. Since then, Sinha has continued her lobbying efforts, advocating to improve transgender health care and campaigning for their right to education, job accessibility, and basic amenities. She travels widely across India, looking to change people's perceptions about trans people, break their prejudices, and encourage a more inclusive approach toward "third genders." More than advocate, Sinha is also a humanitarian leader, establishing her own shelter for abandoned trans people and is a spiritual pioneer, leading the worship of the androgynous Ardhanarishvara—a composite deity who represents the unity of the male and female principles embodied by the god Shiva and goddess Parvati—during Kolkata's annual Durga Puja festival. Profiled by Priyadarshini Sen in this chapter, her story points to some of the new possibilities and leading-from-the-front examples that people like Connor yearn for.

Then there is Andi and Al Tauber, a Mennonite couple who spent more than two decades at Emmaus Ministries in Chicago, Illinois, serving impoverished male sex workers often experiencing homelessness. The married singer-songwriters describe what they call their "ministry of presence," interviewing the men about their lives and turning those life-histories into songs. The result was a musical they called, "Stories from the Streets," which they went on to perform at churches and seminaries around the country, building empathy for the men they served and raising awareness about their situation. Monique Parsons's highly personal profile, which not only describes the Taubers's work in detail but shares some of Parsons's own psychological journey, presents a complicated portrait of their work, pointing out its limitations and liabilities, its exemplary aspects and less-than-desirable outcomes.

Finally, as founder and coordinator of the United Nations Interagency Task Force on Religion and Development and former Secretary General of Religions for Peace International (RfP), Azza Karam brings a unique perspective to the role of religious women across the globe. Working on religion and development with thousands of faith-based and interreligious organizations across the globe, Karam believes what the world needs more than anything else is to listen—*truly listen*—to religious women. When I profiled her, Karam gave me access to her life, and sat for multiple hours of interviews, on one condition: That I share not only her story, but that of other religious women in different parts of the world doing significant work on the ground to bring hope and healing to their communities and contexts (Ela Gandhi, who is also profiled in this book, was one of those women). As the profile in this chapter shows, women and girls are effective and powerful leaders and peacemakers, often playing a critical role in interreligious initiatives across the world. At the same time, and despite advances in gender equality, women and girls still face hurdles when it comes to having a voice in local, regional, and international dialogue. Karam's story, as well as those of women in her orbit, invites us to reflect on how women and girls are involved in interreligious dialogue initiatives across the globe, and how their participation and leadership results in substantial and positive change.

Despite their challenging environments, the exemplars in this chapter are highly resilient. Their beliefs function to reframe their circumstances in a redemptive way, offering a vision of hope and possibility, further reinforced by spiritual practices and deeply held religious convictions. At the same time, religion and spirituality are not distinct qualities that can be separated from the other influences in these exemplars' lives—family upbringing, political structures, interaction with mentors and colleagues, and the supportive network of a community are all factors at play in their present outlooks and activism. But spirituality does seem to be the sea within which these individuals swim and with which they maintain a gritty perseverance in the midst of multiple challenges.

While scholars sometimes make the distinction between intrinsic and fundamentalist religion that is authoritarian, these stories show a more complicated relationship between religion, gender, and sexuality. Included in them are varying levels of privilege and power, each with different implications for socio-economic, health, and social justice outcomes. Interrogating the complex socio-religious and political dynamics at work in each story, the journalists in this chapter show a range of divergent affective tendencies that exist between religion, gender, and human sexuality. Whether those tendencies trend in a direction of justice and increased rights remains an open question. For now, their narratives are a testament to the importance of further exploring, studying, and learning about the multiple ways religion and spirituality will remain key to how gender and sexual identity are going to be understood and experienced in the twenty-first century and beyond—and how deeply held beliefs about gender and sexuality contribute to the interconnectedness of these identifications with the politics and policies that will determine the rights, status, and welfare of billions of humans worldwide.

"Pain Does Not Need to Be Endured Alone"

Ranjita Sinha (Hindu/India)

By Priyardarshini Sen

Sitting in the cocoon of a turmeric-yellow silk sari, head bowed and veiled, activist Ranjita Sinha led ten transgender women in prayer at her shelter home in Kolkata, an Eastern Indian city of nearly five million. Sinha was performing this *puja*—act of devotion or ceremonial worship—in the run-up to the Durga Puja festival. Celebrated with great fanfare across the country, it marks the victory of the Goddess Durga against the bovine demon Mahisasura—a recurrent motif in the Hindu Shakti tradition. But unlike thousands of clay-sculpture idols of the goddess that dot Kolkata every autumn, Sinha's Ardhanarishvara idol was an amalgamation of the Hindu god Shiva and his divine consort Parvati—a synthesis of the universe's masculine and feminine energies. "Our puja challenges the traditional class structure that has kept transgender persons out of socio-religious events for generations," said 48-year-old Sinha, who's been campaigning for the rights of sexual minorities in India over the last two decades.

Shelter for the marginalized

Sinha started the puja to reclaim social space in the city for transgender persons. Later, her venue shifted to Garima Greh, a shelter home for abandoned transgender persons in the suburbs of Kolkata, which she helped set up in late 2021 with aid from the central Indian government. Garima Greh was her dream project.

In 2014, when India's Supreme Court recognized transgender persons as the third gender—marking a major victory for the community—Sinha was at the forefront of the campaigns behind this landmark ruling. But after the ruling, she was disillusioned to see little change in her community's access to jobs, housing, and educational opportunities. The pandemic presented another opportunity to spotlight their fragile lives. So, Garima Greha was launched in the middle of the Covid-19 crisis, when infections in India surpassed global records and hospitals scrambled for life-saving oxygen supplies. Transpersons, who rely mostly on soliciting money and sex work to stay afloat amid everyday experiences of violence and discrimination, were pushed farther to the margins. Sinha felt a shelter home was the least she could do to save her community. "Our shelter could accommodate up to twenty-five people at once," said the outspoken activist in her signature cotton sari and a bright red bindi at the center of her forehead who's fondly called "Ma" or mother by her community members. "It wasn't meant to be a safe space alone, but also a center for counseling and vocational classes."

During the pandemic, transgender people were harassed, driven out of homes, and subjected to correctional rapes—a hate crime where transgenders not conforming to gender, or sexual orientation norms are subjected to homophobic violence to "correct" them. Many came running to Sinha for help at the shelter, where she offered food and utility items, patiently counseling victims on how to deal with violence and ostracization. As the pandemic surged and health systems collapsed, Sinha worked tirelessly with the shelter's residents to reach food and medical supplies in remote parts of the state. She also carried out door-to-door sensitization campaigns to dispel myths about the community as unique carriers of the virus.

When daily wage earners lost their jobs and shelters, Sinha mobilized for funds, setting up a community kitchen to prepare dal, rice, and vegetable curries for up to 100 transpersons every day. She traveled miles to reach them at their doorsteps, freeing up space for distress calls from victims of domestic abuse and gender-based violence. "If I could save even two lives, my life would count for something," said Sinha. "But if I stayed home, who would offer my people food, care, and psychological assistance?"

Sinha tested positive for Covid thrice and was hospitalized once with severe infection, but work kept her motivated despite little support from the government. She lobbied the government to improve transgender health care since sex-reassignment surgeries and hormone therapies were out of reach for most during the pandemic. Access to hospital beds and medicines was also difficult since medical professionals with transphobic views offered little help. But Sinha's persistent appeals to the central and state governments spurred the state health minister to allot separate beds in a government hospital for the care of trans people. It gave her community some hope that transgender health care could extend to remote villages where superstitions and prejudices can run even deeper.

Past experiences

Subhrojyoti Bhowmick, who heads Kolkata's first private health clinic for transgender people, calls Sinha "a groundbreaker with a heart that overflows with empathy. Ranjita should be made part of the government's health committee. Her solutions-focused work will not only help deliver care at the grassroots level where health systems are compromised but also break society's misconceptions."

Sinha's own experiences of victimization have helped her come up with cogent solutions during crises. Growing up in a conventional middle-class family, she was ridiculed for her "feminine mannerisms." At school, she was sneered at, molested, and even forced to "prove" her gender identity. Taunts like "half-lady" and "hijra" (a generic term for transgender persons who live in communities that follow a kinship system in South Asia) not only increased her insecurities but also made seeking out allies more difficult. "I loved wearing makeup from a young age, and my mother appreciated my love for dance," said Sinha. "She bought me anklets to help accentuate my dance steps." Sinha's mother took her to dance school, walled her off from threats, and made space for her to develop her identity as she pleased. But her father and relatives often pressured her to "man up."

Criticisms and lack of validation did not silence Sinha. If anything, they emboldened her to "be as fiery and audacious as Matangini Hazra,"

FIGURE 5.1 Transgender activist Ranjita Sinha at her shelter home for transgender people who've been ostracized by their families in South Kolkata, India, April 2022. Courtesy of Priyadarshini Sen.

the Indian revolutionary shot dead by the British police during the Indian independence movement. Sinha drew inspiration from India's precolonial past as well, when transgender people were revered as demigods and sought out for blessings at social and religious functions. It pained her that colonial anxieties about the community's threat to political authority and public morals had led to a decline in their fortunes since the nineteenth century.

But stories of non-conforming transpersons boosted her confidence. At twenty-three, while interning at an industrial institute in the north Indian city of Chandigarh, near Delhi, Sinha came out as a trans person. She formed a group called "effeminate males" and campaigned widely for the rights of queers, transgender people, and cross-dressers. The campaigns not only shored up her support base but also pushed her to venture into grassroots work. In 1996, she started a community-based organization for the rights of sex workers, truckers, and HIV-positive patients. Dispelling prejudices against them became her focus as she went about sensitizing civil society through dance recitals, picture exhibitions, music programs, and other creative expressions.

Voice for the voiceless

Ten years later, when a sex worker's son in Kolkata committed suicide after his mother tonsured his head for being "too feminine," Sinha made up her mind to fight for the rights of trans persons from Kolkata, her home for several years. As parallel campaigns for transgender rights took off in other parts of the country, Sinha pivoted from local to mainstream protests to verbalize the problems faced by her community. In 2007, she started the Association of Transgenders in Bengal, a community network to campaign for their rights to better education, health, and jobs. She protested the West Bengal Transgender Development Board's decision not to name a transperson as their chairperson and asked why they favored other minorities' access to better jobs. When her dissenters called her anti-national and removed her from the board for her outspokenness, she decided to build her networks independently. Bappaditya Mukherjee, the founder of a youth development organization in Kolkata, says the activist has been a major rallying point in Kolkata and a voice for the voiceless. "Ranjita's courage and fortitude are immeasurable," said Mukherjee. "She's really a movement maker, and without her, sexual minorities would have been left behind."

In 2018, Sinha founded Asthana—a short-stay home for same-sex and interreligious couples fleeing persecution, just a block away from where she founded Garima Greha. She crowd-sourced funds for its upkeep, sheltered couples against social and family pressures, and made it clear that pain does not need to be endured alone. "Our families were opposed to our union because of religious differences," said a former member of Asthana. "But Ranjita Ma gave us the support and kindness to work through our differences since her projects are all about celebrating love."

Sinha's Garima Greha venture also echoed her belief in universal love—that is, until the government withdrew support a year ago due to "practical and financial difficulties." The trans activist's office at the shelter, where she held daily meetings, was an entry point into the tenuous lives of the people living there. Its light saffron walls were covered with photos of family reconciliations, transgender wins in sporting arenas, fashion and dance shows, and sex-reassignment surgeries that transformed lives. Those who Sinha admitted committed to healing through community support and "purposeful living." Sinha welcomed persecuted people from various socio-religious backgrounds. A large poster in the transgender women's quarters forefronted her vision in bold lettering: *Ishwar Allah Tere Naam, Sabko Sanmati De Bhagwan* or "God has given the freedom of choice to every person on this earth irrespective of their religion." It was Mahatma Gandhi's favorite line, woven into a devotional song.

But Sinha's efforts to help her community were diluted when the government turned its back on her shelter last year. She quickly moved her community members to a smaller shelter nearby and went back to the streets to campaign against the government's decision. "I never thought we would be shunned like this," said the activist. "We've been recognized as the third gender, but I'm now supporting my community all by myself."

In 2019, when the Transgender Persons (Protection of Rights) Act was passed by the Indian Parliament to prohibit discrimination against the community with regard to education, employment, and ability to buy property, Sinha was on the streets again, protesting the dilution of civil rights afforded for marriage, adoption, and social security benefits. "It's important that a representative from our community is present in every field of work," she said, openly questioning the act. "Until we raise our voices together nothing will ever get done, and the enactments will have little follow-through."

Grounded in humanism

Sinha thinks the challenges will continue to mount. One of her primary struggles is establishing a hospital dedicated solely to the needs of her community. She wants mobile health check-up vans for trans people who live on the streets and clinics where they can express themselves freely without persecution.

When backlashes increase, she draws inspiration from the life and work of nineteenth-century Bengali poet and Nobel Laureate, Rabindranath Tagore, who emphasized unity through commonalities *and* differences. As a case in point, last year during Eid, Sinha took her shelter's residents on a tour of the richly ornamented nineteenth-century Tipu Sultan Mosque in Kolkata where they engaged with the imam about peace-building campaigns amid recent crackdowns and violence against minorities by the ruling

Hindu nationalist government. During Christmas, they visited a Catholic Church that had not been welcoming of the transgender community earlier and organized cultural events to sensitize underprivileged children. Then, during Durga Puja, Muslim transgender persons joined hands with Hindus to offer sacred food to their deity over five days of worship. Knowing the precarity of the moment, Sinha chose the priest from the community and trained them to carry out rituals a fortnight before the festival began. Sinha encourages the participation of street children, acid attack victims, and those living with HIV. They pray, cook, and eat together without caste or religious discrimination. "These experiences remind us that, despite growing sectarian differences in our country, our gods hold sway," said the activist who draws strength from India's composite culture. "India's pluralistic traditions have helped me resist religious bigots."

Community members have rallied around Sinha as she's moved from one struggle to the next. She relies on their love and respect more than the global recognition she's received or awards from the government. "There's a shared humanity here," says Sinha. "What we want is basic citizenship rights, and for that we're united against social pressures, religious bigotry, and hate."

"Stories from the Streets"

Andi and Al Tauber (Protestant/United States)

By Monique Parsons

The assignment read something like this: For a series on "spiritual exemplars," create a story about Al and Andi Tauber, Chicago-based Mennonites who work at a Christian ministry for male street prostitutes. The couple writes and sings songs about the men, performing their music at churches and Christian schools, many of them evangelical and conservative when it comes to issues of sexuality.

I almost said no. First, as a reporter working the religion beat for more than two decades, I was skeptical about the notion of anything called a "spiritual exemplar." Religion journalists, like all reporters, are doubters by definition. Skeptical by profession. Cynical by calling. And with good cause. "If your mother says she loves you, *check it out*," the old journalism school mantra goes—an ode to rigorous fact-checking (that, it turns out, is itself a misquote).[2] But how do you fact-check a person's spirit? We've all seen much-admired and beloved religious leaders fall from grace—and worse. Then there's the word, "prostitute"—quite the loaded term. There is debate around the criminalization of sex work. Whether it's a legitimate form of labor for consenting adults, who are not victims of sex trafficking, is, for some, an open question.[3] And, I feared that a Christian ministry aimed at male victims of sexual exploitation would have a hidden agenda. Was Emmaus Ministries—founded by a Catholic and supported by a network of Christian colleges, congregations, and individuals—a front for "pray the gay away," anti-LGBTQ programming? Finally, what were Mennonites, religious cousins of the off-the-grid Amish, doing out and about on Chicago's streets in the first place?

Despite my initial skepticism, I forged ahead. Over six months, I learned a great deal about Mennonites out on the streets, male sex trafficking,[4] and what it might mean to live a life that can be a spiritual example for others. I moved in and out of Al and Andi Tauber's lives, collecting hours of audio interviews, church services, meals, musical performances, and ambient sound from the streets of Chicago. I watched them perform their remarkable music and met them in church, at music lessons, at Emmaus headquarters, on the streets doing outreach, at a backyard concert. I watched them perform live and on video, met their supervisors, colleagues, students, and friends. I met Emmaus clients who had a profound impact on the way I approached the story. Along the way, I tried to find answers to the questions that had given me pause. Mostly, however, I listened.[5]

Live songs and simple living

There's so much about a person's story that can't be captured in print. But if you wanted a general overview of Al and Andi Tauber's lives, it would be this: They met in college, began singing and writing music together, and attending different churches before settling with the Mennonites—they both loved the emphasis on music and simple living, as well as the community's social justice commitments. Many Mennonite churches center refugees and their experiences in their ministries, fostering multicultural, multilingual congregations. While their cousins, the Amish, shun modern technology and avoid contact with the "outside world" as much as possible, urban Mennonites intentionally engage with the communities and contexts they are in, albeit with a continued commitment to self-sacrifice and simplicity.

The Taubers once lived in a community in a house in Chicago with other Mennonites, sharing resources and responsibilities. Even after they moved out and lived on their own, they continued to live simply, sharing a single cell phone. Their congregation, Living Water Community Church, meets inside a corner building on Chicago's north side that once housed a discount store. Inside, it's sparse and open; if not for the 8-foot pine cross stuck on a chunk of plywood at the front of the room, a visitor might not guess it's a church.

The first evening I met the Taubers, they were leading an evening music rehearsal at the church. Called the "Monday Night Jam Session," the band members included kids as young as five up to adults in their fifties. Like the congregation itself, the members were a mix of white Mennonite Midwesterners and newcomers from four different continents. They played maracas, ukuleles, guitars, keyboards, and a scratched-up drum kit. With Al leading the way, they stopped-and-started through a song you won't find in a hymnal: "Should I Stay or Should I Go," the 1980s punk rock anthem by The Clash. Wild-eyed and long-haired, Al bears a close resemblance to Warner Salman's much-reproduced "Head of Christ," if Christ shared a cell phone and played electric guitar.[6] Andi, on the other hand, is organized and more reserved, except when she's belting out a tune. She wears glasses and often sports a mischievous grin. On the night I met them, she was gliding back and forth between piano and drums. With joy, optimism, and generosity, the Taubers helped students learn words in new languages, trade instruments, make mistakes, and play on.

Looking for a job, finding a calling

Emmaus Ministries wasn't always their calling. The ministry was founded in Chicago in 1998, with a focus on helping men involved in "survival prostitution"—many of them victims of abuse and trafficking. The founder, John Green, established Emmaus after recognizing a lack of resources and support for boys and men on the streets. The ministry estimates there are 3,000–5,000 of them in Chicago alone. The Taubers didn't start working there because they had a passion for the cause; their friend Green needed help. They needed jobs. They ended up staying nearly twenty years, playing various roles—Al ran an internships program for seminary students and renovated the offices; Andi ran the database and wrote the newsletter. They spent hundreds of nights on the streets, looking for guys to help. "Our guys," they call them. Many grew up with abuse. Many struggled with addiction and mental illness. Many are impoverished, desperate, and lonely. "Most of the men that we work with are selling themselves for food, for money for drugs, often for a place to stay," Al says. "I met a man once who was out selling himself in order to get diapers for his kid."

Gradually, the work became their calling. They started to love it, to love "being with these men." At the ministry center, they shared meals together, played games, helped them get jobs, connected with parole officers, gave them a place to shower and wash clothes. It wasn't about converting anybody—although that was always welcome, Al said. They also didn't focus on the men's sexuality. In a ministry supported by an array of Christian congregations, some of them conservative, sexuality can prove a prickly topic. There was no rainbow flag outside Emmaus's offices when I went there, and they had a policy not to pass out condoms. Some Emmaus clients are openly out; others wrestle with who they are and who they believe God wants them to be. Al described their work as a "ministry of presence." Andi said it felt like being in a family—they learned to be there for each other.

During my reporting, I went out with Al on "outreach" one night. It was almost midnight on a January Wednesday, and it was 33 degrees with snow on the way. Together with a seminary student volunteer named Daniel, Al headed to Halsted Street and a line of popular bars in Boystown, the hub of Chicago's historic gay community. Al's been doing outreach here almost every week for fifteen years. But the men he looks for aren't in the bars; they're lingering on street corners, alleys, and convenience store parking lots. Outside a club known for strong drinks and show-tune singalongs, Al saw a familiar face, a young man with apple cheeks and a shy smile. He was not an Emmaus regular, but Al was pretty sure he was hustling. Al stepped beside him and smoked a pipe as he chatted with the young man, offered him handwarmers, asked after his job and family, asked if he'd seen any other guys out that night. When a man nearby announced he was selling cocaine, Al handed him some hand warmers too, along with a few business cards. He explained his ministry working with male prostitutes and asked him to pass the cards along to anyone who might need them. In time, Al and Daniel moved along, toward the parking lot of a 7-11, looking for more men to help. They don't carry Bibles or religious tracts. In his backpack, Al had granola bars, warm knit caps, and a dose of Narcan, in case he met anyone who overdosed. In all his years on the street, he hadn't had to use it yet, he said.

A musical about male prostitutes

One of the men they met on the streets was Scott Noble, who went on to become a cook at Emmaus. Noble grew up on Chicago's South Side. Rejected by his father, he ran away from home at 16 and started using crack cocaine. He said it took years for the Emmaus folks to coax him off the streets. "I kept running into them; I kept dodging them," Scott says. "But then one day, I was just like, look: I keep seeing you people out here. What do you got to offer me? I'm at the end. You know? So that's the beginning. Then I started coming around." He told me about the good he's seen Al and Andi do. "Going on hospital visits. Care packages. Prayer. They remember your birthday. Jail visits. Just a lot of things that sometimes a person needs. Just somebody to say everything's going to be alright. Or somebody saying, 'You taught me a lot.'"

Some of the men, however, don't make it off the streets. Al and Andi have seen many Emmaus clients die—victims of crime, drug overdoses, despair. They planned too many funerals, and along the way, they realized how hard it is to get people to simply pay attention to these men. And so, they came up with what sounded like a crazy pitch: What if they interviewed the men about their lives, turned the stories into songs, and performed them for live audiences? The program, which took months to put together, included monologues and original songs. They didn't want to shame or exploit the men, so they changed their names to protect their identities and let them read over the drafts to ensure they rang true. Then, they took the show on the road to Christian colleges and congregations. "Basically, we were doing a musical about male prostitutes," Al says with a smile. "Which is just weird."

The songs, it turns out, aren't that weird. The music they created is, instead, poetic and powerful. They called their program "Stories from the Streets," and they performed it dozens of times over the years at places like Goshen College, a Mennonite school in Indiana; the Catholic University of St. Francis in Fort Wayne Indiana; and Asbury Theological Seminary, a Methodist school in Wilmore, Kentucky. One show was about a funeral for a 37-year-old Emmaus client. Others were about abuse and endurance. "Balanced was not a word I'd heard to describe my father. Let's just say he wasn't fair," one song goes. "Still, he tried to divide his time equally in between beatin' me and just not bein' there. Oh, you get used to it. You get used to it."

But Al and Andi Tauber haven't performed "Stories from the Streets" in a few years now. Emmaus Ministries had budget struggles and could no longer afford to pay a troupe of traveling musicians. By the time I was finishing my story, Al and Andi were laid off from their jobs. The ministry needed to hire people with counseling degrees and clinical experience. The Taubers have no formal training like that. They just love serving sexual abuse survivors. When I last saw them, they were trying to make the best of it, dreaming of starting a music school for kids in Chicago who fled war, famine, and the calamitous effects of climate change.

As I reflect on the concerns that almost led me to say "no" to this story, I don't have the answers. Did I walk away wishing Emmaus would hand out condoms and proudly fly that rainbow flag? Yes. I heard the pain in the men's voices as they talked about their sexuality. Perhaps such things would help.

But my story wasn't really about Emmaus; it was about Al and Andi. Are Al and Andi Tauber spiritual exemplars? Many of the people I met—colleagues, clients, friends, interns—answered with an emphatic "yes." Here's how a man they helped get off the streets answers that question, "They're really laboring for the kingdom of God, and they're for real for it." As a journalist, I also came away with two new questions: What would it look like if instead of walking away from the vulnerable people on the street, we walked toward them and listened instead? And, if we value this work, who is willing to invest in it, so people like Al and Andi can do their work, make their music, and inspire us to listen to stories from the streets?

"Listening to the World's Religious Women"

Azza Karam (Muslim/Egypt, the Netherlands, and United States)

By Ken Chitwood

Azza Karam was just about to step up to the podium at the Inselhalle in Lindau, Germany to accept the position of Secretary General of Religions for Peace International (RfP) on August 23, 2019. Shortly before her speech, she spoke offstage with Sonia Guajajara, an indigenous representative from Brazil. Karam was leaning in, listening carefully to what Guajajara had to say about the environment and the need for RfP—a multi-religious platform with the representation of diverse religious institutions and communities—to make a bold statement about climate change. As Guajajara finished, Karam smiled, thanked her, and said, "when it comes to issues like climate change, what the world needs is more women like you."

Perhaps it is telling that before one of the more momentous speeches of Karam's career, she wasn't pacing backstage or making final preparations for the presentation. Instead, she was taking time to hear, and be present with, one of the valued, female members of the organization she was about to accept the leadership of. That, as Karam tells it, is one of the prime directives of her tenure as RfP Secretary General—to raise up women's voices within and across religious traditions and see her fellow females not only "take their seat at the table," but step out in front and lead the way to meaningful change on a range of issues confronting the world today.

To that end, Karam's RfP—with the Foundation Peace Dialogue of the World Religions and Civil Society (Ring for Peace) and supported by the German Federal Foreign Office (Ministry of Foreign Affairs)—convened the first assembly on "Women, Faith and Diplomacy: Keeping the Faith and Transforming Tomorrow." Originally scheduled to take place in November 2020 in Lindau, the event was held online due to the Covid-19 pandemic. Even so, more than 600 participants from ninety countries gathered virtually, with speakers attending in person, to discuss the role of women in the world's religions and their leadership in the realms of faith and diplomacy. Karam said it was an opportunity for representatives from the media, civil society, international development, academia, and religious institutions to celebrate how far they've come in terms of women's leadership on issues of peace and security, sustainable development, and human rights. The whole point of the assembly, Karam said, was to help attendees better "appreciate the breadth and the depth of contributions of women in the realms of faith and diplomacy across the world."

At the same time, it is also an opportunity to wrestle with how far they have to go. Women's leadership—and resistance to it—in these realms is

FIGURE 5.2 Azza Karam addresses attendees at the Religions for Peace International assembly on women, faith, and diplomacy in Lindau, Germany. Courtesy of Religion Unplugged.

something that Karam is intimately familiar with. Over a decades' long career in academia, diplomacy, and interreligious dialogue, Karam has faced impediments to her fierce initiative from a variety of colleagues. Karam said she has frequently faced belligerence from people of faith who would not accept her leadership. "There is a common culture in religious communities, no matter what religion, no matter where they are, where women are not supposed to claim credit for what they do or be up front," she said. "They are meant to serve, be in the background, and not attract attention to themselves. I never learned to fit that mold," said Karam.

Disheartened, but never daunted, Karam pressed on to take on leadership roles as Professor of Religion and Development at the Vrije Universiteit in Amsterdam, Senior Advisor on Culture, at the United Nations Population Fund (UNFPA) and as Chair of the UN InterAgency Task Force on Religion and Development.

Growing up with prayer, devotion, and tension

For Karam, the journey through such positions of influence and leadership in faith and diplomacy started in childhood, growing up in Egypt and India. "The earliest memories I have," she said, "are of my parents praying in our home in Egypt." Right next to these recollections of religious devotion are memories of her "ayah," or nanny, in India where Karam spent her first four years as a child. "Every day, she would do the offerings at her shrine, but never in the house, because my parents would not allow it in their household. And so, I grew up with the value of prayer and devotion," she said, "but also with the awareness of how they can be the source of the greatest contention and tension in communities." It was this dissonance, and at the same time the similarity in sentiment, between her nanny's *puja* and her parents' praying that Karam said set her on a path toward leading people of many faiths into dialogue and common action.

Another set of experiences instilled in her the importance of women's rights. It was the 1970s in Egypt and her aunt wanted to get a divorce. "Laws notwithstanding," it was, in Karam's words, "sheer hell to get a divorce as a woman and, to be honest, it still is." Her aunt was a faithful Muslim, an independent mother, and a public servant. And yet, she struggled for years to get a divorce because of a dispute over property that she herself had purchased. The irony, said Karam, was that this was all going on while Jehan Sedat, the first lady of Egypt, was championing women's rights and reform. "So, here was my destitute aunt with her three children, with laws in her favor to give her the right to be divorced, and people were preventing her from getting the divorce she was entitled to," Karam said, "and much of the resistance came from religious actors." For Karam, this cemented the interest she had in trying to understand the intersection of politics, religion, and gender and how that plays out in everyday lives. "Because it's not a simple black-and-white issue everywhere in the world where people of faith do nothing but good," she said, "it doesn't quite work out that way does it?"

Bringing faith to the United Nations

Those were some of the tensions that Karam brought to her work in intergovernmental work at RfP and the UN. After serving at RfP from 2000 to 2004 as Director of a Global Women of Faith Network and Advisor on Middle East Interreligious dynamics, Karam made the move to the UN, where she found a completely different universe to her work at RfP. "At Religions for Peace it was normal to talk about religion, you don't even think about it," she said, "but the UN was a completely different culture to come to terms with. The general message around the UN was, 'We don't talk about faith. We don't do religion.'"

More than strange, this was nonsensical to Karam. She said, "The UN is supposed to be the quintessential universal culture, and they don't do religion? It was almost a denial of self." While working as Senior Advisor on Culture at the UN Population Fund (UNFPA) Karam worked to bring different religious voices together to create "a certain synergy around how faiths inform us and our politics." She said the problem wasn't with religion, but with the silos that institutions put up between the religious and the secular, the intergovernmental and the interdenominational. Karam saw an opportunity to create a space for UN agencies to learn about spirituality, listen to religious leaders, and understand the beliefs and rituals that motivate people to do both great good and great evil in the world.

The result was the founding of the UN Interagency Task Force on Religion and Sustainable Development (UN-IATF) in 2010. Meant to inform and support actors in the UN universe to understand the why, how, who, and what of religion and engaging with religious actors, for Karam, it was also a matter of the heart. "Yes, when you step through the UN doors, you have no country, you have no religion, you serve all regardless, ostensibly. But how can you serve all regardless if you don't understand what touches other people's hearts?" she said. "We're kind of missing the heart of a human being if we're not talking about their faith." Karam sees understanding a person's religious motivations as an essential step for the UN to form grassroots partnerships. "Religion matters in the work the UN does," she said. "It is the heartbeat of anything that we think we can do to heal the world's problems."

Her legacy in that regard is long. Today, the UN-IATF includes more than twenty UN agencies and provides policy guidance around engagement with faith-based actors. In 2018, the UN-IATF established the Multi-faith Advisory Council (MFAC), an informal and voluntary entity that brings together representatives of thirty-five of the UN's faith-based partners, including religious leaders and heads of faith-based organizations (FBOs) such as RfP. One of the MFAC's members is Rabbi Burton Visotzky, Appleman Professor of Midrash and Interreligious Studies at the Jewish Theological Seminary in New York City. He said Karam was "the mother of us all. Without Azza bringing together these different agencies to talk about religion and listen to representatives of religious traditions, the UN may still have not 'discovered religion.'" Visotzky continued, "and that would be a detriment to the world, because the sad truth is that a lot of incitement to violence and tension comes from religious leaders." He also said he has seen a shift in the UN's operations. "Anytime UN agencies would go to a hotspot or where there is enormous poverty, who would they find already at work there?" Visotzky said. "Religious actors. Whether it's Islamic Relief, Catholic Relief Services, Bread for the World, or the American Jewish World Service or other FBOs, they were the ones working with development organizations to lift people out of poverty and build peace." Now the UN understands that uniting religious leaders around a common cause can lower tensions, and they are keen to partner with MFAC, Visotzky said.

Women of faith often go unnoticed

Oftentimes, Karam is quick to remind, it is religious women who are making the greatest impact on the front lines. That is why, with funding from the Ford Foundation, Karam founded the first Global Women of Faith Network while at RfP before and now, as Secretary General, she convened the "Assembly on Women, Faith, and Diplomacy." Karam said the event was an opportunity to celebrate women of faith doing immense work around the globe. "The work of women of faith is nothing new," she said, "what is new is the collaboration between men and women to bring the voice of women to speak to certain, critical, global truths."

Pointing away from her own immense accomplishments, she highlighted the work of women of faith involved in RfP's network that are making a real difference on the ground. She spoke of Cissé Hadja Mariama Sow, president of Muslim Women of Guinea and RfP co-president, who has worked at the front lines of interreligious peace, reconciliation, and critical issues facing women in West Africa for over half a decade.

A Muslim, she became increasingly involved in politics and interreligious dialogue with other women of faith more than fifty years ago. An advocate for education and equal rights and representation for women, Sow said she worked "to mobilize and organize women in religious affairs" and see women not only read, learn, and memorize their scriptures, but interpret and apply them to the social issues they deem critical. In churches and mosques and multi-faith institutions like the West African Women's Association (WAFA), of which she was president, Sow said that she has witnessed a marked improvement, with women participating in various levels of religious activities. Interpreting the Qur'an for herself—and in concert with the women she works so intimately with—Sow is committed to fighting against religious fanaticism, especially in Guinea, her home country. "Violence has no part in Guinea or Muslims," she said, "we must learn to do better." A mother of eight herself, Sow has also turned her religious energies toward family planning in Guinea. She said, "the effort to develop family planning in Guinea cannot succeed without the full commitment of religious and traditional leaders." Thankfully, Sow said, both the government and religious bodies have listened and are making the changes she and her fellow religious women have advocated so long for.

She also praised the work of Lilian de Jesus-Sison of the Philippines, a Catholic. A chemistry professor for most of her life, Jesus-Sison became Secretary General of RfP Philippines as "a way of giving back," she said. Working with different faith groups, her advocacy took her to the hinterlands of the conflict areas in Mindanao addressing the trauma of internally displaced women and children, working on child protection projects with UNICEF and helping women to respond to issues such as climate change and human trafficking. The results of her work became models for similar efforts in Brazil, Bosnia Herzegovina, southern Thailand, and Myanmar. Similar to Karam, Jesus-Sison found this type of work to be a matter of heart and soul. "I was only able to transcend the darkness in life because of my strong devotion to the blessed Mother. She is my constant companion in generous giving."

At each turn in her long life of learning and service, Jesus-Sison said her faith has remained a constant motivation. Born into an active Catholic family, working at a Dominican university, and taking part in the famous Marian processions of Manila, Jesus-Sison was always grounded in her religion's proverbs and rituals. "If you read the letter of St. Paul to the Corinthians, it says that whatever we do, we do it all for the glory of God," she said, "and that is the one thing that has motivated me and inspired me in all the work that I did." Whether it was actively promoting a "preferential option for the poor" or loving her neighbor through interreligious dialogue and common action, Jesus-Sison said she did all of it "as excellently as possible, because in my view, I'm doing it for the glory of God."

Women like Jesus-Sison and Sow are the reason that Karam and her partners convened the "Women, Faith, and Diplomacy" event—to create a space where "women can discover that they are advocating for very similar things, albeit couched in different religious terms," said Karam. In the midst of a global pandemic and at a time when international cooperation is at its most vulnerable, when the world order is facing a meta-crisis of monumental magnitude, and climate change rages on, Karam believes it is a time for women to take their seats not only around the table, but up front and at the podium. And similar to the gathering in Lindau, Karam does not stand alone. Instead, she brings with her a worldwide network of women like Sow and Jesus-Sison, believing it's time that global leaders start listening to their voices—like she does.

6

Environmental Justice

We were meant to be happy, we were meant to take care of Mother Earth, to protect all life, be it human or animal.

ROSALINA TUYUC VALÁSQUEZ (INDIGENOUS)

There is no way we can consider environmental issues without involving the sacred nature of water, air, land and fire. Our Indigenous teachings tell us that ... we and the Earth are related.

TOM GOLDTOOTH (INDIGENOUS)

My Vietnamese and Buddhist upbringing taught me about interconnectedness and how we need to be concerned ... about how we're connected to everything in the world's ecosystem.

MAI NGUYEN (BUDDHIST)

The eternal tree is vulnerable to our forgetfulness. Forgetfulness causes drought and wildfires and empties the well that feeds the tree. Too much forgetting is an ecological disaster.

ANDREAS KORNEVALL (PAGAN)

We must raise our voices and take actions to heal our planet because of boys and girls who have the right to enjoy it.

CARMEN SANTIAGO ALONSO (INDIGENOUS/ROMAN CATHOLIC)

Introduction

"The road," wrote Spanish poet Antonio Machado, "is made by walking." Often adopted as a metaphor for pilgrimage, Sarah Moring, a climate activist living in Manchester, England, said she journeyed with this quote every day as she joined the Young Christian Climate Network (YCCN) on its relay walk to the United Nations Climate Change Conference (COP26), in September 2021. Stretching over 750 miles and cutting through Cardiff, London, and Oxford, YCCN participants joined a "crusade for climate justice" by walking the route between the end of the G7 meeting in Cornwall on June 13 and COP26's opening ceremony in Glasgow on October 31 that year.

Covering the pilgrimage for *Christianity Today*, I was relatively new to reporting on the intersection between religion and climate justice.[1] When I started on the religion beat writing for *The Houston Chronicle*, there seemed to not be much in it. Houston, for all its multicultural flair, is a city at the center of the global fossil-fuel industry. Many of the people of faith I spoke to at local churches, mosques, and temples were employed at big oil companies and, if they had feelings one way or the other, they knew where their bread was buttered. It was hard to find faith actors who were advocating for a different way, pushing back against theologies and practices that contributed to the adverse effects of climate change.

Those experiences were later informed by Lynn White Jr.'s 1967 essay, "The Historical Roots of Our Ecological Crisis," in which the historian claimed that the Judeo-Christian tradition had promoted anthropocentric attitudes for centuries. Positioning humans as the most important element of existence, this stream of thought undergirded environmentally destructive behaviors across the years, seeding the roots of our contemporary ecological crisis. In the decades following White's essay, some argued that religious communities were becoming more environmentally friendly, what was termed the "greening of religion." Some claimed that, since the mid-twentieth century, the world's predominant religions were becoming more environmentally conscious and thus, contributing more to an environmentally just future. Religion scholar Bron Taylor and colleagues took up this anecdotal claim, surveying theological orientations around divine agency in preventing or promoting natural events. Taylor and his co-authors argued that, in general, religious worldviews and theodicies hindered environmental understanding and mobilization. "On balance [and notwithstanding the generally pro-environmental positions within indigenous traditions]," Bron and his co-authors argued, "we found the thrust of White's thesis is supported, whereas the greening-of-religion hypothesis is not."[2] In other words, the "greening of religion" hypothesis was not panning out.

With my experience back in Texas, I took to his line of reasoning that, with the exception of Indigenous traditions and some nature-based cosmologies, most religious traditions were not prone to pro-environmental positions. Though they left the door open to the possibility of helping religious individuals and groups mobilize more effectively and respond to contemporary environmental challenges, Taylor and his co-authors believed it was not likely. Religious actors, the authors surmised, were not reliable partners in pursuing climate justice. That did not mean there were no religious actors or communities working toward environmental justice. But, they argued, the evidence for positive movement was thin on the ground.

Since encountering their argument over a decade ago, I have gone on to report from locales across the globe where people of faith are coming together to respond to climate change and demand action based on their religious beliefs. I spoke with an interfaith coalition in Rwanda developing a multi-pronged, inclusive approach to strengthen food security; a group of First Nations people and Muslims convening in Canada to address climate justice together; and Anglicans advocating for the Church of England to divest from fossil fuels, which it did in June 2023.[3] Each of these individuals and communities advocate for environmentally friendly policy and plead with institutions, governments, and local communities to take concrete steps to address, and counteract the worst effects of, climate change as an extension of their spiritual convictions. Their examples have not yet convinced me that religion is going green. But they have shown me how it is possible, and vital, that religious actors take climate change seriously and shape their communities, theologies, and practices accordingly.

Such was the case with Rabbi Elias Szczytnicki, who I met in Lindau, Germany, at the 10th World Assembly of Religions for Peace (RfP). While there, I saw Szczytnicki urgently make his way to the front of the crowd after a draft of the assembly declaration was about to be read aloud. It was a document I had spent days preparing on behalf of a committee made up of some of the world's most prestigious religious leaders, people with a long and deep commitment to peace and justice. Addressing a host of issues, ranging from violent conflicts to education, extreme poverty to protecting sacred sites, the declaration was deficient in one detail, Szczytnicki said. While it included a section on "Sustainable and Integral Human Development and Protecting the Earth," the declaration did not go far enough, in his opinion. "The environment has to be the number one priority. It is not enough to make it the last paragraph, it has to be the first," said Szczytnicki, Regional Secretary General for Religions for Peace in Latin America and the Caribbean. "After all," Szczytnicki told me, "if the climate crisis persists at its present rate, we will have no earth to protect, no place upon which we will build our synagogues, churches, or mosques. No shared land to make peace over, no sanctuary at all to pray, worship, or come together in." In other words, Szczytnicki challenged me—and you, the reader—to consider how humanitarian crises, conflict, and other issues of import are not only exacerbated by the deleterious effects of climate change, but if climate change is not addressed, work on those issues will be moot. "What's the point in saving the world," Szczytnicki surmised, "if there is no world left to save?"

This chapter introduces readers to people of faith like Moring and Szczytnicki, individuals agitating for a different kind of future, and perhaps a different kind of religion: One where religious actors partner with everyday citizens, organizations, governmental bodies, and intergovernmental institutions to advocate and plan for ambitious and faith-rooted climate actions to create a livable future for all. The hope is that by hearing their stories, we might come away with a different perspective on the presence—and vital importance—of faith voices in the chorus calling for serious action on climate change.

First is Carmen Santiago Alonso, a Zapotec woman whose blending of Indigenous and Catholic tradition inspired her work as a social and environmental activist, defending the rights of Indigenous people in Mexico. In particular, through her organization Flor y Canto, A.C. (or Centro de Derecho Indígenas "Flor y Canto"), she worked with Indigenous communities in Oaxaca to fight mining activities in order to protect Indigenous water access and search for solutions to reduce the impacts of climate change on Indigenous communities and their livelihoods. Though she passed away in 2022, her legacy lives on in the profile written by Magdaléna Rojo, which speaks to the vital importance of Indigenous voices in the fight against climate change and how champions of environmental justice focus their work on providing interpretations of their faith traditions that support earth-friendly actions, behaviors, and conservation-oriented perspectives.

Then comes my profile of David Rosen, former Chief Rabbi of Ireland and senior rabbi of the largest Orthodox Jewish congregation in South Africa. Speaking with Rosen in Germany and later, from his home in Israel, he told me that of all aspects of his work in interreligious dialogue and education, his greatest passion remains the care of the environment and the need to reform our lifestyles accordingly. "As a religious practitioner, I believe that there is no issue today that is as compelling or imperative for religious people to be engaged with," he said. Drawing on the tradition of the sages of the Talmud—after the Hebrew Scriptures, the central text of Rabbinic Judaism and the primary source of Jewish religious law (*halakha*) and theology—Rosen argues that a vegan lifestyle is the new *kashrut* (or kosher). "There are numerous, important ethical reasons why we should be living according to a plant-based diet," he said, "but from a Jewish perspective, there are specific particular concerns born out of the religious tradition of Jewish practice law that demand we no longer consume in such a way that contributes to environmental degradation and economic injustice."

Finally, in his profile of Gopal Patel in Montclair, New Jersey, Kevin D. Grant finds kinship in a man drawing from his past as he faces an uncertain future—personally, professionally, and on a more global, societal level. Patel is the founder of Bhumi Global, a faith-based environmental movement rooted in Hindu principles. Named for the Hindu goddess who represents

Earth, Patel's organization focuses on the "triple crisis" of climate change, biodiversity loss, and pollution. Born in England and shaped by years of traveling the world teaching the formative Hindu text, the Bhagavad Gita, Pael combines traditional Hindu wisdom and practice with his Western, Indian diaspora identity. He uses this mix to galvanize a diverse community, supporting leadership development and seeking policy change. Patel and those he works with identify biodiversity—the variety of life on Earth—as a strategic priority that is both overlooked in the larger climate conversation and closely aligned with Hindu teachings and values.

Though scholars are right to critique religious communities for their complicity in contributing to environmental degradation, faith-motivated actors are playing critical and multifaceted roles in the movement for climate justice. Not only do they provide long-standing examples of ecologically minded spirituality, they are also often on the front lines of climate-related disaster response. Each of the exemplars in the project focused on environmental justice articulates ecological values within their own traditions and puts their perspectives to work on the ground. Thus, we can infer from the results, a broader coalition of spiritually inspired actors helping populations learn how to live through and confront climate change. Moreover, they are responding in novel and innovative ways. The profiles in this chapter, in particular, provoke us to consider how to move past the marginalization of religious perspectives and practitioners in the fight for climate justice. A more hopeful strategy would align their voices with a chorus of other activists. There are numerous examples of how religious institutions, worldviews, and practices have excused and exacerbated climate change, and continue to do so. Nonetheless, if we are going to avoid climate catastrophe, or navigate our way through it, religious actors must have a seat at the table. Their voices need to be heard.

Building on this notion, religion and environmental studies scholar Victoria Machado argues we need to cultivate new ways of seeing ourselves and our relationship with the world around us. In her research alongside activists working on water issues in Florida, Machado has witnessed how they are trying to shift the narrative so that when we talk about springs, lakes, and rivers, we treat them as living systems rather than commodities of economic value. How do we talk about them as having inherent value and thus, worth saving in and of themselves. She said:

> At a time when young people are filled with climate anxiety—which can be crippling—taking a step back and re-examining the world and themselves can offer a broader perspective, perhaps a more hopeful one that will promote sustainable longer term and effective action for climate justice, rather than apathy and inaction. For me, this means exploring our belief systems (whether or not they are tied to a formal or world religion) and our daily practices. I think there is a lot to be said for taking different directions and offering new perspectives on the world around us and our

> place in it. That not only shifts our language but opens up the possibility of new ideas about what's next.[4]

The stories in this chapter offer some of those new narratives, shifts in language, and the possibility of new ideas about what's next. They are living embodiments of the way toward climate justice being made by walking. Whether it is reframing human relationships to water in Oaxaca, adopting veganism as the "new kosher," or offering the concept of a cosmic dance between destruction and re-creation as a kind of "pastoral care" in the face of a calamitously changing climate, each provokes us to consider how we might both be more hopeful and consider what the path may hold if there is no hope left—or, to riff on Szczytnicki, how we might save the world, even if we feel there might be no world left to save.

"Working Together for Water"

Carmen Santiago Alonso (Indigenous and Roman Catholic/Mexico)

By Magdaléna Rojo

At a pond near Santa Catarina Minas, a municipality in the southern Mexican state of Oaxaca, a few trucks and cars full of people gather before sunrise. The crowd gathering in the nautical light of the blue hours—made up of community leaders from across Oaxaca, representatives of local government and the National Water Commission (CONAGUA), as well as international civil organizations—are there to celebrate World Water Day.

It is March 22, 2019, and I, along with those gathered, am about to join an Indigenous Zapotec morning ceremony. My invitation came from Carmen Santiago Alonso, a Mexican environmental activist and leader of Oaxaca's Center of Indigenous Rights Flor y Canto.[5] Preparations for the ceremony take a few hours, with everything coming together under the soft light of sunrise. As the sun crests the horizon and its first rays pierce the darkness, bathing the pond's water in golden light and slowly warming the soil beneath our feet, four children change into costumes that represent the four elements: water, air, fire, and earth. *Shamans*, *curanderas*, and Indigenous healers prepare a *mandala*—a symbolic circle created with herbs, tortillas, tomatoes, corn, and other native crops, as well as flowers of all colors. In the middle of the gathering circle, there is incense from resin of the copal tree, native to the region, to clean the space before the ritual. People who will perform the ceremony hold different kinds of instruments, from seashells to small, leather-clad hand drums.

We are almost ready for the ceremony. And yet, an ever-growing number of people from Santa Catarina Minas and surrounding communities keep arriving. At the entrance to the *mandala*, local men construct an arc, using palm leaves decorated with red flowers. First, participants cleanse each other using local herbs beneath the arc. Together with Santiago Alonso, I am among the last to enter the sacred circle. She first uses herbs to cleanse my body, and then she asks me to return the favor and cleanse hers. Following her lead, I gently move the herbs across her body in preparation for the ritual ahead.

Dressed in a traditional, embroidered blouse, the Zapotec activist enters the space with the timber of drumbeats and the voices of her fellow indigenous people ringing around her. Her colleague, Beatriz Salinas Avilés, is giving instructions about deep respiration—how we can become increasingly aware of our bodies, so that we might be more "present" during the ceremony.

It takes perhaps forty minutes until we all give thanks to the four elements, to our ancestors and other powers who support us on our terrestrial journey. We then turn to the four cardinal directions, listening to the Indigenous healers' words along with Santiago Alonso's. Together, but not in unison, they stress Mother Earth's importance. Each turn is accompanied by the sounds of the natural world awakening around us and the consistent rhythm of instrumental music. Finally, everybody takes a flower from the mandala to make their way to a chapel by the pond to give thanks to a local saint. They enter a small concrete chapel with a table inside. On the makeshift

FIGURE 6.1 A Zapotec activist, Carmen Santiago Alonso, leads an indigenous water ritual. Photo courtesy of Noel Rojo.

altar, the saint stands amidst flowers decorating the table and surrounding space. Most people kiss the saint and continue to bring one of the flowers from the mandala to the pond. Several people grab a bit of bread or tortilla to eat and pieces of lettuce and other vegetables, some corn, other seeds, or a shot of *mezcal*, bringing their offering to a hole dug just a few meters from the mandala. There, a woman traces a cross in the air and then proceeds to place the food inside the hole—a symbolic act of giving back to Mother Earth, who sustains us. Others follow her lead.

Breakfast is served afterwards, along with a decent serving of *convivencia*—sharing of a moment—before participants make their way back to the village for a day-long workshop about how to protect local water sources like the pond. These are not led by local leaders, shamans, or priests, but researchers from local universities. Each has their role to play—in ceremony or scientific exploration and education—to protect the waters for the people they sustain.

"Syncretism" and an inner, spiritual dilemma

Santiago Alonso grew up in San Antonino Castillo Velasco, a community not far from Oaxaca de Juárez, the region's eponymous capital and most populous city. Her values, she said, came from her parents and grandparents—people with no formal education, but who passed on indigenous knowledge and a sense for community. "The care for nature is an inheritance, a legacy from my grandmothers, from my grandfathers and my father. They taught me to love and to respect the principle from a very young age," Santiago Alonso said. "My grandmother used to say that corn is sacred food, therefore it is very important to take care of it. Love the corn a lot, she used to say in Zapotec." To this, she added:

> As a child, I was only repeating things (after my parents and grandmothers). But when I grew up a little bit more and started working within the Catholic Church—defending the land and territory—only then I understood the teachings of my grandmothers better.

While Indigenous traditions came from her ancestors, Santiago Alonso felt a particular pang of inner conflict when she became an adolescent catechist in her local Catholic parish. In particular, she wrestled with the Catholic Church's prohibition against Indigenous spiritual practices. "I saw that some priests used to say that our practices were not correct and that we should not even speak about them," Santiago Alonso remembered.

Even as she struggled, she enjoyed being part of Catholic rituals. Later on, she decided to become a lay nun. "I had a boyfriend at that time and was about to get married. My parents wanted me to have children, but I decided to change my path." And so, she left her parents and hometown for a vocation that was somewhat uncertain. "We were the first group of seven women that initiated the service for poor Indigenous communities," she said. Santiago Alonso admitted this was one of the most difficult moments in her life. But it was at this stage that Archbishop Bartolomé Carrasco Briseño, a proponent of liberation theology,[6] helped her rediscover her Indigenous spirituality and navigate her way through the dilemma. "Our spirituality is a fundamental part of our people," she said. "I realized that the Catholic theology and the indigenous one are the same in their essence. They both aim to have respect for a divinity because this divinity is a creator of the sky, earth, sea, and all the things that are mentioned in the Bible and that indigenous knowledge mentions, too."

Both spiritual sources helped Santiago Alonso later in life, even amidst the fears and risks that came with her work as an environmental activist. That kind of work, as benign as it may seem, can come with deadly results in Mexico. In 2022, the international nonprofit conservation organization Global Witness documented an increase in lethal attacks on environmentalists in the country. Thirty-one people were killed for defending land and the environment that year—more than half of them Indigenous people.[7]

Before she goes about her dangerous work, Santiago Alonso first consecrates herself to Mother Earth. She said:

> I ask her for help. I also usually go to a chapel that we have in our house for missionaries. The Holy Spirit is there with us. And, I have a spiritual guide with me, a priest who helps me on my spiritual path. I have been lucky during my life as a missionary to meet priests and fellow missionaries that are equally cultured in our Indigenous spirituality.

La Comunalidad

There is one more source that gives Santiago Alonso inspiration to continue fighting for Indigenous peoples' rights: communality or *comunalidad*.[8] Jaime Martínez Luna, a Zapotec scholar based in Guelatao de Juárez, a village in the Sierra Norte region, about an hour and a half from Oaxaca de Juárez, identified four pillars of *comunalidad*: connection to the land, general assemblies, collective work and celebrations. Each of these pillars influenced Santiago Alonso's life and work. "Territory is first and it was here before us," explained Martínez Luna. Around 80 percent of Oaxaca territory is under the control of Indigenous communities. The land is communal, and the community decides on its use together. In Oaxaca, out of 570 municipalities, 417 govern themselves within the system of *usos y costumbres* (customs and traditions), which is guaranteed to Indigenous populations in the Mexican Constitution.[9] Since the era of Spanish colonial rule, authorities have recognized local forms of self-governance and resource jurisdiction, with varying degrees of acceptance and formality. *Usos y costumbres* mechanisms are used by numerous Indigenous peoples in Mexico, Bolivia, Guatemala, and other countries in Latin America to govern water rights, in criminal and civil conflicts, and to elect their representatives to regional and national bodies.

And yet, among many indigenous communities in Oaxaca, there are no political parties. Instead, representatives of all families gather at general assemblies and decide on issues of shared import. "In the assembly, the element that brings us together is the problem or the necessity we need to solve to live happily in our territory. It is the assembly that regulates life and gives it structure," said Martínez Luna. The general assembly has the maximum authority; however, it does not exercise power because it is predicated on the assembly's gathered opinion. Everybody's voice must be heard, respected, and integrated into the final decision. "The agreement is not vertical, it is a horizontal result that resolves the mood, creativity, and capacity of all," Martínez Luna said. The assembly also names representatives of the community as well as people who will provide basic services otherwise provided by the state, such as police officers, finance officers, a mayor. These so-called *cargoes* are typically performed without remuneration.

Collective work, known as *tequio*, is work that community members do together for the community. It can be painting the fences around a local school, collecting rubbish in the community or guarding the forests to protect them from paper companies coming to log the trees. Various communities in Oaxaca were able to protect their territories in the past thanks to such collective work. For example, in Santa María Yavesía, also in the Sierra Norte region, locals remember when a paper company was coming to their forest to log the trees. Local men took turns, spending days and weeks in the forests to prevent the logging.

When such projects come to fruition, *fiestas* or celebrations are a means to celebrate the common work accomplished by the community members. They are also lessons for future generations. In Oaxaca, people are educated to participate in community matters from childhood. "I have learnt to participate … to watch how the elderly do things, to respect their way, to listen to the way of the elderly women too. I believe that when participation is consistent, it pays off. It does have an impact," said Santiago Alonso.

Precedent in Mexico

Inspired by this communal way of life, Santiago Alonso and her organization Flor y Canto supported local communities in winning a precedent-setting case in protecting water sources in Mexico in 2021. Flor y Canto was the driving force in winning a battle with the Mexican government to return control of local water sources to Indigenous communities, with the result that sixteen Indigenous Zapotec communities in Mexico have created over 579 water infrastructure projects, including absorption wells, small dams and water pans, to conserve water in the Oaxaca Valley—a region impacted by recurrent droughts. Despite these significant successes, farmers in the region still struggle to have enough water, making water conservation efforts an ongoing battle.

And so, Flor y Canto still has plenty of work to do. Santiago Alonso had served as the organization's director for more than twenty-five years. Its origins stretch back to October 1995, the result of an eight-year process of "Meetings and Dialogues" between the different Indigenous peoples of Oaxaca, which emerged out of an ecclesial context committed to the life and dignity of Indigenous peoples within the Catholic Church.

At the end of the 1980s, Don Bartolomé Carrasco Briseño—a former Roman Catholic archbishop known as a champion of the marginalized—called on Indigenous communities and pastoral agents in the Catholic Church to talk about how they might commemorate the 500th anniversary of the arrival of the Catholic faith in the Americas. "We had several encounters about our rights as Indigenous communities where spirituality played an important role. We had to share our knowledge and give arguments to society about why we defend Mother Earth and our territory," Santiago Alonso said.

At multiple regional meetings, Indigenous people and Afro-Mexican communities discussed their respective rights and common interests. These communal conversations occurred at the same time the Zapatista movement grew in neighboring Chiapas. An anti-globalization movement for democracy and land reform, the Zapatista National Liberation Front was formed in reaction to the North American Free Trade Agreement (NAFTA) and the economic and environmental burdens it placed on ordinary Mexicans. It was also part of a reorganization of Indigenous communities under way since the 1960s, which empowered Indigenous people to rise up against local governments across Mexico.

With all this occurring in the background, Santiago Alonso gathered with others in her community. The military surrounded the place of meeting, but they continued their consultations anyways. The result was the establishment of Flor y Canto—an organization meant to fight for indigenous peoples' rights and their environment. Six men were appointed to lead the organization along with Santiago Alonso, the sole woman. The organization began to undertake various activities, offering capacity building trainings for communities and devising methods to collect rainwater in dryer regions, while also protesting mining companies' abuses and advocating for Indigenous peoples' rights at the local, regional, and national levels. Today, it is a completely woman-led organization.

For the first decade, Flor y Canto worked tirelessly in the defense of communities for the conservation of their resources, especially on behalf of their water rights. Then, in 2005, many people from the Central Valleys region abandoned their fields as a result of severe droughts. Conservation efforts appeared to have come to dust and thousands migrated, either to other states in Mexico or to *El Norte*.[10] During that time, various farmers from different communities received letters from the National Water Commission (CONAGUA) about fines for the overuse of water, fines which made no sense since they had less and less water in their wells every year.

These farmers approached Flor y Canto, asking for help. The organization discovered that CONAGUA was giving away individual water concessions to municipalities and businesses. No collective concessions were granted to the farmers, in breach of national law. The National Commission was also supposed to take care of the aquifers, which was not happening. Zapotec communities responded by uniting under COPUDA, the Coordinator of People United for the Care and Defense of Water, launching what would become a 17-year-long journey toward control over their water sources. COPUDA members met within irregular general assemblies hosted in local communities across the region to discuss further steps in the legal process against CONAGUA. Flor y Canto assisted these communities during the legal process, organizing training sessions to empower local leaders to stand up for their rights in the face of the government.

Between 2005 and 2007, COPUDA was able to cancel the fines issued to Zapotec farmers. Then, a few years later, a Mexico City court mandated CONAGUA to carry out a meaningful consultation. Between 2013 and 2015, roundtables were set up between members of CONAGUA and COPUDA representatives to discuss the conditions of collective concession. After facing various obstacles and undergoing numerous general assemblies and dialogues between COPUDA and CONAGUA, Mexican President Andrés Manuel López Obrador signed a decree in November 2021, which established a regulated aquifer zone in Oaxaca's Central Valleys. It was a massive victory, but as Mexico continues to face recurring droughts and Oaxaca suffers from annual heat waves, with daily temperatures hovering around 35 degrees Celsius, the fight to keep water flowing—and communities fed and provided for—continues.

Perseverance for our people

I contacted Carmen Santiago in December 2021, inviting her for dinner. "I am having some health problems but will be happy to meet you once I recover," she responded. Two months later she passed away due to cancer. The Indigenous community water titles that she had fought so hard for were subsequently delivered to Zapotec communities in 2022.

In 2023, I revisited various communities in Oaxaca's Central Valleys to see how water rights had changed life there. On the whole, the people Santiago

Alonso fought so long for felt satisfied with their achievement, despite the ongoing challenges brought on by climate change and the subsequent scramble to control precious resources like water, often waged between state institutions, corporate interests, and local communities. As I spoke to men and women who knew Carmen Santiago Alonso over the years, I heard how they all agreed she was, and continues to be, an inspiration and example—especially when it comes to persevering in the face of such adversity. Given the challenges that remain, her legacy will be important for her people for years to come.

"Climate Change and the New Kosher"

David Rosen (Jewish/Ireland and Israel)

By Ken Chitwood

When it comes to the twin issues of climate change and environmental justice, Chief Rabbi David Rosen could not be clearer: "There's no issue more important," Rosen told me during a digital interview at the height of the Covid-19 pandemic. Even as shutdowns became ever stricter and daily life was deeply impinged by an epidemic we had yet to fully understand, Rosen said, "of all the very important things that need to be done in this world, what is it all worth if we are going to destroy the whole thing? It's a critical imperative about life on Earth itself."

Former Chief Rabbi of Ireland and senior rabbi of the largest Orthodox Jewish congregation in South Africa, Rosen is a prominent interreligious leader. He has served as the American Jewish Committee's International Director of Interreligious Affairs and worked with the Parliament of the World's Religions and Religions for Peace International (RfP) on a variety of interreligious efforts aimed at combating the calamitous effects of climate change.

Of all his work in interreligious dialogue and education, his greatest passion remains the care of the environment and the need to reform our lifestyles accordingly. "As a religious practitioner, I believe that there is no issue today that is as compelling or imperative for religious people to be engaged with," he said. He frequently writes, speaks, and is actively engaged with multiple initiatives addressing the importance of climate change. Two of those initiatives include the Jerusalem-based Interfaith Centre for Sustainable Development (ICSD) and the Interfaith Rainforest Initiative—an international, multi-faith alliance that "works to bring moral urgency and faith-based leadership to global efforts to end tropical deforestation."

Planetary piety

For Rosen, this is not just a professional matter, it is deeply spiritual. At the heart of Judaism, Rosen said, is the commandment to care for the cosmos, a reverence for—and safe keeping of—the work of the Creator's hands. "If religion—and this is true of Abrahamic religions and Dharma traditions as well—affirms that the cosmos is in fact a creation, that it is a manifestation of divine power, then how we relate to it and all that is within it, above all other sentient beings, is a manifestation of how we relate to God." He continued, "Any act of disregard, or impiety, let alone a loss of species or degradation is ultimately an offense against God himself."

Above all, Rosen believes his calling is to convince other religious people that this is the single greatest spiritual imperative of our time. To that end, Rabbi Rosen shared his passionate plea with a room full of representatives from across the spectrum of the world's faiths at the 10th World Assembly of RfP in Lindau, Germany in 2019. Underlining the responsibility of religious leaders and communities to engage and lead movements to preserve and sustain the environment—for both pragmatic and altruistic reasons—Rosen did not mince words. "A religion that doesn't care about the environment isn't worthy of the name," he said to applause.

At that same assembly, Rosen saw religious and spiritual leaders affirm the need for urgent and decisive action to end tropical deforestation and combat deepening inequality and climate change by endorsing the Interfaith Rainforest Initiative's "Faiths for Forests Declaration." When it comes to policymakers and scientists working with religious communities on issues like climate change, Rosen believes there has been great progress in recent years. "Once upon a time, there was a normative disregard of religious communities by the diplomatic practitioners who saw religion as part of the problem," he said, "they weren't wrong, but if you don't want religion to be part of the problem the answer isn't to ignore it, you need to make it part of the solution."

More and more, Rosen sees policymakers and the scientific establishment working with religious communities to get good work done. Indeed, Rosen said one of the "silver linings" of the Covid-19 pandemic was "the way in which religion and science have collaborated and the degree to which politicians have increasingly understood the need to engage religious communities. I believe in interreligious dialogue as imperative in and of itself," he said, "but even those who might not appreciate it, they can understand the area of pragmatic collaboration and cooperation. When it comes to the environmental issues we are obliged to address, we are greater than the sum of our different parts." Nonetheless, Rosen believes more needs to be done, both in terms of national and international policy as well as at the local level.

Can veganism count as the new kosher?

On the question of what local faith communities can do, he said mobilizing religious communities to advocate for certain policies, affirming declarations, or promoting "green congregations," is not enough. It is also a matter of drastically changing our lifestyles. In particular, Rosen advocates veganism.

A 2019 report on climate change, desertification, land degradation, food security, and sustainable land management from the Intergovernmental Panel on Climate Change (IPCC) identified plant-based diets as a significant opportunity for mitigating the impact of climate change. Commissioned by the United Nations, the report said that by 2050, dietary adaptations could free up several million square kilometers of land and reduce CO_2 emissions by up to eight billion tons per year. It concluded with a recommendation to reduce worldwide meat consumption.

Rabbi Rosen agrees with such clarion calls. "Changing our diet is more important than recycling or cutting down on our carbon footprint," he said, "and today it's a perfectly feasible thing to do." Speaking to his own constituency, he said in a video produced for Jewish Veg—a U.S.-based organization encouraging Jews to embrace plant-based diets—that veganism is the new *kosher*. Asking people to give up meat—especially those for whom meat is a part of their religious practice—can be a tall task, said Rosen. "When I come along as an orthodox Rabbi and advocate veganism, I'm threatening a system, a system which is of course not only a question of power and position, but also economic interest as well. And that's of course very, very difficult," he said.

Holding to hope

And yet, whether it is urging religious communities to abandon their addiction to meat products or the issue of climate change as a whole, Rosen remains optimistic. "Why does the pessimist see the glass half empty and why does the optimist see it as half full," Rosen said, "the pessimist comes down from on top expecting to see a full glass so therefore he's disappointed by what's missing, but the optimist knows that the glass was originally empty and sees everything in there and celebrates."

This, Rosen said, is his attitude when it comes to the progress made on environmental issues, both within and beyond the global interreligious community. "When you consider how engaged the world was 20 or 30 years ago and where we are today, there has been a dramatic shift. We didn't even have environmental issues on our agenda twenty years ago and now it's a major focus of multi-religious collaboration," Rosen said, "never before in human history has there been as much interfaith understanding, cooperation, and ingenuity on this issue."

The change, Rosen emphasized, has been gradual. Nevertheless, he is convinced we are nearing an Archimedean point, where collaboration and innovation on the issues of climate change and environmental justice will increase exponentially. "Part of the gift of being created in the divine image is the creative capacities to change the universe," he said, "especially with our modern technology we can find a way that we couldn't before, and I guess that's one reason I've got immense optimism. I think that's enough to warrant a positive outlook on the future."

"Taking a Breath at the End of the World"

Gopal Patel (Hindu/United States)

By Kevin D. Grant

Gopal Patel, a Hindu environmentalist and spiritual exemplar, weaves through the crowd gathered at Bryant Park, looking for decent cell phone service beneath the canopy of towering buildings in Midtown Manhattan. Life has been "nonstop" over the last year, he says, stepping away from the WeWork space he occupies during the rare stretches when he is in town, commuting between the city and his home in Montclair, New Jersey. Now the co-chair of two high-profile United Nations efforts—the Decade on Ecosystem Restoration and the Multi-faith Advisory Council—and a leading voice on biodiversity worldwide, Gopal spends much of his life on the road. He's recently been to Davos and given a TED Talk. He's co-founder and director of Bhumi Global, a nonprofit that "seeks to empower people and communities to address the triple crisis of climate change, biodiversity loss, and pollution based on Hindu principles." He advises a litany of interfaith and environmental initiatives including the World Wildlife Foundation's (WWF) Beliefs and Values Programme, the Yale Forum on Religion and Ecology, and the Parliament of the World's Religions.

If that weren't enough, last December, Gopal and his allies came away from the United Nations Biodiversity Conference in Montreal with a landmark agreement to protect 30 percent of Earth's lands, oceans, coastal areas, and inland waters by 2030, while dramatically reducing food waste and government subsidies to businesses that harm the natural world. "It has put biodiversity on the radar in a very significant way, just as the Paris Agreement in 2015, made climate something that people could be more aware of," Gopal says. "Now there's something we can point to and say, 'This is what needs to be done.'"

Despite all his apparent success, however, Gopal is at a crossroads, personally, professionally, and spiritually. "I feel like I'm in a place right now where I can actually make a contribution somewhat on my terms, rather than on someone else's terms," he says.

> And I feel like I can do that because I feel like I know what I want to see manifest. But this is my crisis right now: I just turned 40, I'm divorced and single, you know? Okay, I'm ticking boxes that people can wait their whole careers to tick. But I'm just like, "Well, what do I do next? How do I go up from here?"

A new name

Gopal's faith journey began when he found life-affirming meaning in the pages of the Bhagavad Gita as a high school student in Watford, England. He was so inspired that, at age 21, he left the bucolic setting of his hometown borough on London's outskirts for an ashram on the banks of the River Ganges. There, he studied the Gita in depth before spending the next few years traveling between India and England, leading religious workshops at various colleges and universities.

One key Hindu concept he kept sharing is that people are "born, not built." In other words, people come into the world with certain talents, talents informed by previous lives. And as he was preparing to launch the nonprofit Bhumi Global, named after the Hindu goddess who represents Earth, in 2009, Gopal's teacher Radhanath Swami gave him a new name. The American monk and spiritual activist called him *Gopal Lila Das*—the servant of someone who looks after the planet. "Sometimes it's said that when the guru gives you a name, it means there's a destiny there waiting for you to live up to, but I don't think he knew that" Gopal told me last year when I visited him in Montclair. "It's kind of interesting that my life has turned into trying to care for the environment."

"Eastern traditions and Indigenous traditions are much more comfortable talking about the sacredness of a tree or a plant or a river," he said as we continued our interview, first in the lobby of a trendy hotel and then at an Ethiopian restaurant he'd recommended nearby. "That's why I gravitate to biodiversity work. I felt like in the climate space I couldn't bring my whole Hindu self into that," he said. "All these trees and everything, I can look at them and talk about them in a way that in the climate space, you can't have those kinds of conversations."

As an initiated student in the Vaishnava tradition—one of the major forms of modern Hinduism, devoted to the supreme deity Vishnu, who manifests as Krishna and other deities—Gopal continues to turn to Krishna to help guide his life and work. Krishna is perhaps best known as the divine guide of the epic scripture Bhagavad Gita, advising the archer prince Arjuna ahead of a possible intra-family war. As Arjuna fears the consequences of a bloody battle, Krishna reminds him of his own *dharma*—or duty—to take right action and put his trust in a higher power as one acts accordingly. "The boundary of one's jurisdiction ends with the completion of one's duty," Krishna says. "Do your duty to the best of your ability, O Arjuna, with your mind attached to the Lord, abandon worry and attachment to the results. Remain calm in both success and failure. Such selfless service brings peace and equanimity of the mind."

Gopal's sense of duty shows up when he speaks: animated but focused, confident but introspective and self-aware. The 40-something-year-old leader is bespectacled with an easy smile. His continuous process of self-reflection ("Building institutions, fundraising, I can't do that stuff," he says) seems to act as a catalyst rather than a paralytic. "My meditation has always been, I want to be in the spaces where I can make the most impact as possible," Gopal says. "And I was kind of leaving up to Krishna to open whichever doors he felt like he wanted to open for me. And so, these are the doors that have opened."

A lonely path

Against a backdrop of record-breaking air and sea temperatures, extreme droughts, punctuated with terrifying wildfires and floods that are contributing to further loss of lands and wildlife, Gopal says he has found the path of being a climate change prophet a surprisingly lonely one, with few peers. But he is trying to change that. "I have this mantra, which I'm using right now, which I'm really trying to stick to which is: *cool things with cool people*. I want to do things which I enjoy. And I want to do them with other people," he said. "I don't want to be a one-man band. I don't want to just be in these spaces by myself."

Gopal has earned the trust and respect of a broad range of leaders around the world. When I interviewed Karenna Gore, founder and executive director of Center for Earth Ethics at Union Theological Seminary, she was effusive with praise. "Fundamentally, he loves truth. You can tell his accountability is ultimately to a higher dimension, and he's not one for machinations that would betray that," she said.

Tulasi Srinivas, a professor of anthropology and religion at Emerson College, praised Gopal's work bridging Eastern and Western perspectives. "You need a big tent to do this kind of work. And to mobilize people globally, one can't have technocratic answers only," Srinivas said. "You need Indigenous answers, Hinduism, animism, stuff that we're coming back to in a scientific way—yoga, flow, and balance. Solutions can come from these areas." Speaking to Gopal's observation that he does not have many true peers, Srinivas said, "If you take a Western perspective, there are few Hindus in activism. However, there are local gurus and faith leaders who wouldn't do the kind of activism that one would expect as it doesn't align with Western perspectives, but they create action. They are few and far between, working with limited resources."

But Gopal believes his Hindu devotion is well suited for apocalyptic times such as these, which require a passion for diplomacy and a strong moral grounding. "What Eastern traditions offer to the whole world, which is often framed from a Judeo-Christian perspective, is that the world is not linear. It does not necessarily go from bad to good," Gopal says. "We can offer tools to deal with the ups and downs, the fact that things can get worse before they get better—or always get worse."

The "cosmic dance" in a world on fire

In thinking about his next steps in life, Gopal wonders whether people like him will need to play a role akin to a university chaplain offering pastoral care—but specifically geared toward helping people deal with a calamitously changing climate. "To stay steady in the constant change," Gopal says. "That's how I'm trying to live my life in the age of ecological destruction. Now we can see it, now we're struggling together. How do we stay resilient, stay grounded, keep doing the work?"

The Hindu myth of Shiva's cosmic dance (*Nataraja*), representing both creation and destruction, seems apt to describe Gopal's desire. A popular icon depicts Shiva dancing within a ring of cosmic fire, four arms reaching in all directions, long locks of hair framing his contented face. Speaking in London in 1961, the author Aldous Huxley described the Nataraja in detail, opining, "The whole thing is there, you see. The world of space and time, and matter and energy, the world of creation and destruction, the world of psychology … We [the West] don't have anything remotely approaching such a comprehensive symbol, which is both cosmic and psychological, and spiritual."

A student of the humanities, Gopal is also well aware of moments throughout history in which people have shrugged an apathetic shoulder toward, or even reveled in, others' suffering. Today, Gopal sees this sentiment in the rising tide of right-wing politics and the general message he believes it carries: *People just don't need to worry about the world*. Yet Gopal clearly cares. His candor about all-too-human milestones of hitting middle age, going through divorce, and searching for meaning in one's work both comforts and juxtaposes strikingly with his résumé and the cosmology that governs his life. Speaking with someone who has found his voice on behalf of a planet in peril, someone who has been named a spiritual exemplar for living out his values, someone who feels more like a friend the longer you talk, I found it difficult to believe he feels lonely in life.

A new phase

Interrupting my musings, Gopal returns to the idea that it may be time for him to try something new. "I am thinking I'm at this place right now where

I feel a bit stuck and I'm not intellectually challenged," he says. "You know, so what is going to challenge me, what is going to help make me feel fulfilled and grow? I can build coalitions. I can be in spaces that I have no business being in. I can bring people together. So how do I use those skills?"

There is another dimension to Gopal's decision-making: as "an old-school Hindu," he is thinking about the traditional four phases of life: Brahmacharya (student), Gṛhastha (householder, or married), Vanaprastha (forest walker, beginning to retreat from the world and hand off earthly responsibilities to the next generation), and Sannyasa (renunciate). Though he says these are not hard-and-fast stages, and that even in earlier times they were not necessarily followed, Gopal does anticipate a point in his life when he retreats from the world. At some point, perhaps after many more lifetimes, Gopal believes he will break free from an endless cycle of death and rebirth called *samsara* and achieve liberation, or *moksha*.

But here, and now, at such a time as this, he has more work to do. "Everyone has a contribution to make," he says. "This is just my contribution, there's nothing special about it. I try to stay attuned to what Krishna wants me to do. No guarantees, but it puts me in a better place." And maybe, just maybe, it puts the world in a better place too.

7

Socio-economic Development

God is within the wall to be worshipped. God is beyond the walls to be worked.

CECIL L. MURRAY (PROTESTANT)

I don't want to do this forever; I want to actually solve this problem.

RACHEL SUMEKH (JEWISH)

You cannot say you love God if you fail to love your neighbor.

IDA PULIWA (PROTESTANT)

Love is God's religion and loving is how we practice it.

GREG BOYLE (ROMAN CATHOLIC)

Introduction

Crafting a story is, in principle, pretty straightforward. Whatever the story, we all know the basic building blocks: plot, setting, characters, point of view, and some form of conflict. Of course, as we also all know, it is not that simple, as plots can meander, characters can fall flat, a point of view can be confusing, and the conflict anticlimactic. Similarly, solutions-oriented journalism has three core elements: situation, complication, resolution. As with the elements of a story, however, things can get messy when researching, writing, and sharing that kind of story. There are problems behind the problem, compounding and overlapping issues of concern, and unclear solutions. At no time was that clearer to me than at the heights of the Covid-19 pandemic in 2020 and 2021. As mentioned before, Covid-19 re-exposed the deep inequalities and injustices already present in our societies. Many of those suffering the worst from the pandemic were already vulnerable, often living below the poverty line, subject to the adverse effects of climate change, struggling to make ends meet, without proper access to health care or education, or caught in the midst of civil conflict and violence.

In my own reporting, I not only covered how religious communities were adopting digital technologies or otherwise adapting practices and festivities during the pandemic, but also about the ongoing inequalities and sticky issues of injustice the rampant virus further exposed. There were families struggling to find permanent housing after their shelters closed or significantly reduced their capacities; immigrant parents of first-generation children who wrestled with changes to their kids' education as schools shut down and classes went online; religious communities who were caught blindsided by division and civil strife in their congregations or neighborhoods related to persistent racial inequalities, misinformation, conspiracy theories, and government restrictions on public gatherings.

Writing from my apartment in Berlin, Germany, I felt these stories were important. That they not only pointed to how we were surviving in the midst of major societal, political, and social upheaval, but how we might thrive in the wake of a global crisis. I was not naïve to think my stories, whether about a rabbi in the United States or a priest in India who stepped up to provide frontline care and inspire others in the midst of an unprecedented pandemic, would revolutionize the world. But I did hope they might point to better futures. I did hope incremental change might come as a result of fact-based reporting on the good that religious actors were doing in the midst of so much uncertainty, fear, anger, death, and hate.

Yet, for all the disruption that Covid-19 brought to our lives, not much changed. Inequalities persist. Injustice remains. Nativist nationalism and xenophobia are re-entrenched. In some ways, it feels things have actually gotten worse. As things went back to "normal," I started to wonder whether it was even useful to cover those who were looking to change the world. Their work did not seem to change policies. My reporting did not change how people talked about religion or how it might be used for good. I got into journalism to help people get the information they needed to better understand the world around them and to, perhaps, improve their lives. I was thus discouraged when nothing seemed to shift—despite the attention that I and other journalists put into covering these issues year after year, crisis after crisis, funded project after funded project.

As mentioned already in the introduction to Chapter 1, the solutions approach to journalism provides reporters with tools for covering responses to problems and holding those in power accountable. Though not perfect, the solutions approach offers some of the best changes we have as journalists to write the change we want to see in the world. As a case in point, readers will find in the profiles that follow a range of approaches to sustainable and inclusive socio-economic development—initiatives that provide education and hope to vulnerable youth, guidance and goodness in the wake of city-wide anger and violence, that seek to address student hunger, and deliver hope to the most vulnerable groups (e.g., older adults, persons affected by armed conflict, women, and youth).

First, Arpi Miller profiles the work of Julie Coyne in Guatemala. As Miller writes, "Coyne never planned to leave her native Connecticut, but over time, found herself bound to the community in Guatemala's beautiful but impoverished Highlands region, where she has worked for more than 22 years." Her organization, Education and Hope, provides comprehensive scholarships to more than 200 students at all levels, from kindergarten to university. It also offers an after-school program with daily tutoring sessions, recreational opportunities, and meals, showers, health-care assistance, supplies, and transportation to 100 students. Miller writes, "[w]hile the project focuses on education, Julie's eclectic spiritual life creates a deeply healing environment centering love and compassion, where children and adults can lay down their pain and return to their communities nourished and empowered to navigate very difficult circumstances."

Then, Megan Sweas—channelling her late colleague Nick Street—profiles the CRCC's "in-house exemplar," Cecil "Chip" Murray. An American theologian, renowned community leader, and civil rights champion, Murray was pastor of First AME Church (FAME) in Los Angeles. He not only transformed the congregation from a small, 250-member congregation to a 18,000-member megachurch but developed it into a multi-million-dollar hub for community and economic development that brought jobs, housing, and corporate investment to South Los Angeles. He went to work with CRCC after he retired from FAME, working with his partners in the city to ensure that Black church leaders of the Civil Rights generation passed on their experience, spiritual authority, and political pragmatism to the next generation.

Then there is Rachel Sumekh, the founder of Swipe Out Hunger, a leading nonprofit addressing hunger among college students. According to Hebah Farrag, Sumekh and those she worked with to found Swipe Out Hunger at UCLA in 2010 brought an innovative approach to their work, allowing university students to donate unused funds from their meal plans to food-insecure peers. Replicating this work, they got the State of California to adopt legislation to address college student hunger to the tune of $20 million and similar programs in New Jersey, Maryland, and Pennsylvania. As Farrag writes, Sumekh "credits her upbringing as the child of Iranian Jewish immigrants for her intersectional perspective on doing good in the world."

Finally, Innocent Eteng writes about Helene Babiene Eweni, a youth pastor in Cameroon who works with the poor and vulnerable as an outgrowth of her own experiences as an orphan growing up. She holds the conviction that God will not abandon the disadvantaged and shows an intense devotion to God and the guidance and support she provides to younger orphans in Kumba town in Cameroon's southwest. As she advocates for children's rights, offers free vocational skills training, and spearheads a health campaign bringing sanitary items and antenatal care to displaced pregnant women and girls at no cost, she also shows how her own spiritual grounding is part and parcel to that work.

Each of the stories paints a complex picture of the situations, complications, and resolutions that exemplars contend with in their work to address socio-economic inequalities and injustice. They illustrate the scope of the problems, the various vulnerable communities that are affected, and the overlap of development issues with other predicaments such as access to education or racial prejudice. They outline how solutions to such situations will not be solely secular nor spiritual alone. What is needed, their examples show, is an integrated approach. They also show how the work is not yet complete. In fact, far from it. The issues that each has dedicated their life to persist and are in constant need of addressing. Where success has come, where impacts have been made, others will have to carry on the legacy and pick up where the work has left off so that gains are not lost.

In the end, these stories are also the kind that every solutions-oriented journalist wants to tell. They are the kind of stories that help reporting on vulnerable communities move away from accounts that have created powerful, if ultimately damaging, narratives around inequality and socio-economic injustice. They are the kinds of stories that give us hope that things just might change. They are also the stories of exemplars worth emulating in our own lives and contexts. They are the stories that prompt us to ask: If it is working somewhere else, for someone else, why not here? Why not now? Why not me?

"Creating a Community of Care in Highland Guatemala"

Julie Coyne (Humanist/Guatemala)

By Arpi Miller

On any given afternoon, for more than two decades, Julie Coyne has waited eagerly at the doorway to Education and Hope, green eyes twinkling. Children emerge from the surrounding streets dressed in school uniforms. They line up and are greeted one at a time with a big hug and Julie's signature, full-face smile. "This part never gets old," she explains, a look of sheer delight on her face.

Julie never planned to leave her native Connecticut and move to Guatemala permanently. Yet, her life has become interwoven with the community there, similar to how the two countries are entangled. A steady stream of migrants, asylum seekers and unaccompanied minors from Guatemala have made their way, at great peril and expense, to the U.S.–Mexico border in recent years. Under the Trump administration's policies between 2016 and 2020, migrants have been summarily expelled at the border and deported to their country of origin, many carrying coronavirus with them, or they remain stranded in Mexico with court hearings on pause.

Guatemalans are escaping poverty and violence, searching for survival and new life in a country deeply implicated in both their homeland's instability and the criminal treatment of those who flee it. United States' complicity in Guatemala's painful past,[1] and persistently challenging present, continues to shape the lived reality of many who decide—or are forced—to leave the Central American nation for greener pastures in *El Norte*. But long before the current, so-called, "border crisis"—before children like Jakelin Caal Maquin[2] and Carlos Hernandez Vásquez[3] died in U.S. Border Patrol custody, and asylum-seeking families were told to "remain in Mexico" in dire conditions—locally run Guatemalan projects like Education and Hope have worked to create a microcosm of hope in which families can imagine a future that does not involve migration to the United States. "What we are doing is not flashy," explains Julie, the perpetually jean-clad, vivacious 53-year-old founder of Education and Hope. "We were here before this latest news cycle, and we will be here long after."

Julie's commitment to the unique community she has helped create there is rooted in a spirituality of love—one that is nurtured by the lessons and teachings of a variety of faith traditions, spiritual mentors, and the families she serves.

A place for those living invisible lives

Each day, after being greeted by Julie, students of all ages are welcomed into the building by young Guatemalan staff—almost all former graduates of the program. There are high-fives and hugs, personal check-ins, eye contact, and a moment of being seen. Before tutoring begins, students find a seat in the *comedor*, a light-infused atrium, surrounded by murals from young artists. A team of mothers and grandmothers, dressed in traditional *huipiles* and *traje*, bustle around putting the final touches on a nutritious lunch. Once everyone has gathered and filled their bellies, one can hear Julie's trademark bellow, "*Buenas tardes niiiiños*," followed by a joyous response from the children: "*Buenas tardes Juu-li-uh*!"

Education and Hope is housed in Quetzaltenango, the second-largest city in Guatemala, affectionately known by its Maya name, *Xela*. The city is nestled in a graceful valley in the western highlands, a four-and-a-half-hour bus ride and a world away from Guatemala City, the frenetic capital. Guatemala is a land of spectacular beauty and deep layers of culture. It boasts some of the most impressive volcanoes and fertile valleys in Latin America. It is the bosom of the Maya Cosmovision, a philosophy that articulates the interrelatedness of all life. And it is home to twenty-four distinct languages and sophisticated, historic advances in astronomy, engineering, and agriculture.

Guatemala is also a land of stunning violence and despair. Eighty percent of the indigenous Maya population live in poverty, with 40 percent subsisting on less than two dollars a day. In indigenous communities, four out of five children struggle with chronic malnutrition, and illiteracy for women hovers around 50 percent. Political corruption, targeted assassinations, criminal extortion and femicide are widespread. Education and Hope works to undo those trends. The program currently provides 175 comprehensive scholarships, after-school tutoring and hot meals, as well as sustainable wages for forty-eight employees, almost half of whom are former graduates or the single mothers and grandmothers of enrolled children.

Over the years, the program has provided a million hot meals and graduated nearly 200 children from high school, following each child from early primary school to their logical end—sometimes college, sometimes a job in the project and beyond. In addition to tuition, uniforms, hot meals, and tutoring, the program provides showers, medical attention, and mental health support, classes in art, computers, and physical education, and small loans to families.

The scope may sound small, but in an area where many children will attend school for only a handful of years, if they are lucky, and where malnutrition is the norm, it is anything but. Yet the real goal of the program goes beyond body and mind. "Technically we are an education program," Julie explains, "but that doesn't quite capture it. We provide a safe space for children who have lived their lives invisibly, and often lived them invisibly with great pain." To that end, the project has created an environment where people can "lay it all out on the table, let everything air out," Julie says. "And even if they have to pack it up and carry it back home again, the burden changes and transforms in the sharing. It's never quite as heavy as it was before you unpacked it." José was an early project participant. The year his mother's health was failing, Julie gave her a bed in the building of Education and Hope, where the *señoras* who make meals could nurse her daily as she died. Despite the nurture, José lost himself in despair and delinquency for many years following his mother's death.

There is no quick fix in such a context. You have to follow people all the way, explains Julie. After basic needs are met, trauma can surface, and sometimes kids will begin to act out and do really heartbreaking, self-destructive things. Julie is patient. She has faith that many students have been filled with enough love to eventually cycle back. Such was the case with José. After years on the street, even stealing from the project, he is now regularly found cutting vegetables before mealtimes with the señoras who saw him through his despair. He graduated high school, has taken a position in the after-school program, and is raising a family of his own. "Education is good," José explains shrugging, "but love is much stronger than education."

Julie is not dogmatically religious, and Education and Hope is not a religious organization, but everything she does comes back to her perception of God's love. God made us perfectly and we are all worthy of love, she says. This is a theology Julie brought with her to Guatemala many years ago, but one that is now embodied in the families of the project. "We are all expressions of the divine," she says.

The birth of a project … and a permanent stay

Julie grew up in a Catholic family in Connecticut and felt drawn to the cause of social justice. But she never experienced a clear vision that called her unequivocally to leave her middle-class life and live in Central America. Instead, she fell into her work in Quetzaltenango. After college, she traveled to Guatemala to study Spanish before attending graduate school. As a way to engage with the community where she lived, she volunteered in a soup kitchen for children and at a women's shelter. By her third year in Guatemala, her career path back home seemed even less clear. She had a sense she wanted to help people, but was there a degree for that? Her professors suggested divinity school, but it didn't feel quite right. "From where I was sitting on a dirt floor hut in Guatemala with chickens running around and barefoot kids, illiteracy, starvation and extreme poverty, it just didn't fit. I couldn't see myself in an ivory tower." For her, a degree would have to be earned in the divinity school of the streets.

In retrospect, Julie believes a clear "call" to a life of religious service would have sent her running. Instead, the reality of living in Guatemala permanently was hidden from her until she was so far along the path that there was no turning back. She needed a slow transformation to understand and accept this way of life, so far removed from where she began. She sees God at work in her transformation.

Early on, after giving a talk in her Connecticut church community, a contact offered her start-up funds to support her dream of providing access to education to children in need. With that funding, the seeds of what would become Education and Hope were planted. Julie offered scholarships to a handful of children she knew from the soup kitchen and the shelter. Mission accomplished; she had created an education program. The first semester, everyone bombed their classes. Kids from impoverished families had no one to help with their homework. They had no food to eat. Julie regrouped and invited the kids back to her tiny Guatemala home, a rented, aquamarine block house with a central patio. There she made a big pan of scrambled eggs, the only meal she knew how to prepare for a dozen children. She offered them showers, since they had no running water at home, and they did homework together. Without realizing it, Education and Hope was born.

Even as the young organization began to experience some successes in education, these are not what grounded her in the work, Julie says. Rather,

FIGURE 7.1 Group hug with Julie Coyne after a women's meditation circle at Education and Hope. Photo courtesy of Noel Rojo.

it was sorrowful experiences that bound her heart with this community: a teenager who died from a brain parasite, a mother who died of AIDS contracted from an abusive husband, leaving five children in Julie's care. Then a young man committed suicide, and yet another mother died, this time from cirrhosis. "There was this moment when I was walking in a funeral procession, holding the hand of a young orphan just seven years old, and I had this vision that pieces of my heart, along with everyone around me, were falling into the earth, just falling and being absorbed into the soil, binding me to these people, to this place." "The universe said, 'Oh my God, she thinks she can fix everything. Let's put her in a situation where it is so far beyond her ability to fix it that she'll have to come to the realization that the goal is not to fix,'" she says. "The goal is companionship, community, and connection—and healing through those things. Not healing through fixing; healing through this very experience of love and community." It took a decade for Julie to realize she was staying forever.

What can't be counted

By mid-afternoon, kids in the project have moved to their classrooms. Out in the courtyard, the señoras are taking a break, being led in a Zumba class. "Isn't this Zumba class just the greatest thing you have ever seen?" Julie says through a gurgling laugh, joining in. Funders often want to know what Zumba has to do with the organization's mission. The expectation of financial supporters, who want to see numbers and success stories, often conflict with Julie's approach. Joyful release is a prerequisite for hope, Julie says about the Zumba class. And where there is hope, there is a path forward.

Kids become a part of Education and Hope as young as toddlers tagging behind parents, and preschoolers in the Montessori-style early childhood program. But the program also supports fifteen-year-old mothers in their desire to start first grade or even kindergarten for the first time. And the señoras who have never been given a chance to study are learning to read, beginning with the alphabet. Education nonprofits are often wary of accepting "high-risk cases." As Julie describes, someone will say, "You know what, she's 13 or 14, she's never been to school. Is this really going to make a difference? Culturally she is more likely to get pregnant in the next couple years than anything else." But the transformations that occur in the project are often not quantifiable in a way that "counts" for an annual report. "Isn't this young woman the most important one to give a scholarship to?" Julie asks. "Because one year or two years of reading and writing and that love will go so far in her own development, and then her baby is so much more likely to be nourished, and the focus will be on education." Plus, she will have the extended family of the project forever.

Even as she experiences outward pressures for "success," Julie's love-first approach can also put her at odds with the cultural norms of the area. A youth explained the Guatemalan expression, *Hay que sacarle la verguenza*, meaning "you have to beat the shame out" of a misbehaving child. Sometimes even her own team feels like Julie offers one too many extra chances. "Many of us have never experienced one simple 'I love you' in our homes," explained Jenny, a young woman who began at the after-school program following a childhood of abuse and neglect. "But through Education and Hope," she continued, "we know we have value." Jenny is a definitive success story. This fall, thirteen years after entering the program, Jenny started her first year of study at Berea College in the United States.

To bridge the disconnect between the message children hear at Education and Hope and at home, Julie has introduced tools that travel beyond the organization's walls—including practices such as meditation. At late afternoon snack-time, which serves as dinner for most, Julie stands in front of 150 women and youth in the atrium. She asks them to put their feet on the ground and feel themselves rooting down. After long breaths, she asks them to close their eyes and visualize a source of deep love. They extend this love to friends, to somebody difficult, then to the whole program.

Julie recalls watching an orphan meditate: "I knew he was imagining his mom, with his eyes closed so tightly, he was just working so hard at it. I was filled with that visual of him connecting to this love source that has sustained him and remembering that he could bring it back to himself, even when it's not physically there," she says. "I believe the children and their mothers can witness that they are part of this ability to create change just through summoning love," Julie says.

The sustenance to lead

Practicing what she preaches, Julie returns to her own personal retreat every evening. In contrast to the joyful noise of the project and being physically and emotionally touched all day, her small home is solitary and quiet. It is set on a green hillside in a small community of cabins outside of town. It is an open, mixed-use space with a sleeping loft upstairs. The walls are lined with hundreds of books, both fiction and nonfiction. String lights, candles, and soothing music create a soft ambience. A gaggle of orphaned street puppies lives outside the door.

Few people fully grasp the life Julie leads and the all-encompassing nature of the work she does. People who do community work often live in a liminal world—between being present and thinking big picture; being on the ground in the project and fundraising outside of it. They are with the people but not fully of the people. For Julie, it can be taxing and lonely. Through years of an almost purposeful self-denial, Julie has learned the importance of self-care. She does not have the time or money to take long spiritual retreats. Instead, she builds spiritual practices into her day. She often wakes to a long series of chimes that center her before she begins her workday. And at the end of the day, Julie communes regularly with a host of "saints." Among her saints are Thomas Merton, Dorothy Day, Archbishop Romero, and Mother Teresa. "All those were people who put everything on the table," she points out, "and that, at the end of the day, might not be sustainable."

But there also are contemporary figures, Christian or not, whom she admires: Father Greg Boyle, Ram Dass, Richard Rohr, Pema Chödrön, Nadia Bolz-Weber, and Anne Lamott. "The first time I read *Tattoos on the Heart*, by Father Greg Boyle, it blew off the top of my head, because I saw myself and my Education and Hope family, my people, in every single page," she says. Boyle runs Homeboy Industries in Los Angeles, where he mentors gang members as they find a new way of life. His book gave Julie a language—of connection, community, and radical kinship—to articulate what she does, and this combats isolation. "He also has become a mentor in real life," she says. "He calls me 'kiddo.'"

All these voices—activists, saints, and writers—"have been my salvation," Julie says. She still leans on her Catholic roots but has arrived closer to a Buddhist state of mindfulness. "What I take from so many of these writings is a sense of being present, a sense of humility and grace in brokenness, in the latest calamity, whether it is something going on in the program or with my own health," she says.

> This is just how it is right now. Learning how to trust that there will be a shift, even if I'm not sure what it will be, but knowing it will never stay this bad or stay this good in the next moment. It will all change. Those ideas about transformation give me hope and fuel my thinking. That helps me be self-sustaining.

Julie does not keep her spiritual insights to herself. She recharges and then shares these with the kids and the señoras.

While policymakers fixate on the borderlands, fighting a migration stream that U.S. foreign policy helps to create, microcosms like Education and Hope go on, working to build a context of dignity, where dreams can emerge and pathways to success can take root, pre-empting the need to search elsewhere for a place called home.

"The Prototypical Exemplar"

Cecil L. "Chip" Murray (*Protestant/United States*)

By Nick Street and Megan Sweas

The Rev. Dr. Cecil L. "Chip" Murray was the prototypical spiritual exemplar—a person who provided inspiration for our study on a world of people whose spirituality guides them to be engaged with critical social issues. In his twenty-seven years as pastor, Murray built First African Methodist Episcopal (FAME) Church, Los Angeles into a 18,000-member megachurch. But more than build a church, he brought jobs, housing, services, and economic investment into South Los Angeles. Mayors and city council members who came to him for guidance called him "Los Angeles' pastor" and "the angel of Los Angeles." In the midst of the city's 1992 civil unrest, he stepped into the fray to reconcile rioters and police. Then, in front of city leaders and news cameras, he preached about the injustices that fanned the flames of one of the worst incidents of urban violence in U.S. history. "We set some of those fires, but we didn't start any of those fires," he said, pointing to the transatlantic trade in enslaved persons, disenfranchisement, economic marginalization, and police violence as the real fire-starters.

Donald Miller, the USC scholar behind the Spiritual Exemplars Project, first met Murray in the wake of the 1992 civil unrest, interviewing him for a project on the faith community's role in rebuilding the city. A decade later, Miller recruited Murray to USC. In his retirement from ministry in the AME church, Murray trained more than 1,000 faith leaders in civic engagement and economic development skills at USC's CRCC. When Miller launched the Spiritual Exemplars Project, his work was the reference point for what "engaged spirituality" looked like in practice. Until his death in 2024, he was our "in-house spiritual exemplar."

Murray's achievements—the millions of dollars invested in community development, thousands of congregants and mentees influenced, and his prophetic preaching—certainly made him worthy of inclusion in a project about people who have made a significant impact on human flourishing. But in working with Murray every day, we also experienced the qualities that made him worthy of admiration and emulation not only by his congregants, but also by other faith leaders. As his colleagues, we were able to witness how his discipline, compassion, integrity, humility, and deeply personal spirituality grounded his vision of socially engaged Christianity. In other words, he was an exemplar not only in what he accomplished, but how he led.

Called by God

Murray's tireless efforts to help others emerged from what he described in the introduction of his memoir as a lifelong and constant conversation with God. Murray was born on September 26, 1929, in Lakeland, Florida, notably the same year that Martin Luther King, Jr. was born. Murray's mother died when he was three years old. He and two siblings were raised first by his maternal grandparents on their farm and then by his father and a loving stepmother.

Like a fish trying to describe water, he never thought of himself as poor. In his memoir, *Twice Tested By First: A Memoir of Faith and Service*, he questioned how his generation not only survived but thrived in the midst of the Great Depression and the Jim Crow South. "Trauma in our formative years can push us toward destruction or redemption," Murray wrote, and looking back, he found lessons in his upbringing. From loss, he developed empathy. From poverty, he learned simplicity and hard work. From family, church, school, and the Scouts, he gained a strong sense of personal and communal responsibility. From segregation and racism, he learned to dream, nurturing a fantasy about a model nation called Freeland where all people were equal.

God was a given in this fantasy land where love ruled, as God was in Murray's own life. He served as a youth pastor in high school, and his yearbook predicted that he would pastor a large church in Los Angeles. Yet after graduating from Florida A&M University, a historically Black university, he first joined the U.S. Air Force. During his years in the Air Force, he heard the voice of God speaking to him directly. His airplane caught fire during a failed takeoff, and his hatch would not open. The voice calmed him, guiding him to take off his parachute and squeeze through a small hole in the back of the cockpit. The pilot escaped but was burned trying to rescue Murray and died from his injuries. Murray felt he had to live for two after the accident.

Murray retired as a major after ten years and followed God's call into ministry. "As I matured, as I became wiser, I came to understand you can't change anything from the outside. You have to get on the inside and there, the change can come," he reflected. He earned a doctorate in religion from the Claremont School of Theology and became a minister in the African Methodist Episcopal Church, serving in four congregations until age 75.

Equal rights and economic opportunity

The civil rights movement gave voice and verve to Murray's social and theological perspective. During Los Angeles' 1965 Watts riots, Murray was the pastor of a small AME church in the largely white city of Pomona, California, about 30 miles east of Los Angeles. Sparked by the arrest of a Black motorist, his mother, and brother, the civil unrest resulted in thirty-four deaths and $40 million in property damage. The government commission pointed to economics in addition to police behavior as fostering an atmosphere of disaffection. Black communities in Los Angeles and throughout the United States were experiencing high employment and hiring discrimination, low-performing schools, and segregated and inadequate housing.

In Pomona, Murray was dealing with these same issues as chairman of the Pomona Valley Congress of Racial Equality. The congress met with bankers to push them to give out loans to people of color, but the bankers "said they felt no great obligation to the minorities in the city," Murray said. Murray would be active in similar conversations in Kansas City and Seattle before he returned to Southern California to lead FAME Church, Los Angeles in 1977. The city's Black communities still bore the scars of the 1965 unrest in the form of burned-out buildings, poor housing conditions, and lack of opportunity.

Long before the 1992 civil unrest, Murray saw how Black communities were marginalized through neglect and discrimination. They were, in his estimation, like a tinder box ready for a match. Then came the killing of fifteen-year-old Latasha Harlins, shot in the head by a Korean convenience store owner, and the beating of Rodney King by four Los Angeles police officers. A suspended sentence for Harlin's convicted killer and the acquittal of Rodney King's LAPD assailants sparked a week of fires, looting and violence, leading to sixty-three deaths and more than US $1 billion in property damage.

Murray was devastated but prepared. City leaders, activists, and community members gathered at FAME Church. The church remained open 24 hours a day, housing and feeding people displaced by fires. Murray led the men's ministry to stand between rioters and the fire department. When the fires were quelled, Murray knew he must do more than lead volunteers in sweeping up the broken glass. Murray saw a critical need for economic investment in the communities he served. It is not good enough to give people fish, or even to teach them how to fish, Murray would say, building upon the common refrain. If you taught them how to own the pond, they would have fish for generations and could help others as well.

But bringing practical economics together with faith can be complicated. Murray partnered with corporations that could be found culpable for unfair practices that harmed his community members. Moreover, during his years in ministry, Murray saw the Black church's emphasis shift from civil rights to a gospel of prosperity—the idea that God would bestow blessings (including financial) on those who gave generously to the church.

At USC, Murray counseled other faith leaders to adopt sound business practices and to start community development corporations so that they could tap into grants from foundations and Community Reinvestment Act funds from banks. Yet, he also preached fiscal transparency and told pastors to eschew the temptations to enrich themselves at the expense of the community. The prosperity gospel, in Murray's eyes, was antithetical to the mission of the church.

The "Murray Method"

A strong church, Murray said, focuses on the "five M's"—*mission*, *membership*, *money*, *maintenance*, and *morale*. His students at USC would call this the "Murray Method," though he was too humble to call it that himself. The mission of the church, Murray saw, was to enrich the community by caring for people in their spiritual, physical, mental, social, and economic lives. At FAME, he had the words "Come to worship, leave to serve" painted on the balcony so that congregants would read them as they left the sanctuary on Sunday mornings, said the Rev. Dr. Najuma Smith, who came to ministry under Murray at FAME and now carries on his legacy at the USC CRCC.

On Sundays, thousands of congregants would come to worship at FAME, drawn by choirs and an organ that could rock the rafters of the church, as well as sermons that included a combination of moral remonstrance, social critique, and comfort for the afflicted. He often ended services with a call that harkened back to the fantasy land he dreamt of in his youth, Smith remembered: "If we spend as much time lifting each other up as we spend putting each other down; if we spend as much time holding up the truth as we spend putting down the dirt; if we spend as much time lifting up Jesus, holding up his banner, what a great world this would be!"

His words often fell on receptive ears. In his leadership method, Murray emphasized that the *membership* of the church contributed their time and talent in addition to their tithes. "Is there a place for every member to choose how to serve the Lord?" he asked. Through FAME, members could find their way to serve in up to forty auxiliary ministries, Smith said. Murray systemized service through the men's and missionary societies, recovery programs, free legal counseling, and prison ministries. FAME operated thirteen housing projects with more than 2,000 tenants, including housing for people with physical disabilities or HIV/AIDS, seniors, and low-income families.

In the wake of the civil unrest, the church started a community development arm, FAME Renaissance. As a trusted, local institution, FAME Renaissance would shepherd $400 million in investments into South L.A. It offered business incubation, loans, and mentoring. Workforce development programs with Disney and Vidal Sassoon helped young people get jobs and start careers. Former gang members were employed in a massive program to replace toilets with more water-efficient models.

Murray described himself as a dreamer, but his practical side came through in his emphasis on *money* and *maintenance*. He extended a strong sense of personal discipline to the church, demanding sound budgetary practice and the upkeep of the church's physical environment.

When he was training pastors at USC, his students decided they would beat Murray to class one day. They showed up early, only to find out it was not early enough, recalled Rev. Frank Jackson, Jr., one of his mentees. Murray was already there, in a cleanly pressed suit, collar-starched, ready for the class to arrive. Appearances are not enough, though. Murray's fifth M, *morale*, requires ministers to cultivate authentic spiritual lives. "Whose you are determines who you are," Murray often said. "If you are God's, you will have morale."

Murray's many children

Well into his 90th year, Murray was the first person in the CRCC office in the morning, just as he had been the first person at FAME every morning. He would unlock the office's front gate to a steady stream of visitors seeking his counsel, and as he did at the church, he gave everyone who entered his undivided attention, advice, and words of encouragement, whether they were experiencing homelessness, leading a megachurch, or launching a social movement. But that does not mean Murray did not challenge those he sat with and counseled. One mentee, the Rev. Kelvin Sauls, remembers Murray did not offer easy solutions. After Sauls shared his ministerial challenges during one visit, Murray told him, "Don't grow weary in well-doing," Sauls recalls. "Those are words that continue to ground me."

Murray's magnetism went beyond his way with words. Murray had a direct line to God, said Herb Wesson, former president of the LA City Council at Murray's 90th birthday party. Wesson shared how his son recovered from a nearly lethal car accident after Murray prayed over the boy in the intensive care unit. Congregants included celebrities and city leaders, such as Wesson and Mayor Tom Bradley, Los Angeles's longest serving and first African American mayor. Murray's rolodex included Rosa Parks, Nelson Mandela, presidents from George H.W. Bush to Barack Obama, and celebrities like Barbra Streisand, Oprah, and Arsenio Hall. His access to wealthy and powerful people allowed Murray to advocate for and spur investment into his community.

But Murray's care was not reserved for the prominent. A woman once stopped her car in the middle of a busy road to flag down the then-retired Murray, said Jackson, who was going to lunch with him at the time. "That's my pastor!" she shouted, before sharing about the time Murray picked her up at 3.00 a.m. to drive her to a prison three hours away so she could visit her son. Countless people claim to be Murray's sons or daughters, Smith said at his retirement party, laughing along with Murray's family. Murray and his wife Bernadine had one son as well as a niece and two nephews, in addition to hundreds of spiritual sons and daughters. His plethora of spiritual children was evidence of Murray's ability to be present and connect with people, Smith said. "He would challenge us, when someone came into your office, to 'see the people' by seeing to their needs. He wanted to make sure that no one felt that they went unseen."

Murray's efforts to drive economic investment and change systems were both grounded in his connection with community members. The long hours and significant needs of those who came to him for help might have tired others, but his ministry seemed to energize Murray, Smith said.

In the wake of Murray's death in April 2024, a congregant shared a story that was emblematic of his dedication to others. A three-year-old girl had been at the hospital all night, her face swollen by an allergic reaction to spider bites. On the way home at 5.00 a.m., the girl insisted on seeing "Papa Murray." Her parent drove by the church to prove he would not be there—but there his car was. When he opened the office door, Murray looked at the parent sternly while asking the girl, "Who did this to you?" She answered, "a spider." Murray burst into laughter in the hallway, the congregant wrote. "They went into the office and had orange juice. He listened while she told him all about her night."

"Prophetic Judaism"

Rachel Sumekh (*Jewish/United States*)

By Hebah Farrag

I sat down with Rachel Sumekh, one the youngest humanitarians profiled in the Spiritual Exemplars Project, ten and a half months after she made a life-changing decision. Rachel, the founder of Swipe Out Hunger, one of the most impactful organizations working on issues related to higher education reform and poverty alleviation in the United States, had decided to step down.

Rachel helped to found Swipe Out Hunger in 2009,[4] stewarding the organization from a small organization addressing student homelessness and hunger on campus at the University of California, Los Angeles to being named a Champion of Change by the Obama administration. All this before she even graduated from the school. Highlighting the hidden cost of college across the United States, Rachel moved the organization's strategy beyond *simply* providing meals to food-insecure college students to advocating for legislative change. In 2018, she authored the Hunger Free Campus Bill, which has since allocated over $112 million to campus food security efforts across ten states.

During the Covid-19 pandemic, when it became abundantly clear just how much students rely on campuses to provide food, housing, and basic needs,[5] Rachel scaled the organization up yet again. In 2019, Swipe Out Hunger provided 2 million meals on eighty-three campuses in thirty-two states. By 2022, they were on over 550 campuses in all fifty states, providing over 4.8 million meals to food-insecure students. It was then, at the height of her success, that Rachel decided the time had come to pass the baton. In August 2022, she named Jamie Hansen the new executive director, walking away from the nonprofit she affectionately calls her "baby." For Rachel, this was an essential step in proving her worth as a leader; for the organization to survive without her at the helm. It was also what she saw as the essential next step for her own progression, allowing her to focus on solving strategic problems related to alleviating hunger with a direct focus on the Jewish community.

For me, it was the fulfillment of prophecy. The very first time we spoke in 2019, Rachel told me, "I don't want to do this forever." Forecasting the bold action she would take three years later, Rachel said the problems Swipe Out Hunger was trying to address were systemic. She knew she would one day need to pursue righteous social change at a higher level. "Policymakers have defunded higher education, leaving our universities in a position to have to make everything profitable, starting with food," she said. Unhappy with simply providing aid and what she felt like were stop-gap measures, she said, "I want to actually solve this problem."

Enough is enough

When I asked Rachel if it had been difficult to transition leadership in the organization she gave birth to, she immediately replied, "I've never lost a night of sleep. I feel so much confidence in the team, the organization. They've already raised half a million dollars, and the fiscal year hasn't even started yet." She credits the ability for the organization to not only grow but thrive under new leadership as her "biggest personal success."

Overcoming what is often termed "founder's syndrome," a disease that plagues nonprofits, for-profits, and faith-based organizations alike, is indeed more than just a professional success. Charismatic leaders, let alone founders, don't often like to leave their organizations. Those that do don't tend to do it well. Many don't think of legacy at such an early stage, nor succeed in scaffolding the infrastructure of organizations in such a way that they can outlast their vision, charisma, and influence. In some cases, as Naree W.S. Viner wrote, a founder, "has been in the position for so long that people outside the organization can't imagine it existing without them."[6] Rachel's success in guiding Swipe Out Hunger to its next phase of leadership is a personal victory. But Rachel also counts it as a spiritual one as well.

It was during Passover one year when her executive coach shared one Hebrew word with her, *dayenu*. Meaning "enough," it is sung as part of a song of gratitude during Passover. Leading up to that *Pesach*, Rachel was struggling with a "sense of obligation" to the organization. Hearing the word *dayenu* was a reminder to be grateful for the miracles provided. A reminder of Pharoah's stubbornness to recognize the injustice before him, "even the first plague should've been enough, slavery should've been enough," she said.

Rachel understood that what she knew was enough to make her decision. "When I decided to remove myself from my organization, I very intentionally wanted to model for people that this work is not about you. God forbid I get to the point where I'm so obsessed with my status and power," she explained. "I've seen so many nonprofit CEOs stay in their roles forever, build a board that doesn't know how to function without centering the CEO, without centering themselves, without centering some legacy for the organization." Enough was enough, she decided. *Dayenu*.

Prophetic action

While Swipe Out Hunger continues to grow under its new leadership, Sumekh herself has homed in on her next chapter advising philanthropies and philanthropists, mostly Jewish, on how to better alleviate poverty with their strategic giving. Her mission remains the same in this role: To end hunger and meet people's basic needs. She also continues to play the role of excavator, unearthing the reality of Jewish poverty that defies the stereotypes of affluence that the Jewish community is so often labeled with.

In March 2023, Rachel addressed a standing-room-only crowd at the Jewish Funders Network conference. The title of her session was, "Moonshot: Ending Jewish Poverty."[7] In her presentation, she reminded the crowd that one in five American Jewish households are designated as "financially insecure," meaning they have an average combined household income of less than $50,000.[8] As the child of Iranian immigrants who relied on government assistance in her early life, alongside resources offered from faith-based organizations like Jewish Family Service, Rachel said it was important that the Jewish community commits to solving problems like hunger and poverty.

This is what Rachel calls "radical prophetic action." It is an integral part of what she calls her, "grounding philosophy"—the reasoning that drives all her thinking. Rachel firmly believes that, "we as a society have everything we need to solve big problems like education, injustice, income inequality, hunger, housing. We have abundance in society right now and it's not a lack of knowledge that's holding us back. It is a lack of will." If you ask Rachel what provides her with her own abundance of will, she will tell you that all her work emanates from a spiritual core. For her, Judaism is best when it is practiced in its prophetic form. "There is a difference between rabbinic Judaism and prophetic Judaism," she said, almost as a parable:

> Rabbinic Judaism says: "Let's sit in synagogue and meet." Prophetic Judaism says: "Let's go and spend Yom Kippur out on the streets, having a festival feeding people who are hungry." On Passover, you're supposed to open the door and say: "All who are hungry, come and eat." The fast I want is the one where you feed people on the street every day. It's the one where you pay your employees on time, where you dress the naked, where you house the homeless. That's what I want.

Rachel wants the next chapter of her life to be filled with such prophetic action—like "the Freedom Seders that happened during the civil rights movement," she told me, "where Black and Jewish activists came together and said, 'What if we had a Passover Seder that was actually about freedom in this moment?' I think that whatever happens next, I'm excited for the way prophecy and more radical actions can capture people's attention."

Tehrangeles

Where does that strong social and religious ethic that Rachel describes as her motivating force come from? As religious scholars observe the continual rise of "the Nones"—people who select "none of the above" when asked about their religious beliefs—Rachel's beliefs may seem a bit of an outlier. Rachel was born and raised in the San Fernando Valley in Los Angeles, California to parents of Iranian Jewish heritage. It would be easy to credit Los Angeles, a city with vibrant Jewish and Iranian communities, as the place where a bold, intersectional identity could flourish, but Rachel very much represents a newer iteration of Tehrangeles's story.

Indeed, Los Angeles is home to one of the largest populations of Iranians outside of Iran. Exact population numbers are hard to come by, but it is estimated that there are anywhere from 100,000 to 1 million people of Iranian heritage living in Los Angeles today. Iranians in Los Angeles are diverse, both ethnically and religiously, and have come to the United States in three major seasons of immigration.[9] The first season began in the 1960s with Iranians coming to study at institutions of higher education, often staying as employment opportunities presented themselves. The second season began in 1979 with the Iranian Revolution and subsequent Iran–Iraq war, which served as a catalyst for a mass exodus from the nation.[10] The third season of Iranian immigration is ongoing, beginning in 2001 after 9/11, when the number of migrant and refugee visas issued to Iranians decreased significantly.

Rachel's father came that first season, in the mid to late 1960s. Born in Abadan, in southwestern Iran to an Isfahani family, he had international connections due to a history of working in petroleum. He came to the United States for the first time to study, completing both a bachelor's and a master's during his time in Oklahoma. Rachel's father spent time not only in the United States, but also in the UK. Along the way, he incorporated Buddhist practices into his Jewish faith—a "JewBu" of sorts, part of a trend in mid-twentieth-century America.[11] "My dad says he 'graduated' from Judaism to Buddhism. He has *sangha* [community], he meditates every morning. If I'm ever at my parent's house, if you wake up at like, 6:30 a.m., he's sitting on his little meditation pillow, staring out." Rachel's mother arrived later, in the mid-1980s, from Shiraz, a city in south-central Iran, known for its literary history and world-renowned gardens. Smuggled out of Iran on the back of a camel through Afghanistan where she received her visa to immigrate to Israel as a refugee, Rachel said that even though her mother has spent three decades in the United States, "her Hebrew is better than English ... even though she can speak English, she never embraced it."

Rachel has more of a third season mentality, you might say. As the immigration of Iranians to the United States slowed following 9/11, younger generations of Iranian Americans worked to found and foster institutions, participate in governance and civil society, and create art all while redefining their ethnic, religious, and political identities. In response to what they found to be an increasingly hawkish foreign policy toward Iran and hate-motivated bias toward Iranian and Middle Eastern communities in the United States, younger generations of Iranian Americans worked to create institutions, participate in governance and civil society, and create art, all while redefining their ethnic, religious, and political identities. Rachel is an embodiment of this ethic, a woman who, as religious adherence declines, has carried her beliefs and connections with her into civil society—letting it define her and her contributions to the country she calls home.

When Sumekh was named a changemaker by Repair the World, a faith-based organization with a mission to mobilize Jewish community toward public service, she was asked what role Jews should be playing in advancing food justice. She responded by saying:

> If you see someone who is naked, clothe them. And if you see someone who is hungry, feed them ... the rabbis say that ... as Jews, we live on the edge between being insiders and outsiders. From that perspective, we can see things from both sides and have the opportunity to build bridges. That is our obligation.[12]

Today, the conservative Synagogue where her parents were married—and where she and her siblings were Bat Mitzvahed—has been converted to condominiums because, as Rachel puts it, "Conservative Judaism is dying." But, at least in Rachel's circles, her vision of Judaism is growing.

Quoting Marshall Ganz, another prolific Californian dedicated to understanding ethical leadership as part of his take on theologian Walter Brueggemann,[13] Rachel explains where her hope comes from: "Young people come of age with something called prophetic imagination. They have a critical eye and a hopeful heart. And it's a critical eye and hopeful heart that make change possible ... I'm excited for how radical action and prophetic action are going to present themselves in this next generation."

"Finding a Way in the Wake of War"

Heline Babiene Eweni (Protestant/Cameroon)

By Innocent Eteng

In the summer of 2019, an armed conflict between the Cameroonian government and Ambazonian separatist groups in the English-speaking Northwest and Southwest of Cameroon raged. And every Tuesday during that conflict, a youth pastor named Heline Babiene Eweni snuck into the thicket of the forest near her home to deliver free feminine care products and clothes to displaced pregnant women or women who had been raped and were hiding for fear of their lives. It is estimated that the conflict displaced at least 712,000 Cameroonians, with thousands fleeing their houses for safety in the bushes because both the militants and government troops were picking people from their homes and assaulting them, especially those in rural communities.

Eweni lives in Kumba, often referred to as the largest town in Cameroon's southwest. The bushes of Kumba hosted many of the locally displaced. It was these bushes Eweni snuck into to deliver the products. When the 28-year-old was not making her way through the forest, she hid and delivered packs of food items to households impoverished by the ongoing conflict, enlisting teenagers from her church to help. She was also appearing on radio shows appealing to rebel fighters to allow kids to return to their classrooms. But every Tuesday since 2021, her focus has shifted to education. And this time, it's her very own.

Today, Eweni can breathe in the soothing air of relative safety and freedom as she travels one and a half hours by road from Kumba to the University of Buea, in the region's capital. There, she is pursuing a master's degree in education administration. Ever committed to her hometown, Eweni returns to Kumba on Saturdays to spend the weekends with her four orphaned brothers. Daring that distance in the region three to five years ago would have been suicidal. The brutal civil war made life unsafe, grounding free movement to a halt. As a result of the crisis, most businesses failed, thousands lost their lives, and almost every home or family felt the crisis's savage sting. "Either your family member was killed, or someone was abducted," Eweni said.

Changing attitudes among Anglophone Cameroonians have helped reduce the intensity of the conflict in the region since 2021. And now, civilians have a chance to mourn their dead, come out of the bushes where they have been hiding, heal their wounds, rebuild their homes, and return to their farms, businesses, and schools. But this tenuous calm also introduced other problems that forced Eweni to reimagine her approach to advocacy and shift her work's focus. What, after all, constitutes an activist's life when the direction of their work shifts due to changing societal factors?

The war many didn't expect

With nearly six million people, southern Cameroonians comprise 20 percent of the country's 27.2 million population inhabitants. They consider themselves highly under-developed and marginalized by the larger French-speaking population, led by 93-year-old President Paul Biya, who has ruled the triangle-shaped central African country since 1982. But when lawyers, teachers, and students from southern Cameroon took to the streets in late 2016, protesting the imposition of the French language on courts and schools in their regions, not many imagined it would lead to violence. When a government crackdown on demonstrators, however, angered youths from Anglophone Cameroon, they picked up arms and fought back. They joined distinct but united separatist groups fighting to actualize Ambazonia, a breakaway state comprising the two English-speaking regions.

As the conflict intensified with government troops responding with greater firepower, the rebels' frustration took hold and they resorted to committing abuses, including the rape of young girls, abducting and killing fellow southern Cameroonians, enforcing lockdowns, and shutting down businesses and critical public institutions and schools. They aimed to hurt the national economy, which partly relies on natural resources and considerable agricultural businesses in the minority regions. Government troops have also been reported to have committed abuses, which Human Rights Watch said include restricting humanitarian aid from reaching about 2.2 million Anglophone Cameroonians, the rape of women and girls, and attacking civilian populations after accusing them of supporting the rebels.

At least 4,000 to 6,000 people have died since the crisis started seven years ago, with over 700,000 more displaced, including nearly 100,000 who crossed borders to neighboring Nigeria as refugees. Comprehensive data on the actual number of rape victims since the conflict started is hard to come by, but in 2020 alone, the UN documented at least 4,000 cases of rape and gender-based violence. In separate reports in 2020 and 2023, respectively, Amnesty International and Human Rights Watch said justice remains elusive for most victims.

Distressed orphan turned activist

Eweni was orphaned at age 20, in 2015. Being the firstborn among five siblings with limited means of survival, the burden of caring and providing for her four younger brothers fell on her. With a degree she obtained in curriculum studies a year before, the pastor of about fifty teens at the Town Green Road branch of Christ Embassy (the global ministry of Nigeria's popular Pastor Chris Oyakhilome) in Kumba since 2020, Eweni picked up a teaching job at a local primary school to supplement her income and support her brothers. But because the pay was still meager compared to her responsibilities, Eweni's usually stern mental resolve began to break down. At her worst, she began to wrestle with depression and thoughts of suicide. She was still mourning and battling mental distress when the war broke out, rendering her jobless.

In frustration, she started advocating for children's education rights, calling on the separatists to allow schools to reopen. She appeared on local radio shows with her message, sometimes angering separatists, who warned her to stop her crusade or risk abduction and torture. By 2018, the Anglophone Cameroonians had gathered about fifteen teenagers to form the Exceptional Youth Initiative. Together, they promoted community service and canvassed for the financial strengthening of communities directly impacted by the conflict. In early 2019, the group started raising funds to pay the prenatal care bills for ten girls aged 13–19, who became pregnant after being raped and could not afford their bills. They also distributed clothes and feminine care products to about 300 pregnant displaced women. By December 2019, the Future Africa Leaders Foundation noticed her work and awarded her $35,000 as the star prize winner of its Future African Leaders Award.

Following the 2020 Covid-19 lockdown, which further exacerbated the already harsh realities of the civil war, Eweni used the cash to provide sacks of foodstuffs to households in Kumba, reaching a total of 130 families. She also gave grants of 50,000 francs (nearly $100) to ten women to support their small business start-ups. When schools reopened in early 2021, her group renovated a primary school affected by flooding and organized back-to-school campaigns, providing uniforms, school bags, shoes and books to hundreds of impoverished children.

Difficult economic times prompt a shift in focus

Local sources confirm that the suffering civilian population in southern Cameroon bears credit for the reduction in the intensity of the conflict. Many of them, desperate to break free from the dominance of Francophone Cameroon, supported the rebels in 2016, emboldening them to pick up arms and fight. But as the separatists gradually became abusive, the support died out, hitting demoralizing levels in 2020 when civilians started criticizing them openly and violently attacking their camps. Many have since given up fighting in the southwest, unlike in the northwest, where the rebels still command popularity and have continued to fight vigorously. "People are really fed up in this area; they no longer support their [rebels'] actions like they were doing before," Eweni said.

Still, irregular attacks in some southwestern rural communities and the continued observation of lockdowns on most Mondays mean the conflict is not entirely over. This is why "more internally displaced people fled from their rural communities" to towns like Kumba and Buea for safety, said 23-year-old Jani Bertha Bate, one of Eweni's volunteers. The implication is that the relatively calm areas are becoming overly congested, over-stretching surviving infrastructure amid job and food shortages, worsening poverty levels, and skyrocketing living costs.

This has hurt Eweni's work. Raising local funds has become increasingly challenging as most people can barely feed their households, let alone spare a donation. And Eweni's attempts at international funding applications have not yielded hoped-for results. "Since 2022, I have organized only one campaign. Things have risen in the market, and production isn't as high as before. What I could do with 100,000 francs, now I can't. I have to cut the number of people or kids to contact," she lamented. Given this challenging economic situation, in 2021, Eweni decided it was time to shift focus to herself. Not necessarily "to herself," she said—but to educate herself to better respond to the region's current social problems by gaining new leadership skills and tools.

A master's program in education administration at the University of Buea was her answer. Aiming to complete the program by the end of 2023, she already knows in her heart what she is called to do following her studies. "Jesus taught that you better teach men how to fish instead of giving them fish. So, when I finish my program, I will start soliciting funds to build a school," she said. "It is my new vision—to build a school where children aren't taught theoretical knowledge but where kids, even from a tender age, can have computer, cyber security, web development, and other digital or tech skills. I'm looking at the level at which the society is changing and growing and the job market," Eweni said.

Even though it is her vision, she feels it is too big to carry alone. And her faith has informed her search for a partner to help bear the load. "You know the Bible says it is not good to be alone," she mused. "I'm planning to settle down (get married) in 2024. I feel that I need somebody that can complement this vision. And with the right person, we can do better and touch more lives. Somebody has made his intention known already, but I'm still contemplating." This much planning and partnership are required because, according to her, she is seeking to compel a multiplier effect with her project where the rise of one child with the right skills and resources means a change in the fortunes of their entire families.

With a steady rise in inflation (from 2.27 percent in 2021 to 6.5 percent in 2022) fueled by production shortages amid a 44 percent multidimensional poverty rate and a 3.5 percent unemployment rate, she believes skills that allow young people to earn working in companies outside Cameroon will make a difference and contribute meaningfully to changing the socio-economic situation of Cameroonians on a large scale. "If you have that knowledge [skills], no matter how young you are, you can start doing something for yourself and your family. We must focus on helping young people develop skills that will benefit them, their families, and our society," she said.

Eweni feels excited about her dream project now that a certain sense of calm has returned to Kumba and the southwest region.

> I feel good and feel like I'm gradually stepping into my point of fulfilment. You know, there's this peace. [Until now] before you move or travel, you have to think whether the road is good or not for you to pass. You know that fright. But now, I don't have to worry about what I want to do or when I want to do things.

Only in a peaceful atmosphere can she fulfill her burning vision, she said. "For now, there's this peace," she said. "So yeah, I feel good."

8

Interreligious Dialogue and Peacebuilding

When we talk about chaplaincy ... if I'm not taking care of myself, I cannot take care of my other people.

SABRINA SOJOURNER (JEWISH)

Multi-faith prayer helps me control the anger. It's some sort of anchor, to help me build resilience. It's helped me get over the pain, even though you never really get over [it].

ELA GANDHI (HINDU)

Systemic change is built on the collective consciousness, which changes by the rubber hitting the road, and people really transforming their way of daily living.

TRUE DEDICATION (BUDDHIST)

The church is not a place. It is a community on a journey.

JACQUES MOURAD (SYRIAC CATHOLIC)

Introduction

We live in a world defined by diversity and difference. Every day, from New Delhi, India to Dayton, Ohio, layers upon layers of peoples, cultures, histories, traditions, philosophies, rituals, objects, and bodies bump up against one another, come into conflict with each other, or fuse together into new coalitions or combinations as they compete for social, cultural, political, and economic capital. In this age, even if you wanted to, you cannot escape "the Other." The Other—the person, place, idea, or thing you imagine as different from you—is constantly there. Or, rather, "They" are *here*. Whoever "They" are—or, more accurately, whoever we define "Them" to be—they are on our television sets, filling our social media feeds, in our email inboxes. They are sitting next to us on the airplane, detained at the border, working in our fields, handing us our pay checks, serving us our meals, moving in next door, occupying our media screens, entering our worship spaces.

Though humans have always lived alongside, or at least in proximity to, those of varying identifications and struggled with notions of belonging and co-becoming, the everyday contact between "Us" and "Them" in the present era has been exacerbated by the ongoing effects of late-modern globalization. As sociologist Peter Berger, one of the progenitors of the "secularization theory," wrote:

> Modernity is not necessarily secularizing; it is necessarily pluralizing. Modernity is characterized by an increasing plurality, within the same society, of different beliefs, values, and worldviews. Plurality does indeed pose a challenge to all religious traditions —each one must cope with the fact that there are "all these others," not just in a faraway country but right next door.[1]

In effect, if pluralization was a latent process and product of the last five hundred years, it became even more extensive, fluid, and energetic in the waning years of the twentieth-century and at the start of the twenty-first. It is the pluralization of modernity in flowering bloom. And in modernity's spring, nobody's conceptual, physical, or spiritual space is immune from the involuntary juxtaposition and encounter with that of Others.

This has led to almost constant contact with the Other, the different, the foreign—what German sociologist Ulrich Beck called, "banal cosmopolitanism": the experience of "globality" embedded in the mundane experiences of everyday life.[2] As a result of this "banal cosmopolitanism," our ideas about being and belonging (what a "place" or who our "people" should or could be) are constantly under threat and in flux. Regardless of our religion, we do not live in a "modest, familiar, local, circumscribed and stable" shell, but in a world that is a "playground of universal experiences … of encounters and interminglings or, alternatively, of anonymous coexistence and the overlapping of possible worlds and global dangers."[3]

It is little wonder, then, that interreligious dialogue has been enjoying what historian Howard Thomas Albert calls, "a booming heyday."[4] Interreligious dialogue has antecedents and lineages in the "dialogues" between Christians, Jews, and Muslims in the Middle Ages. It also has precedent in the more ancient "dialogue" between faith traditions that shared not only villages and cities across the millennia, but ideas and practices related to the divine, community, and the fate of everyone who ever lived, shaping modern religions into the hybrid traditions we know today. Contemporary interreligious dialogue efforts often trace their origins back to the 1893 Parliament of the World's Religions at the World's Columbian Exposition in Chicago, Illinois. Often seen as the birthplace of the modern interfaith movement, the parliament has since been followed by an ongoing series of initiatives and institutions, congresses and collaborations, as well as messages and meetings aimed at fostering dialogue and peace-building between the world's faith communities.

Even so, the challenges of religious diversity and difference remain. The shared problems that many interreligious dialogue efforts over the last century were supposed to solve, or at the very least address in a substantive manner, persist and thrive. Perhaps, as Azza Karam, former Secretary General of Religions for Peace International, opined, the problem is that such events do not trickle down to the lived realities of rank-and-file believers and practitioners. She wrote, in frustration, how:

> [a] global emerging elite of "experts" [have] permeated … four and five-star hotel meeting rooms, gave business to caterers and conference centres as they traipsed the "conference circuits" from north to south," expressing "common values, to uphold the good in public service."[5]

Karam, who was also founding convener of the United Nations InterAgency Task Force on Religion and Development as well as its Multi-Faith Advisory Council, concluded in disillusionment, "[w]e are not living in better democracies now, in spite of all that business. Will we have more faithful societies? Will people pray more, for one another and serve more selflessly now that 'religion' is in? Somehow, I doubt it."[6] The problem, in Karam's estimation, is that as global elites leverage "religion" to enhance the perception of dialogue, they often do so without the engagement of religious actors engaged in the work of everyday peacemaking. Those at the dialogue table are often not themselves engaged in acts of service, gifts of charity, and the defense of human and civil rights. Without such bona fides, Karam openly wonders what—if any—"good" interreligious dialogue in its current, popular forms can do.

This chapter features interreligious actors of another kind. The kind, you might say, that Karam wants to see more of at the dialogue table. Each comes from a different religious community: they are Muslim and Christian, Buddhist and Hindu-*ish*. Each hails from, or works in, a different part of the globe: Syria and South Africa, Indonesia and Belgium. And each has their own slant on what it means to identify with one religion or another, to say one "belongs" to a particular community or not. What they share is a commitment to interreligious belonging and co-becoming, a fidelity to tangible justice and the expansion of human rights. Moreover, each in their own way is dedicated to challenging the binaries and boundaries that exclude "Others" whenever humans decide who to include and who to exclude when they say "We" or "Us."

From the Middle East, Stephanie Saldaña reports on the everyday dialogue taking place between Christians and Muslims in Palestine and Syria. Whether it's sharing cookies during a holiday or saving lives during a brutal civil war, Saldaña's stories introduce exemplars whose spiritual lives, like her own, "are enriched by engaging in conversation and in the dialogue of daily life with people of other traditions." Profiling Huda Abu Arqoub and Jacques Mourad—the one Muslim, the other Syriac Catholic—Saldaña shows how each found their calling *because* of interreligious encounters, not *despite* them. Their stories are examples of lived plurality, which offers multiple possibilities for relationality that are often not seen in terms of either/or and Us/Them, but of both/and or We. Their biographies and vocations, Saldaña suggests, prompt us to consider that there is no "Other." That instead of seeing ourselves as this religion or that, we might instead foster interreligious identities in the "fertile soil" of everyday relationships.

In South Africa, I profile the legendary Ela Gandhi. More than granddaughter of Mahatma Gandhi—or Gandhiji, as she calls him—Ela Gandhi is an exemplar of how interreligious dialogue is more than a matter of talk, but of embodied justice. From her efforts at undermining and resisting white South Africa's Apartheid regime to saving money to buy groceries for those who cannot afford them or funneling funds to local causes she believes in, Gandhi channels the principles of her grandfather's "religion beyond religion" to make the world a more just, verdant, and secure place for her neighbors, no matter their religious background or racial identification.

Then there is Alissa Wahid, a trained family psychologist who is perhaps more widely known for her work in interreligious dialogue and the promotion of human rights and democracy. With a focus on training the next generation of interreligious leaders, Wahid directs the Gusdurian Network Indonesia (GNI), named after her late father, President Abdurrahman Wahid, better known as "Gus Dur." GNI hosts thousands of grassroots-level activists in more than 100 cities in Indonesia, working to promote interreligious dialogue and active citizenship in one of the world's largest democracies. Channeling the legacy of her forebears, Wahid works hard at fostering integrity and building trust across intra- and interreligious divides, knowing that if you do not show up for others at their time of need, then promises made at the table of dialogue are just that: talk.

Finally, readers are introduced to Bart Weetjens, a Buddhist monk in Belgium who wants to save the world by teaching meditation to one entrepreneur at a time. By training CEOs to connect with something in the universe bigger than the bottom line, he believes they will not only become happier humans but create more compassionate companies and economies. But his real target is social entrepreneurs—those who sacrifice their time, talent, and treasures to battle global ills like poverty, disease, violence, and other human-made problems and disasters. This is a constituency he knows well, having come to prominence as founder of the well-known nonprofit HERO Rats, which trains rats and dogs to sniff out landmines in countries such as Angola, Azerbaijan, and Cambodia. In her profile of Weetjens, Kimberly Winston reflects on how his latest goal might be to target not business leaders and humanitarians, but a journalist who visits his meditation center in Belgium. Winston shares how, slowly but surely, she starts to see how Weetjen's plans just might work, not only improving her journalism, but perhaps making the world a better place in the process.

The world, wrote theologian Love Lazarus Sechrest, "is entering an era in which our capacity to find leaders with gifts for managing diversity will determine our society's ability to persist and thrive."[7] The exemplars profiled in this chapter can perhaps be considered such leaders. Their gifts are diverse, ranging from meditation to everyday peacemaking, leadership development to a soft-spoken pursuit of justice. But each has contributed what they can to bring peace to a world so often divided by diversity and difference. They are not perfect. They have flaws and foibles like the rest of us. But their stories remain invitations to lean into a future defined by interreligious relationality and a shared effort to heal and repair the world.

Their stories are also a fitting capstone for a book that has featured many such leaders. This book has been a testament to telling the stories of individuals who have pursued solutions to some of the world's most intractable problems through a combination of spiritual ideals and religious practices, drawing not only on their own faiths, but also on those of others along the way. As readers may have noticed, many of these exemplars have engaged in interreligious dialogue as part of their work pursuing environmental justice, expanding educational access, or advocating for cultural empowerment. Thus, in many ways, this chapter is not just about a few exemplars, but about what it means to be a spiritual exemplar on a larger scale.

"Finding a More Interreligious Identity"

Huda Abu Arqoub and Jacques Mourad (Muslim and Syriac Catholic/Syria)

By Stephanie Saldaña

I live in Bethlehem in the West Bank next to a small church, where my husband happens to serve as the Syriac Catholic priest of the local parish, about a ten-minute walk from the Church of the Nativity. The place where tradition says Jesus was born. My daily life is as one would expect it: weddings and prayer services and baptisms, visits with parishioners, preparations for Easter and Christmas, all to the regular tolling of church bells.

That is, except for the fact that our immediate neighbors are Muslim. They run "The Manger Bakery" right next door. They guard our doorway, and we buy our bread from them every morning, as well as the cakes we serve after church on Sundays. Our afternoons are enhanced by the call to prayer, and the smell of freshly baked goods, wafting through the churchyard. I walk to the market and buy from villagers selling fresh mint and cucumbers from the surrounding villages, each one of us calling out greetings that inevitably have some mention of God. If you were not from Bethlehem, you would have no idea who belongs to what community—Muslim or Catholic or Orthodox—for we are all interwoven within the same fabric of everyday life.

It is in living here that I know that religious identifications are complex, expansive even. I think of my neighbor Nahida, who is a member of our church and who also owns a bakery. She specializes in baking *ma'moul*, the date-filled pastries served on special feast days. A few years ago, when Easter and Ramadan overlapped, she was swamped with work—first making *ma'moul* for local Catholics, then for local Orthodox Christians who have a different liturgical calendar and so celebrated their Easter a week later, and finally for Muslims celebrating Ramadan. Nahida is deeply Catholic, and yet part of her expression of her Catholic faith is in serving members of other religious communities during their feast days.

In living next to people like Nahida, I've come to understand that it is possible to be simultaneously rooted in one's own religious tradition and to live life differently because of daily, deep interactions with people who identify with the traditions of other faiths. I have come to think of this as, "interreligious identity." People in the Middle East who live in religiously diverse cities often take deep pride and express great care in these interfaith relationships.

It is in between the *ma'moul* and the *adhan*, the tolling of church bells and cakes served on Sundays that I wanted to profile spiritual exemplars from the Middle East who have an expansive sense of their own faith lives—those whose spiritual lives, like my own, are enriched by engaging in conversation and in the dialogue of daily life with people of other traditions. What I didn't expect to find was that they first experienced their vocations—or callings—precisely *because* of those interreligious encounters. Something in these meetings led them to become more deeply themselves—to discover who they are in the fertile soil of day-to-day diversity and difference.

Our father

Jacques Mourad grew up in Aleppo, Syria in the Syriac Catholic community. As a boy, he was initially hesitant to engage in dialogue with Muslims because of his community's difficult history. That history included what are known as the *Sayfo*—or Assyrian massacres. At the beginning of the twentieth century, in what is today southeastern Turkey, Syriac Christians were deported and killed. After discerning he was called to the priesthood, Mourad entered seminary in Lebanon, where the legacy of the Sayfo led many of his teachers to be critical of Muslims, even advocating for violence in the context of the Lebanese Civil War.

Then, in the early 1980s as the Lebanese Civil War was at its fiercest heights, Fr. Jacques visited a monastery in the Syrian desert called Deir Mar Musa, 80 kilometers north of Damascus on the eastern slopes of the Anti-Lebanon Mountains. There, an Italian priest named Fr. Paolo Dall'Oglio was restoring an ancient monastery from the ruins and creating a community of Christian monks and nuns dedicated to dialogue with Muslims—to understand them and their faith on their own terms. Mourad became a monk there. In the following years, while he was still studying in Lebanon during his novitiate in preparation for his ordination, he would return to Mar Musa during the summers. That is when his "conversion" began, he said. "That's where I started slowly meeting Muslims, from the bakers making bread in Nebek, to the ice-cream man, to the people who were working with us," he told me. "All of them were kind people and generous."

It was in these everyday friendships that Mourad began to reconsider his relationships with Islam as a whole. Yet the transformation truly came after his ordination, when he was invited by the local bishop to restore the nearby monastery of Mar Elian in the village of Qarytein, Syria, an oasis in the desert between Homs and Palymrya. It was a village that Mourad did not know well, consisting of a mix of Muslims, Orthodox Christians, and Catholics. In Qarytein, like my neighborhood in Bethlehem, interreligious encounter was a fact of everyday life.

Yet for Mourad, what made the village unique was that all the inhabitants, Muslim and Christian, believed that the monastery of Mar Elian he was now entrusted with was a *sacred* place. Muslims referred to the saint buried there as *Ahmed al-Houri*, the Christians as *Mar Elian* (St. Elian). Seeking a cure for bodily ailments, both Muslims and Christians visited the grave, believing that it was a site of *baraka*, or blessing. Carved into the monastery's stone were scribbles of graffiti left behind by pilgrims, including Stars of David and Arabic script. The building also bore an inscription stating the monastery was under the protection of a local Muslim ruler, Emir Sayfudullah, reflecting the peaceful coexistence of Muslims and Christians living in the region around the fifteenth century.

Mourad initially arrived in Qarytein unsure whether he would stay for more than a short period of time. But as he started restoring the monastery, Mourad was inspired to the vocation by Mar Elian, the saint buried there. He noticed that St. Elian did not differentiate between Muslims and Christians who came to the monastery to pray in front of his tomb. He bestowed blessings on both. Perhaps there was something to learn in the expansive love that he felt God was calling him to.

While continuing the work, he found he needed a sieve. And so, he headed to the market to buy supplies. A shopkeeper, who happened to be Muslim, asked him why he needed it, and Mourad mentioned that he was in Qarytein to restore the ancient monastery. The man could not believe that this young man, covered in dust, was a priest! He immediately sent his son with him to the blacksmith to get supplies, insisting on paying for everything as it was being used for the church. "This trust—according to me, was something strong, and really made an impact on me," Mourad said. "How could one give his small child to a stranger? With one he didn't know? According to me, this was a sign from God that these people were worth coming to live among," he said. Mourad was touched by the community's common love for Mar Elian, and for the fact that this man had shown such remarkable generosity to someone of another faith who he had only just met. He experienced this not only as a sign from God, but as a sacred lesson about the holiness of inter-communal hospitality.

It was Mourad's belief that God speaks to us in simplicity, and that God was speaking to him through this Muslim shopkeeper and his son. The shopkeeper's simple trust, his ability to love, to be generous beyond his own community, and his dedication to the monastery were all qualities that Mourad aspired to. Later, he would tell me of God speaking to him through the Muslims and Christians who left their doors and their hearts wide open in Qarytein, always ready to receive guests. Mourad saw in these humble acts a parable for God's love for everyone, his heart always open and available to all.

An even greater conversion came later, as Muslim villagers came to call Mourad "Abouna," which means "our father." The more he heard them, the more he understood that God was calling him to love everyone equally, to understand that God does not play favorites—that God loves Muslims and God loves Christians, which is to say that God offers all love. In short, the people of Qarytein were helping Mourad understand God as "our father," in a more universal way.

Siblings

If one were to think of Mourad as a "spiritual exemplar," it is usually considering what came later, however. The Syrian Civil War broke out in 2011, and Mourad decided to open the monastery to everyone, both Muslim and Christian, creating a sanctuary where they were safe from harm. As rival factions wreaked havoc across the region and homes in the village were destroyed amidst the fighting, he sought funds to restore them, insisting on repairing the homes of Muslims and Christians alike. He worked with *sheikhs* and priests, all of them engaged in the daily work of peace-building and restoration, hospitality, and mutual help in times of need.

Eventually, however, Mourad and the Christians of Qarytein were kidnapped by *al-Dawla al-Islamiyya* (a.k.a., Islamic State, IS, or ISIS). Mourad, imprisoned for five months and facing the possibility of death each day, maintained his faith, praying for those who kidnapped and tortured him. Despite the circumstances, Mourad said he was able to see the image of God in every person, even those who took him, a fact that he later said, "liberated him."

Most importantly, he said, this disastrous event did nothing in his heart to obscure the powerful relationships he had built with Muslims over the previous decades. In the end, Mourad and his parishioners were rescued by their Muslim neighbors from Qarytein, who carried them out of the town in groups—in disguise and concealed in the backs of trucks. Based on years of living side-by-side, giving one another mutual aid, devoted to the same saint and the blessings they believed he bestowed, they did not consider Mourad and his parishioners the "Other." They were siblings of the same "father," whom they were meant to protect.

Mourad is often lauded as "exemplary" for his actions in this period. His strength and generosity. His consistent faith amidst captivity. His unending love for others. But he himself is careful to give credit where he believes credit is due: to God *and* his Muslim neighbors. He said it was they who taught him how to live his faith by calling him "Abouna." It was they who rescued him. He noted that his decision to help everyone in the village, "emanated from

FIGURE 8.1 Father Jacques Mourad greeting Sister Friederike at the monastery of Maryam al-Adhrah in Iraqi Kurdistan. Photo courtesy of Stephanie Saldaña.

my faith that God called me to be there for all of the people, not only for a part." In other words, his exemplarity is the result of relationships—everyday peacemaking in the ordinary and mundane moments of life together.

Bread-loaf-by-bread-loaf

From my perspective back in Bethlehem, situated amidst its bakeries and living every day with its religious diversity, I believe this adds much needed nuance to our discussions of interreligious dialogue (IRD). Dialogue is framed at its most basic level as how communities can coexist and learn about one another. Too often, however, IRD practitioners and experts are removed from the communities they intend to benefit. They are not embedded in the life-on-life contexts where interreligious dialogue is baked and shared, bread-loaf-by-bread-loaf.

The way Mourad understands his calling, his work in IRD, opens up the possibility that the very act of living with people of other faiths can not only lead us to a wider vision of what constitutes dialogue, but can open up new horizons for how we understand ourselves and who we are called to love. The "teachers" in this story, the interfaith experts, are not trained theologians or diplomats, facilitators with fancy degrees or even faith-leaders, but neighbors—those people who Mourad himself credits with being the true "spiritual exemplars" in the story. He notes this explicitly, saying: "When I want to know about dialogue with Islam, I'm not going to ask a professor at the Gregorian university or at Yale to teach me dialogue. I'm going to ask a local bishop from Idlib, or I'm going to ask someone who lives in a Muslim neighborhood in which all of his neighbors are Muslims to teach me dialogue," he said.

A Muslim finding faith among Mennonites

Huda Abu Arqoub, a Muslim peace activist who was born in Jerusalem and raised in Hebron in the West Bank, grew up during the First Intifada, a time when there were regularly Israeli tanks stationed outside her home. The daughter of a father rooted in a Sufi tradition and a secular mother, the first exposures to her faith taught her that if God was anything, God was love. But as violence increased around her, Arqoub watched as Islam was politicized and radicalized, as some political groups responded to the crisis with rage and violence in her own neighborhood. Arqoub found herself rejecting the anger and her faith entirely, feeling "there was no one witnessing what was happening to us." By "no one," she meant God. For despite the faith of her childhood, she now had difficulty conceiving of how a God of love could exist and yet stand by as she, her family, and her neighbors suffered.

It was only later, when she traveled to the United States on a Fulbright Fellowship to study peacekeeping at Eastern Mennonite University, in Virginia's Shenandoah Valley, that she felt called back to her faith. Yet, perhaps unexpectedly, her Mennonite classmates were not responsible for her conversion to Christianity, but her reversion to Islam. As Arqoub witnessed her classmates reading the Bible, holding up Jesus as a model for peacemaking and social justice, she was able to reclaim "the narrative of religion as one of liberation instead of one of oppression." In their use of circles, in which students gathered and spoke about what was in their hearts, listening to one another, her spirit was reignited, she said.

Then, when she decided to fast during Ramadan that year, her Christian classmates fasted with her. They led her to a local mosque attended by recently resettled Iraqis, who had escaped the war in their own country. She recognized her life in theirs, touched by their vulnerability and connection to God despite their exposure to war and violence. Arqoub reread the Quran, this time finding inspiration in the verses on light, rereading them with the relationships she had found in the Shenandoah close to her heart and mind. Through all of this, Arqoub felt, God might be calling her to transform conflicts, rather than sidestepping them.

She would later return to the West Bank and become a peacemaker on the front lines of the conflict there, working with bereaved parents, former combatants, and thousands of Muslim, Christian, and Jewish women seeking to interrupt the cycle of violence and find a path to peace. In the Holy Land, Arqoub discovered that the expansive, interfaith identity that formed her vocation in Virginia was not only still possible elsewhere but is a vital component in creating the deep relationships that make conflict transformation possible. This is more than "tolerance," or "coexistence," she said; it is the belief that in the context of interfaith relationships, a new world can be made possible. Her Mennonite friends have been vital in this process, she said. "I have to admit," she told me, "if I ever go to heaven, it will be because of the Mennonites."

Today, Arqoub's calling as peacekeeper is sustained by her practice of prayer and fasting during Ramadan. She is inspired by the Virgin Mary in Islam, strong Muslim women like Khadeeja, the prophet's first wife, and the Prophet Muhammad himself, whom she sees as a social justice activist. This strength has allowed her to remain steadfast in a society that often criticizes her work in conflict transformation.

Beyond Christian, beyond Muslim

In 2017, Huda Abu Arqoub was awarded the Laudato Si' Award from the Vatican for her peace-building work in the Holy Land. In 2023, Fr. Jacques Mourad was ordained Archbishop of Homs in Syria. In light of these very public recognitions, six years apart, it becomes clear that they are not exceptions or anomalies in their societies, but individuals who reflect something deep about the hopes of the communities they come from and represent. Both deeply rooted in their respective faith, each also feels called to act on behalf of a wider multi-faith community. Through the twists and turns of violence and exclusion, community and everyday relationship, they have fostered an interreligious identity that transcends the "Us"/"Them" politics that so often divide.

To categorize them as simply "Muslim" or "Christian" exemplars diminishes this particular aspect of their story. Perhaps it is best to call them "exemplars of dialogue," or exemplars who belong to *everyone*. Arqoub insists her identity is that of living in a "shared community," and that she is "part of something bigger than just being a Muslim." For his part, Mourad said his identity is rooted in his vocation to love all people, as God their father loves them, without preference.

Both stories highlight how ordinary people—neighbors and students—are spiritual exemplars, people whose examples change the lives of supposed "Others" for good. They also challenge us to a more expansive notion of religious being, belonging, and co-becoming—and what that might mean about discovering who we really are, as humans in relation to other humans.

"A (Not So) Quiet Commitment to Justice"

Ela Gandhi (Gandhian/South Africa)

By Ken Chitwood

There is a temptation to underestimate Ela Gandhi. With her soft, fluttering voice, attentive nature, and reserved demeanor, you might think Gandhi is placidity personified. On that, said her friend and biographer Susan Easterbrooks, you would be wrong. "Behind that sweet demeanor," she said, "is the heart of a lion. It's a gentle heart, it's a respectful heart, but it's also a no-holds-barred kind of heart."

Beyond being one of Mahatma Gandhi's—or *Gandhiji's*—granddaughters, Ela Gandhi has become a symbol of social justice in her own right, living a life of quiet—and sometimes not so quiet—resistance over the last eighty years. Her life is a testament to the slow-working power of engaged spirituality over the long haul. Growing up in Phoenix, one of the oldest Indian settlements in South Africa, Gandhi later went on to serve as a social worker engaged in non-violent protests and activism, fighting on behalf of the oppressed. Along the way to helping South Africa transition to a post-Apartheid state by sitting on the Transitional Executive Committee in the South African government and as a member of South Africa's Parliament (1994–2004), Gandhi faced house arrest for nine years and lost her son, who was killed in the struggle for justice. Now retired, Gandhi remains committed to the pursuit of justice and to building interreligious harmony. She founded and still chairs the Gandhi Development Trust, is a member of South Africa's Religious Affairs Committee and works with international organizations, including Religions for Peace International, to bring peace through dialogue.

From the streets of Phoenix to the halls of parliament

Most people who know Phoenix, South Africa today know it as where the infamous Gandhiji's philosophy of passive resistance developed in embryonic form, before he employed it in India to free his homeland from British colonial rule. Ela Gandhi simply knows it as "home."

It was on Phoenix's rolling green hills and meandering dirt streets that Gandhi grew up running next door to borrow *ghee* (clarified butter) from the neighbors, picking vegetables in the shared market gardens, joining in communal prayers and hymns, or sharing parcels of homemade sweets for Christmas, Diwali, or Eid. Following Gandhiji's principle of self-sufficiency, Gandhi's parents Manilal and Sushila—married in India in 1927—ran the Phoenix settlement's printing press thereafter. They built the brick home she grew up in by hand and tended to the mango and lemon trees that her grandfather himself planted. There, Gandhi learned "the confluence of spirituality that makes up Gandhian values." To Ela Gandhi, those values were not coupled with any particular tradition but embraced many. They may be Hindu-ish, in other words, but decidedly multi-faith in outlook and practice. "Our neighbors accepted what we were doing, and we accepted what they were doing," said Gandhi. "We would have a Christian prayer, a Muslim prayer, or Hindu prayer. People spoke different languages—spiritual and literal."

That interreligious approach to her own spirituality guided her throughout her life. Over the years, Gandhi gleaned lessons for life from multiple traditions, such as the principle of *satyagraha* (non-violent resistance), theologies of liberation, and practices of self-discipline. Her formal education started in her parents' brick home before her mother launched a racially integrated school at the Gandhi house for about 200 children when Ela was 8 or 9-years-old. Not too long after, an inspector from the Apartheid government warned Sushila not to educate Black children. Under Apartheid, the government passed a series of laws enforcing separate and unequal education for each of South Africa's racially classified groups: White, Black, Colored (mixed race), and Indian.

It was then that another kind of education began for Gandhi. "This is where I first became aware of racial oppression," she said. By age 12, she was marching with her father as part of the Defiance Campaign—a large non-violent resistance campaign from 1950 to 1952, featuring boycotts, strikes, and civil disobedience. Gandhi went to the Brook Street library, an all-white institution where "Coloreds" were not allowed. She went in anyway, she said, walking with her brother, sisters, and friends. She also went to African townships where Indians were forbidden to go by law.

Then, she went to university and studied for two bachelor's degrees at Natal University. As a student, Gandhi said she learned a lot leaving the Phoenix settlement and stepping out of her comfort zone. "In a way, my parents protected me from Apartheid, but then I get to university, and they have separate buildings, one for whites, one for others," she said. "It's the same university, but you can't access all the facilities simply because you are not white. It was then that I started to understand the extent of oppression and it made me angry." She channeled her anger into "more positive behavior," she said, taking part in placard demonstrations against unequal access at the university.

Later, as a social worker in the Inanda District of Durban after school, Gandhi saw the "absolute poverty" of her community and her righteous rage was rekindled. So, she not only sought to ameliorate the day-to-day suffering of people in her community, she said, but also sought to fight the system that kept them down. In the 1970s the Natal Indian Congress (NIC)—a political organization established by her grandfather in 1894 to fight discrimination against Indians in the Natal Colony, and later Natal Province, of South Africa—was revived at a convention at the Phoenix Settlement on October 2, 1971, Mahatma Gandhi's birthday. "Seeing the power of the Apartheid regime and fearing that it could continue to split us apart, we started to organize politically," Gandhi said.

Her then husband, Mewa Ramgobin, was meant to be president of the NIC, but had been banned, meaning that he could not attend the convention. Instead, Chanderdeo "George" Sewpersadh served as NIC president and Ela was elected vice president. She was also an active member of the Detainees Support Committee in Durban, assisting people who had gone to prison and fasting in solidarity with those who were arrested by the Apartheid regime.

Fearful that Blacks and Indians would be divided, Gandhi and the NIC were driven by the motto, "Think Black, not Indian." While it was practically difficult to organize on a non-racial basis, Gandhi and others did it anyway, feeling that if not everyone was liberated, no one was liberated. This would be tested in 1984 when the apartheid government promised peripheral representation to Indians and "Colored people" in separate but unequal chambers of parliament. Blacks were to be excluded. During the campaign, Indians asked what Gandhi would have done if he were faced with that choice. "Non-cooperation with the oppressor until universal franchise on an equal basis is accepted," replied Mewa. Eighty percent of the Indians boycotted the election. The NIC also committed to a principled resistance that eschewed violence. "Violence is destructive," Ela told the weekly magazine *India Today* in 1989.[8] "Hate won't solve our problems, principled opposition is what counts." These perspectives, she said, were no turning point or sudden revelation, "but more of a natural progression from the Gandhian values we were already living in Inanda."

Her reputation as an agitator for justice became so well known that Apartheid authorities took notice. For taking in those who had been arrested by the authorities and organizing alternative labor societies when unions were banned, Gandhi was put under house arrest for nearly ten years along with Ramgobin. Subjected to harassment from the state, her house was constantly under watch, and she was prevented from going to meetings, barred from leaving her home on weekends, and under curfew from 7:00 p.m. to 7:00 a.m. every day. Even so, for the nearly nine years that Ela was banned, she worked underground. "We used to run camps, discuss various issues, take part in the Black Consciousness movement, the Freedom Charter, the education system and all that; we also did simple things like helping people in the neighboring community to re-build their homes after a flood."

Her role models in this work went beyond her father and grandfather to include a who's who of Black and Indian luminaries and leaders in the anti-Apartheid resistance, including Chief Albert Luthuli, Nelson Mandela, Walter Sisilu, Govan Mbeki, Monty Naicker, and Yusuf Dadoo. Inspired by their various forms of resistance—and their multiple faith traditions and perspectives—Gandhi said, with a bit of a twinkle in her eye, "I broke the banning order and house arrest many time." Careful to cover their backs, Gandhi said it was then she began to appreciate how activism works at the grassroots. There, she said, one learns what it is to participate in democracy. "It is to consult, to value opinions of people, not to have a judgment, not to make up your mind in a drawing room or something. To go out in the community and experience what the community is experiencing and work with them and listen to what they are saying."

Upon her release in 1983, Gandhi served as the executive of the Natal Organization of Women and became involved in the anti-Apartheid United Democratic Front (UDF)—a multi-racial coalition of civic, religious, student, and worker organizations. For Gandhi, the UDF was a watershed in resistance to Apartheid. "Coming from a home where we respected our Hindu tradition but did Christian prayers, Parsee prayers, and Muslim prayers, I thought UDF was a defining moment—when all the religions came together. The UDF brought all the religious groups, all the civic organizations, all the races together in one united front," she said, "that's the only way you can break oppression: together."

It was during this politically active time, however, that her son Kush, 29, was killed—shot in the back in his home in the Durban suburb of Verulam, on December 16, 1993. The circumstances around Kush's death were never cleared up. While police Major Bala Naidoo described it as an apparent robbery at the time, the murder was also linked to ongoing political violence in the area. Amidst the pain and the sadness of losing one of her five children, Gandhi also felt anger. In her darkest times, she would draw on the repertoire of multi-faith prayers she learned as a child. "It helps me controlling the anger, it's some sort of anchor, to help me build resilience," she said. "It's helped me get over the pain, even though you never really get over losing a child."

Through prayer and the encouragement of others, Gandhi once again channeled her anger into activism, sitting on the Transitional Executive Committee and serving in South Africa's first democratically elected parliament, focusing on welfare programs and support for single mothers. Along with Nontsikelelo Albertina Sisulu ("Mama Sisilu")—founding co-president of the UDF—Gandhi was one of the people who met with Nelson Mandela and other UDF leadership the day before the future president and Nobel Prize Winner was released from Pollsmoor Prison.

Legacy and lessons learned

During her life, Gandhi worked hand in hand with some of the most prominent figures within the anti-Apartheid movement, from Nelson Mandela and Mama Sisilu to Archbishop Desmond Tutu and Steve Biko, founder of the Black Consciousness Movement in South Africa whose brutal death while under police custody in Pretoria in 1977 made him a martyr for the anti-Apartheid cause. "There were some blockbuster events in my life, you know," she said, "but I've never been one for glitzy events. I would rather hide away in some corner."

Oddly enough, Gandhi doesn't have many physical tokens of these friendships and interactions other than her memories and the history books written about them. There are no framed photos of her shaking hands with leaders or standing together at galas. "I don't even have a single picture of me with Mandela," she said. "I just don't think of taking photographs, because they don't mean as much to me as interaction with people, learning from other people through conversations." Instead, Gandhi said, she carries intangible proof of these encounters in how she continues to use her voice for the vulnerable and to advocate for justice, even in the later stages of life.

It is also, said Easterbrooks, a testament to Gandhi's effusive humility and the desire to deflect attention to those she interacts with. When Easterbrooks first traveled to South Africa as part of a partnership between her U.S. university and the Durban University of Technology, little did she know that it would spark a long-term friendship between her and Gandhi. Reflecting on her time with Gandhi in her book *My Time with Ela Gandhi*, Easterbrooks said, "my editor says to not use the word 'humble.' But she's just very humbling. As soon as you meet her and talk to her, the next thing you know, she has taken your request to the next level on your behalf." Easterbrooks said Gandhi left a profound influence on her, particularly when it comes to her engaged spirituality. "Gandhi's life shows us that in constructive action, you can turn people from their personal frustrations and help them see a broader, higher perspective," said Easterbrooks. She said that no matter how many times Gandhi was banned, barred, or thrown into jail, she continued to gather women around her struggling with their own issues—whether it was the cost of housing or not being able to sit on certain benches because of Apartheid's unjust laws. "Ela inspired people not only to protest, but to consider how you can sit back and complain about things, or you can take action and by your actions demonstrate a better way of being," Easterbrooks said. "She helped people create a better reality. And in creating the better reality, they felt more empowered, and in feeling more empowered, they could continue to create more." Repetition.

A still vibrant spirit

Gandhi is still not done. Amidst the global unrest and upheaval of the Covid-19 pandemic, she continues to work toward sustainable local activism and inclusive intercultural and interracial justice. "In my mind, I'm still an activist," Gandhi said. And so, as she often did throughout her life, Gandhi channels grand goals into her local, everyday life and with the people around her that need her help the most. Since her time in parliament, Gandhi has gone on to develop the Gandhi Development Trust, is a member of South Africa's Religious Affairs Committee, and set up a 24-hour domestic violence support organization.

Her spirituality, which she said draws from a broad stream of practices, perspectives, and prayers, motivates her efforts on behalf of human rights. One misperception many have, she said, is that she does not belong to any formal religious group. "I was brought up in the tradition of my grandfather, who was a universalist and drew from many traditions," Gandhi said, "and so I promote the Ghandian values I learned from my family."

"For me, it is all about people," said Gandhi, "getting to know people at the grassroots and changing their lives from the ground-up, no matter their religion, their background, the color of their skin."

Like many members of the well-known Gandhi family, Ela could be seen regularly on the front lines of the global interfaith movement in recent decades. And, in 2019, she served as a draftee of the Declaration of the 10th World Assembly of Religions for Peace in Lindau, Germany. She wrote, along with other leaders in the world of interreligious dialogue, how, "the burdens of the human family are well-known to us. We know too well war, how it kills, maims, and destroys the lives of the innocent. We know the crushing weight of extreme poverty, how it stunts, humiliates, and plunders."

Each of these could be plucked from Ela Gandhi's own biography of pain and division, poverty and violence. But so too could lines from the end of the statement, in which the declaration reads: "We take heart that multi-religious actors and institutions are working to build just and harmonious societies with a vibrant spirit of care and commitment to justice. We commit to continued common action to tackle injustices ... We commit to instilling the respect, mutuality, and solidarity that are essential to promote, build, and sustain just, harmonious, and diverse communities."

Since the onslaught of the Covid-19 pandemic, however, Gandhi's own commitment to tackle injustice from her multi-faith perspective has been taking place closer to home. "Before the pandemic, I used to travel often," she said, "but now staying at home, I am saving money." Instead of using that money for herself, Gandhi has been buying groceries for those who cannot afford them or funneling the extra funds to causes she believes in. She shared this not to draw attention to what she is doing, she said, but to inspire others "to change things to make the world more secure." In a time of upheaval and uncertainty, Gandhi said that pursuing equity and generosity for others might be a way through the chaos. It was, she said, always the case for her over the course of an active and often tumultuous life.

Thinking back to her early days as a social worker in Durban, she said it was always the "grassroots people" that sustained her. Today, it's no different. "When I go out and work in the community and try to make their lives better. That's what sustains me," she said. "I'm not doing many things, but the little that I can do—even if it's for a few people—it makes me happy." Together, the little acts add up, she said. Speaking to all those pursuing justice from a multi-faith perspective, Gandhi enjoined, "do what you can, where you are, with what you have."

"A Legacy of Social Transformation"

Alissa Wahid (Muslim/Indonesia)

By Ken Chitwood

Carrying a father's legacy is never easy—especially when that father is widely considered a hero in the world's third most populous democracy. When President Abdurrahman Wahid—popularly known as "Gus Dur"—died in 2009, millions of people visited his grave in the remote East Javanese town of Jombang. Even now, twelve years later, the East Java Tourism Agency reports that half a million pilgrims visit the shrine each month, making it one of the most heavily frequented pilgrimage sites in the world.

While only president of Indonesia for two tumultuous years, Gus Dur's legacy is broader than his time in office. Upon his passing, people from across Indonesia's religious and political spectrums felt a deep, personal sense of loss for a much-loved humanitarian whose compassionate activism transcended religious boundaries. Philip Bowring, who wrote his obituary for *The New York Times*, said Gus Dur, "was the single most important figure not merely in Indonesia's transition from Suharto's centralized autocracy to a decentralized democracy, but in ensuring that the new democracy was committed to religious and ethnic pluralism."[9] In short, Gus Dur's legacy in Indonesia—and globally—is long.

For Alissa Wahid, being the daughter of the first democratically elected Indonesian president in a generation, and granddaughter of one of the founders of Nahdlatul Ulama—the largest Muslim organization in the world, with between 40 and 60 million members—it is also quite the

FIGURE 8.2 Alissa Wahid poses in front of a portrait of her father Abdurrahman Wahid—more popularly known as Gus Dur. Courtesy of Alissa Wahid.

legacy to live up to. "You can imagine what kind of expectations I was born into," she said with a portrait of her father hanging behind her, "it was this huge burden to step into the shoes of the giants before me."

Even so, she has channeled her family's legacy into a pioneering interfaith dialogue movement of her own: the Gusdurian Network Indonesia (GNI). Founded in 2010, GNI works with grassroots-level activists across Indonesia to promote interfaith reconciliation, active citizenship, democracy, and human rights. As its National Director, Wahid has been at the forefront of fighting for the rights of religious minorities in Indonesia, promoting a vision of interreligious exchange between Muslims and non-Muslims, and seeking to build on, and extend, her forebears' legacy.

Indonesian scholar and GNI member Aan Anshori said, "Alissa is not only Gus Dur's biological daughter, but an ideological one. I've learned many things through her work: integrity, modesty, and courage." He continued, "she is a spiritual leader for us, showing us the path that requires sacrifice for defending the oppressed." In that, Anshori said, she carries the legacy of her predecessors well.

For Wahid, the journey to being the public leader of a movement with chapters in over 114 locations across Indonesia—and international chapters in places like Malaysia, the United Kingdom, Saudi Arabia, Germany, the Philippines, and Egypt—was not self-evident. While her sister Zannuba Ariffah Chafsoh, popularly known as Yenny, went into politics and took up the mantle of directing her late father's research center (The Wahid Institute), Alissa initially shunned public service. During her father's presidency, Wahid said she lost trust in the political system. "I was discouraged and distrustful," she said, "I became convinced that politics left no chance for the kindhearted." She instead chose social work with at-risk teenagers and being a mother.

Then, when her father passed away in 2009, representatives of various religious minorities started coming to Wahid's house to pay their respects. They would also share their struggles and ask her to intervene. "They said things to me like, 'now that your father has passed away, who should we come to when we suffer? Who will protect us?'" she said. "In those moments, I thought back to what my father always told us—'you have to realize your capacity,'" said Wahid, "he always said we could live whatever lifestyle we wanted, but we could not abandon our calling." And so, Wahid "came out of retirement from the public eye," she said, founding GNI to extend her father's work and create collaborative spaces for interreligious dialogue.

It is hard to measure the full extent of the organization, as they have no formal membership structure, but the group enjoys nearly 300 thousand followers on the social media site X and Wahid herself more than 500 thousand. On Instagram, they have a combined followership of more than 200 thousand and various "fan" accounts that share, promote, and disseminate their content on peace and justice. That extensive, organic network has allowed Wahid to not only promote pluralism in Indonesia on a large scale but mobilize people locally to protect marginalized communities when they come under threat.

For example, in 2010, Wahid was sipping on a latte in a coffee shop near her home when she received a notification that a village in West Java was coming under attack. The village was inhabited by many Ahmadis, part of a denomination considered "non-Muslim" by religious hardliners. As part of a spate of vicious attacks across Indonesia, extremists descended upon the village and the Ahmadis feared for their lives. The message Wahid received from 500 kilometers away not only communicated the danger but expressed the hope that Gusdurians would come to the Ahmadis's aid. "They wrote, 'at times like this, we regret that Gus Dur passed away,'" Wahid said, "I had to do something, anything." She sprang into action, finding Gusdurians close to the village and getting them connected to village residents. The network not only responded, they formed a protective, human barrier around the village—literally standing up for the ideals of religious pluralism and freedom Wahid's father championed. It was a tipping point for the organization. And for Wahid. "I realized then that this work isn't just nice talk," said Wahid, "this is about defending freedoms, protecting people, especially vulnerable groups."

Since those early days, the network's work has not only continued but expanded. Wahid and GNI have been at the forefront of high-profile religious freedom debates, from the case of a Christian high school student in Padang, West Sumatra obligated to wear a veil, to efforts to counter the growth of religious extremism online. The prominence of the organization, and the conviction of Wahid, have led her to wade back into politics—not with reticence, but with determination. The rise of religious extremism in Indonesia has many members of government worried and, in recent years, they've increasingly called on Wahid to help address the popular shift to the right. Since 2017, Wahid has been working on projects with the government to "not only promote peace," she said, "but to advance religious moderation."

Although she admits that there is still a long road ahead, she is pleased to see how her father's ideas and legacy are not forgotten but perhaps thriving more than ever before. "At the highest levels of government, we have been talking about interfaith cooperation, about respect, about bringing a more just perspective into religious lives," said Wahid, "the real achievement will be to take that talk and establish social, physical, and psychological space where people can come together based on principles of justice and humanity."

While more work lies ahead, others have recognized what GNI has already accomplished. In 2018, GNI received Taiwan's Asia Democracy and Human Rights Award and in 2020, they were named the best social media movement by one of Indonesia's largest news agencies. Manjid Achmad, a professor at Gadjah Mada University in Yogyakarta who researches interfaith dialogue in Indonesia, said GNI and Wahid are prime examples of how to promote religious pluralism and effectively protect minority rights. "The mission of concern is not fighting against or solving these common problems by [themselves] but how to inspire others to solve them," he said. Pointing to how Catholics, Protestants, Hindus, Buddhists, and others are all part of the network, Achmad said, "the more actors that are doing this, the better for Indonesia." Achmad also praised how GNI focuses on real problems rather than intellectual or theological debates. "I think this is why it attracts so many young people in particular," he said, "they are interested in social activism, and they need to feel they have a role in solving real problems. GNI does that for them."

Nonetheless, Wahid and GNI continue to face opposition from traditionalists and hardliners in Indonesian society and government. The battles that her father fought are persistent, said Wahid, and she knows they will not go away without perseverance. "You don't have to like the work, just focus on the result you're trying to get," said Wahid, "politics is like dancing: One step forward, two back. Justice is elusive, but always around the corner."

Asked about her own legacy, and how it sits with that of her father and grandfather before her, Wahid said, "social movement, social transformation, to make sure that the Indonesian people live in a society that brings quality of life in a comprehensive way based on the fundamental values of justice, spirituality, and universal values. Those are the things that would make me happy when I'm retired from the work." On when that retirement might be, Wahid laughed and said, "I don't know, probably never. There's so much more to be done. I may not see results in my lifetime." Perhaps then, she said, someone else will have to inherit her legacy, as she decided to do with her father's more than a decade ago.

"Do Good: What I Learned from a Rat Monk's 'Fortune Cookie Philosophy'"

Bart Weetjens (Buddhist/Belgium)

By Kimberly Winston

Not long after I met Bart Weetjens, my interior skeptic started making noise. Crucial to every good journalist, she stood up on her tiptoes, waving every red flag within her reach. "This guy cannot be for real!"

"He's too selfless! Too caring! Too accomplished!"

"He's just too … perfect!"

On paper, Bart is an exemplar's exemplar. He uses seated meditation to train rising social entrepreneurs across the world in compassionate mindfulness, both for themselves and for their colleagues, in an effort to help them avoid personal and professional burnout. And while he was still a university student, he co-founded a nonprofit called Apopo that successfully trains rats (yes, *rats*) to save lives in Africa and Southeast Asia. The first stage was training rats to locate deadly landmines. With over sixty countries—like Angola, Cambodia, Myanmar, and Mozambique—still contaminated with hidden landmines and other explosive remnants of war that cause tragic accidents and hamper communities from developing their productive land, the team at Apopo trained "HeroRATs" to sniff them out. Meanwhile, slow and inaccurate detection methods make tuberculosis the world's most deadly infectious disease; 10.6 million new people contracted TB in 2022 and a further 3.1 million went undiagnosed, with 1.3 million dying from the disease. Those numbers led Bart and the Apopo team to train the same species of rat to sniff out tuberculosis. They use dogs too—"HeroDOGs" no less—but it was the rats that got my attention.

Shortly before joining the Spiritual Exemplars Project as a journalist fellow, I had seen a television news report about Apopo and the work it was doing on landmines in Cambodia. Since its founding 25 years ago, Apopo has found and cleared over 155,000 explosive devices from 87 million square meters of land. The report was full of glamour shots of Apopo's African Giant Pouched rats, harnessed up and digging around fields for mines. Bart did not appear in the report.

Then, a couple of months later, when the spiritual exemplar fellows met for an orientation, I was less than excited about many of the people the project organizers had listed as possible subjects for long-form profiles. Many had been profiled by journalists before, and others were notable for things they had done in the past, making them a harder sell for editors who want the "new" and "now." But the social scientists leading the project were open to ideas from journalists. And that's when I remembered the vague outlines of the news report about Apopo. I googled "landmines," "rats," + "Cambodia." A couple of hits down, I found Bart, listed as a "changemaker" on the website of Ashoka, a nonprofit that fosters social entrepreneurs.

Now, I have been a religion reporter for thirty years, and I have a theory: Religion is everywhere. If you look hard enough at an issue, you will find a religion, faith, or spiritual angle. So, I was not surprised that when I clicked on Bart Weetjen's profile on the Ashoka website I saw that in addition to being a landmine-sniffing rat whisperer, he is also Buddhist monk. Boom, I had my first spiritual exemplar. How easy was that? But I soon realized I was in for more than the standard profile when I emailed Bart from my home in California. In my message, I laid out the parameters of the project and asked if he'd be up for me trailing him for a few days. Usually, this requires some negotiation—who among us wants a total stranger following them around and reporting what they see to the entire world? But Bart just replied, "Yes, of course. And would you like to stay in my house in Belgium?" That was it. No get-to-know-you phone call, no request for my published work or references to vet me; no big questions about me or the project. Just total acceptance and warm welcome. How nice, I thought.

Then my skeptic piped up—what's the deal with this guy?

Is this guy serious?

In today's strained journalism environment, I don't often get to travel. Or, if I do, it is to spots that are not exactly international tourism magnets (Dresden, New York for a story about a tiny museum) or the scene of great tragedy (Las Vegas after the Mandalay Bay shooting). So, I was very happy to have an assignment that would take me to Europe.

In my excitement, I ignored my niggling worry about why my subject was so accommodating and unquestioning. I booked my flight, packed my bags, and traveled from San Francisco to Antwerp, Belgium, where Bart has lived since childhood. I met his wife, a nurse, and the youngest of his two daughters. I ate with them; I shopped with them; I watched and took notes while Bart donned his monk robes and led a seated meditation via a Zoom call. We looked at family photos, we talked about the variety of religious icons displayed in his home—a statue of the Virgin Mary, a portion of the Qur'an, a figurine of Kuan Yin, the *Boddhisatva* of compassion. He also told me every personal, candid detail about his rather dark childhood, his teenage drug use, and his eventual stint in a mental hospital.

Not satisfied with his rat sniffers, we talked about Bart's current plan to change the world. It was, as I was later to write, "the ultimate in trickle-down economics—Improve [a leader's] inner well-being and their 'well-doing' will improve, too. And, the hope goes, so will the world." Or, as Bart summed it up for me: "Don't do bad. Do good. Do good for everybody. Do good every day."

I went to bed that night in a lovely bedroom on the second floor—the first time I have ever slept in a subject's home—and thought to myself, *that's it?* Do good? What is that for a world-changing project? I could write that on a *fortune cookie*. How am I going to write 2,000 words about, "do good"? As I drifted off to sleep, I thought, again, *is this guy serious?*

To meditate or not to meditate?

On the morning of the second day, I rode shotgun while Bart—a surprisingly aggressive driver for a Buddhist monk—drove us two hours south to La Lobbe, France, where he had a retreat house called La Grande Terre, or "The Big Land." I asked Bart what I should expect, as this would be my first Buddhist retreat. He explained that he was taking his belief in compassion's power to change the world to a group of businessmen and businesswomen in the hope that it would create kinder organizations and happier employees.

"Great," I said as we zipped past the green pyramid memorial marking the site of the Battle of Waterloo. "I'll just sit on the side and watch and ask questions after, maybe at lunch or dinner."

But Bart would have none of this. His one and only condition to me following him like toilet paper stuck to his shoe was that I must participate in the retreat. I must sit in silent meditation five times a day for three days, on the hardwood floor in the midst of his paying students.

Now, here's a pickle: How do you maintain your journalistic objectivity if you become part of the story? Another pickle: throughout my career as a religion reporter, Buddhism has been the one set of beliefs that I just can't quite grasp. I can't parse the teachings, I don't understand the nuances, I get confused about the different strains and teachers. Now I would have to practice it, if only for a weekend? Worse, to me, was the requirement to sit still. I am notorious for multitasking—cooking and talking on the phone, drawing and watching television, knitting in the bathtub. How could I sit still with no thoughts, not activity, for up to half an hour, five times a day? Torture! But here I was, 5,500 miles from home in a car heading to a retreat with total strangers. I could not say no.

The first day was awful. I felt sore and bored and was completely disgusted with myself because I could not silence my thoughts. I resented Bart for making me do this and I was furious with myself for agreeing too easily. In every post-meditation discussion, Bart reiterated his fortune cookie message—do good, don't do bad. My notebook is filled with these quotes. I went to bed on my mattress on the floor under the eaves of La Grande Terre that first night in a major funk of anxiety and self-doubt.

Do something

Then, on the second day, I made a deal with myself. Give over, I told myself as we sat in the chilly October morning on the cold, bare floor. Giving over and being in *one* story will not compromise your career. And what's the alternative? Be miserable for two more days? So, I tried, for the first time in my life, to *really* meditate; to turn off the incessant interior monologue we all have—our "monkey brain," in Buddhist-speak—and just be present.

It was difficult, but over the course of the day I managed a few, luminous moments when I experienced a stillness—a true stillness—and with it, a kind of quiet serenity that I have almost never known. These were just flashes or scraps of peace; but they were revelatory. With this newfound stillness came a new ear for Bart's teaching. What seemed overly simplified before now seemed visionary; what had felt trite suddenly felt profound. Why not *do good*, and do it every day? What's the alternative? Do nothing? I choose to do something.

And, since I met Bart, I try to make that something good. When the Covid-19 pandemic hit four months after I returned from Belgium, my husband and I took great solace in some of the small acts of kindness we were able to do and that we were on the receiving end of. Bart gave me—a skeptical journalist—a way to light a candle in an extremely dark and frightening time. I think after writing about Bart I have become generally less pessimistic and more open; where I once may have rolled my eyes at the Spiritual Exemplars Project's goal to suss out and highlight *do-gooders*, I now see it differently. Profiling people inspired by faith, spirituality, or a powerful sense of morality to make this dingy little world a little brighter is a way to call others to care for our world and our fellow human beings. It's a way of not giving up in the face of all the evils we in journalism write about every single day—natural disasters, famine, war, duplicity, and environmental collapse, to name just the front-page stories I saw this morning.

So now, I embrace what I once thought of as Bart's "fortune cookie philosophy" and make it my mantra for journalism and life—"Don't do bad. Do good. Do good for everybody. Do good every day."

Afterword: How Then Shall We Live?

"I'll be honest, the future freaks me out," said Reginald, a pastor of a 100-member congregation in Leimert Park, a neighborhood in South Los Angeles. As we talked in the back of a sanctuary after an event addressing the advent of mass-market artificial intelligence (AI), the 40-something pastor, dressed in a black bomber jacket, Nike shoes, and a snapback hat, said, "I'm not sure I'm ready for what's next or able to help others make sense of what's coming at them."

Reginald and I had both just listened to experts in information science, ethics, theology, and education share how people of faith—or no faith at all—could navigate rapid technological shifts and their effect on culture, religion, politics, and the economy. They shared deep background on the development, capabilities, and limitations of AI and stories of how various institutions, organizations, and individuals were using the technology to do good … and not so good. Nevertheless, and despite the cogent replies and robust conversations that followed, Reginald still felt a palpable sense of fear about the future. As I spoke with others that evening, I found he was far from alone.

The event was part of a three-part series called, "How Then Shall We Live?" Held in conjunction with the CRCC and First Lutheran Church in Venice, California in summer 2024, the series addressed three prominent issues facing communities in Southern California and beyond: climate change, political polarization, and AI. The series not only helped attendees identify and understand the pain and problems they felt in their contexts and communities, but listen and learn, dialogue and discern how they might continue to live, and lead, when the world feels like it is on fire. While attendees felt the events were insightful, even helpful, there was a sense that the future remained far from certain and their ability to face it fledgling.

In the months to come, many who were part of these events felt that chaos and concern palpably and personally, as their city was left devastated by multiple, real-life fires in Pacific Palisades, Altadena, and elsewhere across the Los Angeles metropole. In the wake of the firestorm, communities of faith across the Southland asked once again how they might encourage and direct care for victims, find solidarity in the face of climate catastrophe, protect the dignity of vulnerable populations in the community, and reimagine and rebuild more just communities in the wake of disaster. They were inspired to do so but also weary and frustrated—unsure whether they had enough in the tank to face all that was burning down around them—literally and figuratively.

In the introduction, I invoked the great American essayist Joan Didion as a pioneer and paragon of a new kind of journalism and fresh form of storytelling. But within Didion's essays and reporting were also a range of revealing reflections on, and critiques of, the search for societal transformation that took the 1960s and 1970s by storm. Profiling the British writer Doris Lessing, a Nobel Prize for Literature winner, Didion chafed at what she called her generation's "cognitive frenzy for answers."[1] Through the lens of Lessing's life, Didion bemoaned the promising starts, disappointing downfalls, and false pledges of a range of proposed solutions to the world's worst problems.

Though Didion was profiling Lessing, writing about how the famed novelist had seen multiple movements come and go—environmentalism and organized politics, Freudian determinism and post-colonial protest, psychedelic drugs and feminism, racial reconciliation and ecumenism—she could have also been painting a disenchanted portrait of her own experience. Emerging out of the firm 1950s and rebellious 1960s, by the time Didion wrote the Lessing profile in 1971, she had shifted into the cynical 1970s—rolling her eyes at the unending quest for answers to the overwhelming complexity and urgency of the problems facing the world. Finding her own fleeting hopes and unending frustrations with naïve fools trying to save the world against all odds in Lessing's biography, Didion wrote how she had "been betrayed by all those answers and more, and yet, increasingly possessed, her only response is to look for another." Not only seeing herself, but all of us, in Lessing, Didion concluded that the British author, "is scarcely alone in this possession ... the impulse to final solutions," which Didion characterized as "the guiding delusion of her time." With a sideward glance and nihilistic whisper, Didion winks to let us know it might also be the guiding delusion of our own as well.

Nonetheless, Didion closes the profile by extolling—if not embracing—Lessing's tenacity in the face of the world's persistent pain and problems, even as she poignantly fingers the futility of our attempts to fix them. Didion wrote how "there is something finally very moving" about those who are driven by a sense of immediate responsibility to commit their lives to healing the world's brokenness and sacrificing themselves for the greater good. If I may be so bold, Didion may have even found such fools to be *exemplary* in their willing ridiculousness to try and address the greatest crises of their age.

Which brings us to the close of a book about how a great many of these individuals are inspired, sustained, and driven by the wisdom of their religious traditions and spiritual practices to give it a go—to try and actually heal the world. And if, like Didion or Reginald, we find ourselves a bit skeptical, a bit worn out, a bit panicky, or a bit fried on the idea of doing any good in a world that feels on fire, how might what we encountered in these stories lead us to live differently and do good in our own corner of the world? What might we take away from the stories in this anthology? What inspiration or resilience might we find in tales of engaged spirituality?

Spirituality's social role

First, this collection makes spirituality's social role palpably evident. The stories in this anthology feature a range of religious actors motivated, sustained, and challenged by precepts, texts, traditions, rituals, communities, and practices to pursue solutions to the most intractable challenges facing humankind. It is not revelatory that religious actors can be, and often are, catalysts for change. What this book shows, however, is how wide-ranging and widespread that impetus is. A Buddhist in Sri Lanka inspired by his "karmic worldview" to provide free medical, educational, vocational, and recreational assistance to thousands; a surgeon from Egypt driven by a Quranic imperative to save lives, who risks his own on the front lines in Syria, Yemen, and Sierra Leone; a campaigner using Ifá-inspired meditations to inspire abolitionist futures in Los Angeles; an activist performing puja to advance the cause of transgender rights in India; and a priest praying for peace amidst the ongoing, dehumanizing plight of migrants crossing the Mediterranean Sea. In each chapter, religion and spirituality in multiple forms prove powerful resources in the lives of people working for social change.

Thus, we might rethink religion and spirituality as critical features in the lives of those who dedicate themselves to serve humanity. Expanding earlier research focused on the United States, this project shows how the kind of engaged spirituality these exemplars embody empowers individuals across the globe "to act upon the palpable tension between the current state of the world and the way they believe it should be."[2] Though religion is imbricated within the social, political, economic, geographic, and cultural constraints of their practitioners' contexts, there seems to be a widespread use of spiritual resources to inspire, inform, and sustain work for the common good. It is not solely a means of ameliorating feelings of chaos or pain, an internal process of self-exploration, or a pathway to transcendence (those things, after all, are not practically measurable). Instead, religion and spirituality are active, ongoing processes "directed outward with the intention of making a discernable difference in the [...] world."[3]

In addition, it seems to take more than just "spirituality." While readers may appreciate how individual exemplars such as Ela Gandhi or Julie Coyne draw from a wide well of spiritual sources and cannot be so easily categorized as followers of one religious tradition or another, the combined stories in this book reflect the power of explicitly religious institutions, traditions, practices, and narratives to help people do good. There is a tendency in contemporary Western discourse for "spirituality" to be painted with a generally positive brush, given greater leeway in its ability to add value to the world. As critiques of religious institutions have increased and people have become warier of claiming institutional religious identifications, saying one is "spiritual, but not religious" has become a way to wipe our hands of the bad things religious people, institutions, and traditions have done. In a word, "spirituality" is good, "religion" less so, or even possibly bad. In this framing, spirituality is not an accurate descriptor of a particular set of phenomena, but a way to distinguish between religion you like and religion you don't like.

Yet, spirituality is not always what it is cracked up to be. As religion scholar Liz Bucar argues, our own smorgasbord spiritualities, picked and chosen from the buffet of options on offer in a plural religious context, can often be predicated on racial, cultural, economic, and other forms of inequality and exotic Othering.[4] Moreover, as the stories in this anthology show, religion in a more traditional sense can be, and often still is, a force for good. In fact, one ironic aspect of this project, and this collection in particular, is that we often referred to those profiled as *spiritual* exemplars. But many could be just as easily referred to as *religious* exemplars. On the one hand, regardless of tradition, the exemplars share a common wellspring of spirituality, which includes several common aspects: personal and collective experiences that connect them to socially constructed yet individually meaningful ideals, entities, or higher powers; acts, rituals, and other practices that put them in communication or communion with divine entities, values, or higher powers; and the experience, practice, and implementation of these perspectives and practices in the course of their daily efforts toward justice. That is to say, they share an array of spiritual experiences, values, and practices across their specific traditions and identifications.

On the other hand, these spiritualities are funneled through the constraints and contexts of their specific *religious* identifications and communities. Certain exemplars aside, most identify with one tradition or another. They are Buddhist or Muslim, Sikh or Catholic, Hindu or Jewish. Though some may appeal to a broader spirituality or hold to more universalistic ideals, some would even find the beliefs, practices, and material cultures of other exemplars offensive, incorrect, or abhorrent. They would disagree with one another. They would not always appeal to their highest shared values. They would not always see eye to eye when it comes to things like the divine or the ultimate fate of everyone who ever lived. And that is okay. It does not preclude their individual ability to contribute to the common good nor necessarily prevent them from working together toward it.

Expressed another way, despite religion's capability to create, foster, and deepen division, it is not necessarily so. Many of the exemplars featured here claim one religion or another and yet do good for others beyond their specific communities. They find in their lives, dedicated as they are to social change and doing good, that religion is a ballast for balancing the mismatch between the scale of the threats we face and our very real limits as human beings. To inspire, establish, extend, and sustain their work, they turn to religion as a means of looking beyond the world as it is. Concepts like surrender and long-suffering, postures of humility and courage, practices like prayer and meditation, come up again and again in their stories. It is my inclination that this is not by accident.

That is why, in an age of right-wing populism and post-truth politics; rising political and social polarization; Othering and xenophobia; as well as anti-Muslim, anti-Semitic, and other forms of anti-religious hate crime and violence, this book stakes the claim that telling exemplary stories is necessary. Necessary not only because they encompass and embody a different kind of narrative about religion and spirituality than often presented, but because telling these stories, in this way, gets the complexity and details of contemporary religion and spirituality right. It tells their stories in all their multidimensional complexity, encompassing religion as daily practice and as social engagement. It reflects texts and traditions exemplars interpret and draw from. It details the political dimensions of their work as well as the conflicts they confront both within their communities and without.

Not letting religion off the hook

At the same time, I am not suggesting we let religious individuals, institutions, or communities off the hook. Although religion can be a source of inspiration and positive change, it can also be used to advocate for harmful practices, support prejudiced systems, or excuse injustice. This is often the case when religious teachings are used to justify hateful behaviors or attitudes toward certain groups or when religious texts are used to warrant discrimination and marginalize individuals or whole communities.[5]

I am not, by nature, an optimist. I am a critic. A realist. Sardonic and on my worst days, a cynic. I do not hold too much hope for humanity. Based on my observations as a journalist, scholar, and everyday human, we too often fail each other. Our vaunted heroes hide stories we would rather not know, but which always seem to come out. Our histories are marked with the legacies and lingering impacts of systemic injustice, corrupt power, and divisive violence. Religious actors, institutions, and communities have often been at the forefront of these "bad news" stories and histories. Over the last fifteen years of covering religion across the Americas, Europe, the Middle East, Oceania, and Africa, I have reported on a range of the worst. Just this week, I wrote an article about the imperial nature of Western evangelical mission work, even as those same evangelicals delivered emergency aid to the hungry, the impoverished, and the displaced. I then wrote another piece about interreligious violence in West Africa. Right before working on this afterword, I was hearing from Christians in Germany who are anti-migrant, anti-LGBTQ+, and anti-Muslim. Finally, a year before this book was released, one of the exemplars profiled as part of the project—Imam Muhsin Hendricks, the world's first, openly gay imam—was murdered in South Africa. All of this is a painful reminder of religion and spirituality's capacity to undergird, feed, and protract hate, violence, and Othering.

As readers would have also noted, spiritual exemplars are not always *exemplary*. They do not always do good. They are finite and fragile. They sometimes contribute to the very problem they attempt to address. They have ailments (physical, psychological) and limitations (poverty, geography, social marginalization, etc.) and shadow sides (egos and more). They struggle with the weight of their humanity and, sometimes, they falter and fail. In the words of my own tradition, each of these exemplars is simultaneously righteous and wicked, holy and profane, *saint* and *sinner* (*simul iustus et peccator*). In other words, this anthology is not made up of case studies in perfection. Nor is it an anthology meant to make the argument that religion is inherently good for the world. Religious actors and spiritual leaders need to be held to account. They need to be investigated. They need to be interrogated and critiqued. I will continue doing that work of critique and interrogation and I hope other scholars, journalists, activists, and readers will as well.

However, if the project shows us one thing, it is that there is still value in emphasizing the exemplary; sitting with good stories; knowing narratives of hope; dwelling with dispatches from better worlds and different futures. You may, like me, be a skeptic: Critical of religious institutions, actors and communities. But after encountering their stories, I hope you see how religion and various forms of spirituality can be, and often are, a force for good. As I wrote in the introduction, this book tried to tell a more complicated story—of imperfect human beings doing good things because of, and bolstered by, their faith. The fact they are imperfect should not discourage us. Far from it. It should inspire us. Because if these exemplars are like you and me, it means that *ordinary* people can pursue *extraordinary* goals. They can weave a storyline of grace, goodness, and generosity in the world, despite the limitations around or within them. They can leave a legacy of good work in their wake when they are gone. Perhaps, they can even make the world a better place—if not on the macro scale, at the very least in the places where they live or among the communities where they are called.

The best argument is a good story

Thus, these stories help *orient us to the good*, as philosopher Charles Taylor put it. As Taylor wrote, "this sense of good has to be woven into my understanding of my life as a story," because, "we grasp our lives in a narrative."[6] These stories show how a little help can transform lives and, in turn, inspire readers to write their own accounts of exemplary humanitarianism in thought, word, and deed, according to their own religious convictions and spiritual practices, and in their own contexts.

Through these stories, and in the way they are told, the storytellers help us see that the key to change lies in unleashing potential. They make clear how so many people have helped to do just that, and how we can each do our part. Telling that global story is not only the right thing to do; or a clever way to make an argument; it might also be a sound strategy for bringing a salve of healing to the worst in our world. Because if the best antidote to counteract the bad is to do something good; perhaps in this case, it begins with encountering, or discovering, something good.

By telling spiritual exemplars' stories—and those of the journalists who profiled them—this book is meant to do more than make an academic intervention; it is to ignite readers' minds around the idea of religiously inspired humanitarianism and, in turn, promote the common good. For people of all faiths (or no faith), it offers a thoughtful perspective on questions around how to create a more open, just, and compassionate world; one that promotes human flourishing in all its forms. It is also an encouragement for activists and those desiring to do good who may be struggling with meaning and purpose by providing them with a mosaic of images and a diverse range of perspectives on how to live the "good life" through values-driven, spiritually inspired humanitarian work. Telling their stories with complicated, nuanced, and touching texture is not to abandon the critical nature of journalism or scholarship. Instead, I believe, this anthology testifies to quality work in both fields, following the facts and reflecting the world as it is—in all its complexity—with balance, accuracy, and insight.

In conclusion, I suggest *good* religion stories help us look beyond—beyond the suffering and limitations of human life on Earth, beyond the horizon of what we know or can apperceive, beyond the limited view often offered about religion in the news media. As suggested in the introduction, we not only need *better* stories told about religious actors, institutions, and communities, but stories about religion—or religious actors—*doing* good. Good religion stories help us imagine a new repertoire of the possible, for ourselves and the world around us. "Every crisis," wrote essayist and cultural historian Rebecca Solnit, "is in part a storytelling crisis."[7] Writing about the need for new stories on nature and the environment in order to pursue new solutions to address the common challenges that a changing climate confronts us with, Solnit wrote:

> We are hemmed in by stories that prevent us from seeing, or believing in, or acting on the possibilities for change. Some are habits of mind; some are industry propaganda. Sometimes, the situation has changed but the stories haven't, and people follow the old versions, like outdated maps, into dead ends.

Her words resonate well beyond the current climate crisis. They could be easily applied to any of the crises and challenges addressed by exemplars in this anthology: expanding access to health care and education, cultural empowerment, gender equity, migrant and refugee rights, economic justice, land rights, prison reform, protection against sexual violence, racial reconciliation and reparations, persistent socio-economic disparities, interreligious conflict, and other forms of internecine violence. The answers we produce to our shared challenges do not come from nowhere. They come from the stories we tell, about ourselves and the world around us. The stories we know, or think we know, about each determine the ways we approach them and contribute to their persistent ubiquity and tenacity, despite our hopes, desires, and dreams to pursue a more just, true, and verdant world. If we are to find better futures, I echo Solnit in believing we need better stories to pursue them.

As the CRCC team, its researchers and journalists, worked through this project, we often wondered what it would mean to put all these stories out into the world. We contemplated what difference such in-depth, nuanced, and solutions-focused journalism would make when capital "J" journalism too often offers something different. The verdict is still out. The end of this project's story still not written. We are unsure what difference the project, and the stories it allowed us to tell about religious actors of various kinds doing good in contexts around the globe, will or will not make.

That is where you, the reader, come in. This anthology, and the stories contained therein—these narratives of resilience, inspiration, and pursuing the common good—are no longer our own. They no longer belong to the project (if they ever did). They were out there in the world, making a difference at local and regional scales. All we have done is put them into conversation, so that you might join the dialogue. It is up to you now, to tell us how these stories will end.

In fact, perhaps the next chapter begins with you knowing your own story. In the research team's running notes from the beginning of the project, we often reflected on how exemplars' understanding of their own path, their journey to where they were when the journalists met them, and their ability to tell that story served an essential role in their ability to engage and lead. As we came to the end of the project, we appreciated how a person's leadership, their sustenance, and their ability to influence others often comes from their understanding of and ability to communicate their stories. Knowing their life's narrative allowed them to communicate the values that motivated the choices they made and invite others to do the same. This is more than talking "about" values or practices or experiences but telling a story that embodies them. There is other research that echoes our conclusions in this regard.[8] That is, a person's ability to lead and influence others often comes from their understanding of, and ability to communicate, their own stories. That means that in order to motivate others to join us in making change, we need to identify and articulate our shared values in a way that spurs us to take action together. The most effective way to do that, such research suggests, is by telling better stories.

So, what story do you have to tell? How might you address, and appreciate, your own path? What kind of community were you born into? What kind of relationships made you who you are? Were you baptized or otherwise initiated into a faith? Or were you raised with no faith at all? What new perspectives are you encountering right now? What questions do you still have? What hate do you harbor? What prejudice has been passed on to you? What is your perspective on this whole religion and spirituality thing? What problems do you feel compelled to address? What issues keep you up at night? Who is suffering right now in your neighborhood? What things weigh heavy on your heart? What might you do to address them? And how might your religion or spirituality act as a resource to help you do so? Learning your own story, and then cultivating the courage to tell it, demands the bravery of introspection, and even more strength to share what you discover. I encourage you to try anyways. It will not always be perfect. You will make of a mess of it sometimes. You will falter, fumble, and fail along the way. Most things will be okay eventually, but not everything will be. Sometimes you will put up a good fight and lose. Sometimes you will hold on really hard for a long time and realize in the end there is no choice but to let go. But the world we live in invites, even demands, that you (and I) try. Together, when faced with the question of how we might live in a world on fire, let us begin by listening for the good. Then, let us lean into the good and, when given the opportunity, look for opportunities to write and tell and embody different kinds of stories.

NOTES

Introduction

1 Joan Didion, *The White Album* (New York: Simon & Schuster, 1979), 1.

2 Peter Berger, *Sacred Canopy: Elements of a Sociological Theory of Religion* (New York: Anchor Books, 1967).

3 Hannah Arendt, Zwischen Vergangenheit und Zukunft: Übungen im politischen Denken, 1 (München: Piper Verlag, 2012).

4 Katherine McKittrick, *Dear Science and Other Stories* (Durham, NC: Duke University Press, 2021), 6–7.

5 This project emerged out of earlier research conducted at the CRCC. See Gregory C. Stanczak, *Engaged Spirituality: Social Change and American Religion* (Brunswick, NJ: Rutgers University Press, 2006).

6 Kendall Cotton Bronk, "The Exemplar Methodology: An Approach to Studying the Leading Edge of Development," *Psychology of Well-Being* 2, no. 5 (2012). Available online at: https://doi.org/10.1186/2211-1522-2-5; Mona M. Abo-Zena and Pamela Ebstyne King, "Finding the Extraordinary in the Ordinary: Case Studies of Spiritual Exemplars," *Journal of Humanistic Psychology* (June 2021); Pamela Ebstyne King, Mona M. Abo-Zena, and Jonathan D. Weber, "Varieties of Social Experience: The Religious Cultural Context of Diverse Spiritual Exemplars," *British Journal of Developmental Psychology* 35, no. 1 (2017): 127–41; Pamela Ebstyne King, Casey E. Clardy, and Jenel Sánchez Ramos, "Adolescent Spiritual Exemplars: Exploring Spirituality in the Lives of Diverse Youth," *Journal of Adolescent Research* 29, no. 2 (2014): 186–212; Kendall Cotton Bronk, Pamela Ebstyne King, and M. Kyle Matsuba, eds., "Exemplar Methods and Research: Quantitative and Qualitative Strategies for Investigation [Special issue]," *New Directions for Child and Adolescent Development* 142 (2013): 1–12.

7 Bronk, "The Exemplar Methodology."

8 Several of the exemplars have since passed but were interviewed and profiled before their deaths.

9 M. Kyle Matsuba and Lawrence J. Walker, "Young Adult Moral Exemplars: The Making of Self through Stories," *Journal of Research on Adolescence* 15, no. 3 (2005): 275–97. See also Bronk, "The Exemplar Methodology."

10 Hebah Farrag, "Who Are Spiritual Exemplars? A Cross-Sectional Exploration of 100 Spiritually Engaged Humanitarians," SSSR+RRA Annual Conference, Baltimore, MD, November 12, 2022.

11 The literature on this theme is broad, but a helpful overview is provided by Laurie Patton, "Defining Hinduism," in *Oxford Bibliographies Online*. Available online at: https://www.oxfordbibliographies.com/view/document/obo 9780195399318/obo-9780195399318-0015.xml (accessed February 7, 2025).

12 Victoria S. Harrison and Rhett Gayle, "Self-transformation and Spiritual Exemplars," *European Journal for Philosophy of Religion* 12, no. 4 (2020): 9–26.

13 Ninian Smart, *Worldviews: Crosscultural Explorations of Human Beliefs* (Upper Saddle River, NJ: Prentice Hall, 1995).

14 William Damon and Anne Colby, "Why a True Account of Human Development Requires Exemplar Research," *New Directions in Child Adolescent Development* 142 (2013): 13–25.

15 Don Miller, "'Spiritual Exemplars' Change the Media Narrative about Religion," Religion News Service, March 10, 2023. Available online at: https://religionnews.com/2023/03/10/spiritual-exemplars-change-the-media-narrative-about-religion/ (accessed August 13, 2024).

16 Miller, ibid.

17 Anne Marie O'Connor, "Emergence of a Hybrid Culture," the *Los Angeles Times*, April 29, 1997. Available online at: https://www.latimes.com/archives/la-xpm-1997-04-29-mn-53610-story.html (accessed August 13, 2024).

18 Rosecrans Baldwin, *Everything Now: Lessons from the City-State of Los Angeles* (New York: MCD, 2021).

19 Stephen Prothero, *Religious Illiteracy: What Every American Needs to Know—and Doesn't* (San Francisco, CA: HarperOne, 2007).

20 Costica Bradatan and Ed Simon, eds., *The God Beat: What Journalism Says about Faith and Why It Matters* (Abergavenny, UK: Broadleaf Books, 2021).

21 Kenneth L. Woodward, *Getting Religion: Faith, Culture, and Politics from the Age of Eisenhower to the Era of Obama* (New York: Convergent Books, 2016), 4.

22 Woodward, *Getting Religion*, 400.

23 For more on this theme, see Ken Chitwood, "Ethnographic Journalism and the Public Understanding of Religion," *Bulletin for the Study of Religion* 52, no. 3 (2024): 88–101.

24 Randolph Filmore, "Anthro-Journalism," Center for Anthropology and Science Communications, 1995.

25 Anne Kirstine Hermann, "Ethnographic Journalism," *Journalism—Theory Practice and Criticism* 17, no. 2 (2016): 260–78.

26 Mario Luis Small and Jessica McCrory Calarco, *Qualitative Literacy: A Guide to Evaluating Ethnographic and Interview Research* (Berkeley, CA: University of California Press, 2022).

27 Howard S. Becker, *Telling about Society* (Chicago, IL: University of Chicago Press, 2007).

28 Walt Harrington, "What Journalism Can Offer Ethnography," *Qualitative Inquiry* 9, no. 1 (2003): 90–104.

Chapter 1

1 Patrisse Cullors, born in June 1983, is an artist, organizer, best-selling author, educator, and self-proclaimed "abolitionist" living and working in Los Angeles. Cullors founded Dignity and Power Now in 2011 and has since founded at least three other nonprofit organizations in Los Angeles: Reform LA Jails, JusticeLA, and the Crenshaw Dairy Mart. Patrisse is a Fulbright Scholarship recipient, was named 2007 Mario Savio Activist of the Year and received the Sidney Goldfarb award. She earned a bachelor's degree in religion and philosophy from University of California, Los Angeles and a Master of Fine Arts from the University of Southern California. Patrisse was dubbed by the *Los Angeles Times* as one of the nation's top civil rights leaders and the NAACP as a History Maker. She is best known as a co-founder of Black Lives Matter, which grew from a hashtag coined in 2013 into a global movement. She served as the executive director of Black Lives Matter Global Network Foundation until 2021. The Black Lives Matter movement was a nominee for the 2021 Nobel Peace Prize before she stepped down. As an artist, Patrisse's work has been featured at the Hammer Museum, the Broad, Frieze among other galleries. In January 2018 Patrisse Cullors published her memoir, *When They Call You a Terrorist: A Black Lives Matter Memoir*. Her memoir became an instant *New York Times* Bestseller.

2 Hebah Farrag and Ann Gleig, "Far from Being Anti-Religious, Faith and Spirituality Run Deep in Black Lives Matter," The Conversation, September 14, 2020. Available online at: https://theconversation.com/far-from-being-anti-religious-faith-and-spirituality-run-deep-in-black-lives-matter-145610 (accessed March 13, 2025).

3 Daniel Taylor, "Morning Start: #BlackLivesMatter Started with a Love Letter," *Vernon Morning Star*, June 2, 2020.

4 One example of the discussions of that era is evident in a series produced by The Immanent Frame in September 2016 entitled "Religion, Secularism and Black Lives Matter," in which eleven academics produced academic think pieces dissecting the secularism of the BLM movement. Available online at: https://tif.ssrc.org/2016/09/22/religion-secularism-and-black-lives-matter/. Another poignant example is Kenneth D. Johnson's "#BlackLivesMatter as a Secular Black Political Theology: Ethical and Practical Implications of the First New Black Social Movement of the 21st Century," TELOSScope, February 8, 2016. Available online at: https://www.telospress.com/blacklivesmatter-as-a-secular-black-political-theology-ethical-and-practical-implications-of-the-first-new-black-social-movement-of-the-21st-century/ (accessed March 13, 2025).

5 According to the U.S. NIH National Center for Complementary and Integrative Health, Reiki is a complementary health approach in which practitioners use light touch with the goal of directing energy to facilitate the person's own healing response. Reiki is based on Eastern beliefs connected to energy and natural healing abilities within the human body.

6 I first published on this topic on June 24, 2015, for Religion Dispatches in the article, "The Role of Spirit in the #BlackLivesMatter Movement: A Conversation with Activist and Artist Patrisse Cullors." The article was

reprinted under the title "The Spirituality of Resilience," by Krista Tippett's On Being on February 25, 2016. These two works "broke the story" on the religious elements and faith-based quality of the Black Lives Matter movements. Hebah Farrag, "The Role of Spirit in the #BlackLivesMatter Movement: A Conversation with Activist and Artist Patrisse Cullors," Religion Dispatches, June 24, 2015. Available online at: https://religiondispatches.org/the-role-of-spirit-in-the-blacklivesmatter-movement-a-conversation-with-activist-and-artist-patrisse-cullors/ (accessed August 27, 2023).

7 Available online at: https://dignityandpowernow.org/about-us

8 Stacy Chen, "What Is Healing Justice?" Good Morning America, July 24, 2020. Available online at: https://www.goodmorningamerica.com/culture/video/healing-justice-71932989

9 Patrisse Cullors, "Abolition And Reparations: Histories of Resistance, Transformative Justice, And Accountability," *Harvard Law Review* 132, no. 6 (April 2019).

10 Carol Hanisch, "The Personal is Political," February 1969. Available online at: carolhanisch.org (accessed August 27, 2023).

11 Scholars like Chidi Anslem Odinkalu, Makau Matua, and Bahey El Din Hassan have written extensively about the "colonial residue" of IHRL, which sought to "civilize the non-Western world" while turning a blind eye to colonial powers' crimes. Odinakalu points out that it is impossible to believe that many who drafted the UDHR could have believed they were drafting a rule applicable to all of humanity, considering that they, as colonial powers, were opposed to the idea that colonized peoples were capable of exercising their will, especially in choosing their own government. Experts like Hassan, Stork, and Paul have discussed a favoritism the United States has with human rights records, preferring to ignore the records of countries it most enjoys intimate relations with (e.g., Saudi Arabia and Israel). Especially in the "War on Terror" era, the relationship between the United States and human rights has been strained by incidences like Abu Ghareb and places like Guantanamo Bay. Chidi Anslem Odinkalu, "Globalizing Rights, Africanizing Wrongs: Africa and International Law in a Changing World," Edinburgh: Remaking Law in Africa: Transnationalism, Persons and Rights Conference, May 2003; Makau, Mutua, "Savages, Victims, Saviors: The Metaphor of Human Rights," *Harvard International Law Journal* 42 (2001): 201–45; Bahey El Din, Hassan, "Regional Protection of Human Rights in the Arab States in *Statu Nascendi*," in *Human Rights: International Protection, Monitoring and Enforcement*, ed. Janusz Symonides (London: Routledge, 2003); James Paul and Joe Stork, "The Middle East and Human Rights," *Middle East Report* 149 (November/December 1987).

12 Patrisse Cullors, *When They Call You a Terrorist: A Black Lives Matter Memoir* (New York: St. Martin Griffin, 2018), 160.

13 Mapping Police Violence database. Available online at: https://mappingpoliceviolence.org/ (accessed August 28, 2023).

14 Los Angeles Police Department O.I.S. Shootings and Critical Incidents online database, 2023. Available online at: https://www.lapdonline.org/office-of-the-

chief-of-police/professional-standards-bureau/critical-incident-videos/2023-o-i-s-shootings-and-critical-incidents/ (accessed August 28, 2023).

15 Patrisse Cullors, *Abolitionist Handbook* (New York: St. Martin's Press, 2022), 8.

16 Ibid.

17 Maxine Wally, "Patrisse Cullor's Abolitionist's Handbook Puts Change in its Readers' Hands," *W Magazine*, January 20, 2022. Available online at: https://www.wmagazine.com/culture/patrisse-cullors-book-abolitionists-handbook-interview (accessed March 13, 2025).

18 See: Hannah Strohmeier and Willem F. Scholte, "Trauma-related Mental Health Problems among National Humanitarian Staff: A Systematic Review of the Literature," *European Journal of Psychotraumatology* 6, no. 1 (2015): 28541; Robert I.S. Macpherson and Frederick M. Burkle Jr., "Humanitarian Aid Workers: The Forgotten First Responders," *Prehospital and Disaster Medicine* 36, no. 1 (2021): 111–14; Gemma Houdley, *The Vulnerable Humanitarian: Ending Burnout Culture in the Aid Sector* (London: Routledge, 2021).

19 Libor Jany, "LAPD Officers Involved in Keenan Anderson Death Found Out of Policy," *Los Angeles Times*, October 25, 2023. Available online at: https://www.latimes.com/california/story/2023-10-25/lapd-officers-involved-in-keenan-anderson-death-found-out-of-policy (accessed March 13, 2025).

20 Jonathan Griffin, "For Two Los Angeles Artists, the Spiritual is Political," *New York Times*, March 23, 2023. Available online at: https://www.nytimes.com/2023/03/23/arts/design/patrisse-cullors-noe-olivas-artists.html (accessed March 13, 2025).

21 United Nations High Commissioner for Refugees (UNHCR), "Refugee Statistics." Available online at: https://www.unhcr.org/refugee-statistics/ (accessed September 13, 2023).

22 *The Migrant Priest*, directed/produced by Linda Freund (2022; Voice of America (VOA News)), 52 Documentary. Available online at: https://www.youtube.com/@VOANews. Produced as a journalism fellow for the University of Southern California Religion and Civic Culture's "Spiritual Exemplars: A Global Project on Engaged Spirituality."

23 Italian and Maltese Coast Guard email records (2011–23).

24 Stephanie Saldaña, *What We Remember Will be Saved: A Story of Refugees and the Things They Carry* (Minneapolis, MN: Broadleaf Books, 2023).

25 "This Syrian Catholic priest was kidnapped and tortured by ISIS. He still has hope in humanity," *America Magazine*, February 19, 2020. Available online at: https://www.americamagazine.org/faith/2020/02/19/syria-catholic-priest-kidnapped-tortured-hope-humanity (accessed September 13, 2023).

26 Kristi M. Wilson and Tomás F. Crowder-Taraborrelli, eds., "GIs Documenting Genocide," *Film and Genocide* (Madison, WI: University of Wisconsin Press, 2012), 170–86.

27 Katy Fallon and Ravishaan Rahel Muthiah, quoted in "This is Europe," a panel hosted by ON FRONT LINE, a UK-based journalist platform, July 25, 2023. Available online at: https://www.youtube.com/watch?v=wwAKL3Dgs7I (accessed September 13, 2023).

28 Images that show a different facet of the refugee crisis can wield an immediate impact on policymaking. Take, for instance, the viral 2015 photograph of two year old Alan Kurdi, a Syrian who drowned while trying to cross the Mediterranean and was found dead on the shoreline. This image sparked global policy discussions and a notable upsurge in contributions to organizations aiding migrants and refugees.

29 Maria Heim, *Theories of the Gift in South Asia: Hindu, Buddhist, and Jain Reflections on Dana* (New York: Routledge, 2004), 37.

Chapter 2

1 Phil Alexander, *Sounding Jewish in Berlin: Klezmer Music and Contemporary City* (New York: Oxford University Press, 2021), 5.

2 Alexander, *Sounding Jewish in Berlin.*

3 Ibid.

4 Ibid., 12.

5 Alexandria Neason, "How Hawaiian Came Back from the Dead," *Slate*, June 8, 2016.

6 In Georgia, several generations often live under the same roof.

7 The interview was conducted in Georgian. Most Kists are bilingual and speak Kist—a Chechen dialect—and Georgian.

8 Even though there are currently no risks associated with traveling to the Pankisi, foreign governments are reluctant to suppress this notice.

9 During the Second Chechen War, Moscow accused Tbilisi of turning a blind eye to the presence of Islamic fighters in the valley and increased pressure on its southern neighbor. After 9/11, the global war on terror pushed the Pankisi Valley even further into the spotlight. Western media reframed the Chechens' struggle for independence from Russia as terrorism, which had dire local repercussions for the Kists.

10 An interesting read on this issue: Maia Barkaia and Barbare Janelidze, *Under the Security Gaze: History, Religion and Politics in the Pankisi Gorge* (Tbilisi: EMC, 2018).

11 Rayhan Demytrie, "Jihadist Shadow Hangs over Georgia's Pankisi Gorge," BBC News, April 21, 2016.

12 Reuters, "Moscow Accuses Georgia of Aiding al Qaeda in Russia," October 13, 2009.

13 Traditionally in the Caucasus, a host would not accept money from a guest.

14 Vincenc Kopeček, "Welcome to My Neighbour's Funeral: Pankisi Kists and International Tourism," in *The Scale of Globalization: Think Globally, Act Locally, Change Individually in the 21st Century*, ed. Přemysl Mácha and Tomáš Drobík (Ostrava, Czechia: University of Ostrava (2011)), 157–65.

15 He remained in power until 2013 although the last year of his rule was marked by a cohabitation with the Georgian Dream party which won the

2012 parliamentary election and is still in power now. The Georgian Dream government has a more ambiguous stance on Georgia's integration with the West and is often accused of holding a hidden pro-Russian agenda.

Chapter 3

1 Don Miller, "Tom Catena: Choosing Joy over Happiness," Religion Unplugged, June 14, 2022. Available online at: https://religionunplugged.com/news/2022/6/10/choosing-joy-over-happiness-why-an-american-catholic-doctor-stayed-put-in-sudans-civil-warnbsp (accessed August 20, 2024).

2 World Health Organization, "World Health Statistics: Monitoring Health for SDGs, Sustainable Development Goals," (2024), 3.

3 Ken Chitwood, "Ethnographic Journalism and the Public Understanding of Religion," *Bulletin for the Study of Religion 52*, no. 3 (2024): 88–101. See also Anne Kirstine Hermann, "An Ethnographic Journalism," *Journalism—Theory Practice and Criticism* 17, no. 2 (2016): 260–78.

4 Procés Constituent, "Manifesto." Available online at: https://www.procesconstituent.cat/qui-som/manifest/ (accessed September 15, 2023).

5 "Procés Constituent Propone Construir la República Catalana," *La Vanguardia*, October 13, 2013. Available online at: https://www.lavanguardia.com/politica/20131013/54391867607/proces-constituent-construir-republica-catalana.html (accessed September 15, 2023).

6 Dean Dettloff, "The Radical Benedictine Sister who Fought for Catalan Independence," *America Magazine*, July 11, 2019. Available online at: https://www.americamagazine.org/politics-society/2019/07/11/radical-benedictine-sister-who-fought-catalan-independence (accessed October 3, 2023).

7 In this manifesto, Forcades contends that pharmaceutical companies pose a threat to public health, citing drug patent issues between pharmaceutical companies and developing countries: Teresa Forcades i Vila, MD, OSB, *Els Crims de les Grans Companyies Farmacèutiques (The Crimes of Big Pharmaceutical Companies)*, *Cristianisme i Justícia*, 2006. Available online at: https://www.cristianismeijusticia.net/sites/default/files/pdf/en124.pdf (accessed March 13, 2025).

8 "Colegio de Médicos inhabilita a la monja Teresa Forcades por defender clorito," *La Vanguardia*, April 13, 2023. Available online at: https://www.lavanguardia.com/vida/20230413/8893491/colegio-medicos-inhabilita-18-meses-teresa-forcades-defender-clorito.html (accessed October 3, 2023).

9 Diane Winston, *Righting the American Dream: How the Media Mainstreamed Reagan's Evangelical Vision* (Chicago: The University of Chicago Press, 2023), 29.

10 This range of acceptable ideas is commonly called the Overton Window, as coined by Joseph P. Overton, "The Overton Window," Mackinac Center for Public Policy. Available online at: https://www.mackinac.org/OvertonWindow (accessed March 13, 2025).

11 Joanna Moorhead, "Alternative Catholic Synod to Push Case for Ordination of Women Priests," *The Guardian*, September 24, 2023. Available online at: https://www.theguardian.com/world/2023/sep/24/alternative-catholic synod to push-case-for-ordination-of-women-priests (accessed October 3, 2023).

12 Teresa Forcades i Vila, *La Teologia Feminista en la Història (Feminist Theology in History), Fragmenta Editorial*, 2007.

13 I discuss Forcades's feminist liberation theology in this feature article: Linda Freund, "Meet a Catholic Nun Who Smashes the 'Pro-life' Patriarchy." *Smashboard*, September 27, 2022. Available online at: https://smashboard.org/meet-a-catholic-nun-who-smashes-the-pro-life-patriarchy/ (accessed October 3, 2023).

14 Singulars, "Teresa Forcades," June, 16, 2009. Available online at: https://www.ccma.cat/tv3/alacarta/singulars/teresa-forcades/video/1313539/ (accessed March 13, 2025).

15 Reuters, "Pope Says Abortion Is Murder; US Bishops Should Not Be Political." Available online at: https://www.reuters.com/world/europe/pope-says-abortion-is-murder-us-bishops-should-not-be-political-2021-09-15/#:~:text=%22Abortion%20is%20murder (accessed March 13, 2025).

16 I discuss this radical proposal in the following editorial: Linda Freund, "What I Learned after Meeting a Catholic Nun Who Supports Abortion Rights," *Independent*, August 2, 2022. Available online at: https://www.independent.co.uk/voices/abortion-rights-catholic-teachings-vatican-church-b2136442.html (accessed October 3, 2023).

17 The Canadian Press, "Baxter Admits Flu Product Contained Live Bird Flu Virus," *The Canadian Press*, February 27, 2009. Available online at: https://www.ctvnews.ca/baxter-admits-flu-product-contained-live-bird-flu-virus-1.374503 (accessed October 3, 2023).

18 Júlia Partal, "Teresa Forcades: 'No pot ser que domini el negoci farmacèutic enmig d'una pandèmia'," *VilaWeb*, April 30, 2021. Available online at: https://www.vilaweb.cat/noticies/entrevista-teresa-forcades-covid-vacunes/ (accessed October 3, 2023).

19 Nicholas Casey, "A Nun and a Doctor, She's One of Europe's Longstanding Vaccine Skeptics," *The New York Times*, April 23, 2021. Available online at: https://www.nytimes.com/2021/04/23/world/europe/spain-covid-vaccine-nun.html (accessed October 3, 2023).

20 Immanuel Kant, "An Answer to the Question: What Is Enlightenment?" *The New York Public Library*. Available online at: https://www.nypl.org/sites/default/files/kant_whatisenlightenment.pdf (accessed October 3, 2023).

21 "Japan's Child Population Falls Further to 14.4 Million," Nippon.com. Available online at: https://www.nippon.com/en/japan-data/h01670 (accessed May 18, 2023).

22 Julian Ryall, "Can Anything Be Done to Stop the Population Decline?" *Deutsche Welle*. Available online at: https://www.dw.com/en/japan-can-anything-be-done-to-stop-population-decline/a-6643282 (accessed March 8, 2023).

23 "Masue Katayama," Ashoka, accessed September 18, 2023. Available online at: https://www.ashoka.org/en-us/fellow/masue-katayama (accessed March 13, 2025).

24 "Social Welfare Corporation Shinko Fukushikai," Social Welfare Corporation Shinko Fukushikai, accessed September 18, 2023. Available online at: https://www.shinkoufukushikai.com/skfch_international/languages/english/index.html (accessed March 13, 2025).

25 "Funerals in Japan," Nippon.com. Available online at: https://www.nippon.com/en/features/jg00039/ (last modified July 5, 2015).

26 "Statistics of the Catholic Church in Japan," Secretariat, Catholic Bishops' Conference of Japan Social Communications Division, August 2022, 1. Available online at: https://www.cbcj.catholic.jp/wp-content/uploads/2022/08/statistics2021.pdf (accessed March 13, 2025).

27 "Masue Katayama," Ashoka. Available online at: https://www.ashoka.org/en-us/fellow/masue-katayama (accessed September 18, 2023).

28 Yomiuri Shimbun, "Foreign Care Workers in Japan Increased Fivefold Amid Pandemic," *The Japan News*, June 21, 2023. Available online at: https://japannews.yomiuri.co.jp/society/general-news/20230621-117300/ (accessed September 18, 2023).

29 Shintoism (or Shinto) is an ancient religion of Japan whose followers believe that spiritual powers exist in the natural world.

Chapter 4

1 UNICEF, "Education: Every Child Has the Right to Learn." Available online at: https://www.unicef.org/education (accessed February 13, 2025).

2 Max Roser, "Talent is Everywhere, Opportunity is Not. We Are All Losing Out Because of This," 2019. Available online at: https://ourworldindata.org/talent-is-everywhere-opportunity-is-not (accessed February 13, 2025).

3 Ken Wytsma, *Pursuing Justice: The Call to Live and Die for Bigger* (Nashville, TN: Thomas Nelson Publishers, 2014).

Chapter 5

1 Landon Schnabel, Eman Abdelhadi, Katherine Ally Zaslavsky, Jacqueline S. Ho, and Angie Torres-Beltran, "Gender, Sexuality, and Religion: A Critical Integrative Review and Agenda for Future Research," *Journal for the Scientific Study of Religion* 61, no. 2 (2022): 271–92.

2 Susy Schultz, "Let's Change This Journalism Motto," Medium, February 13, 2018. Available online at: https://medium.com/@Susys/lets-change-this-journalism-motto-because-if-your-mother-says-she-loves-you-check-it-out-a953b9a8d96c (accessed March 13, 2025).

3 Debra M. Haak, "What Are We Talking about when We Talk about Prostitution and Sex Work?" The Conversation, January 14, 2018. Available

online at: https://theconversation.com/who-are-we-talking-about-when-we-talk-about-prostitution-and-sex-work-88123 (accessed March 13, 2025).

4 Sara Ann Friedman, "And Boys Too: ECPAT-USA Discussion Paper about the Lack of Recognition of the Commercial Sexual Exploitation of Boys and Young Men in the United States," ECPAT-USA, Brooklyn, New York, 2013. Available online at: https://humantraffickinghotline.org/sites/default/files/And%20Boys%20Too%20-%20ECPAT%20USA.pdf (accessed March 13, 2025).

5 And I wasn't alone; the result was a radio piece for KALW's Spiritual Edge podcast, with editing and invaluable guidance by Cheryl Duvall and Spiritual Edge creator Judy Silber and audio mixing by Tarek Fouda. Religion News Service, which had commissioned the piece, published a print version of the story.

6 Anna Swartwood House, "The Long History of How Jesus Came to Resemble a White European," The Conversation, July 17, 2020. Available online at: https://theconversation.com/the-long-history-of-how-jesus-came-to-resemble-a-white-european-142130 (accessed March 13, 2025).

Chapter 6

1 Ken Chitwood, "UK Christians Walk 750 Miles to Urge Action on Climate Change," *Christianity Today*, October 21, 2021.

2 Bron Taylor, Gretel Van Wieren, and Bernard Daley Zaleha, "Lynn White Jr. and the Greening-of-Religion Hypothesis," *Conservation Biology: The Journal of the Society for Conservation Biology* 30, no. 5 (2016): 1000–9.

3 Ken Chitwood, "Evangelicals Rejoice at the Church of England's Fossil Fuel Divestment," *Christianity Today*, July 13, 2023.

4 Ken Chitwood, "What Is Religion's Role in Climate Justice and Environmental Action?" Patheos, November 4, 2024. Available online: https://www.patheos.com/articles/what-is-religions-role-in-climate-justice-and-environmental-action (accessed May 9, 2025).

5 "Flor y Canto," Flor y Canto. Available online at: http://cdiflorycanto.org/web/ (accessed September 19, 2023).

6 Olivia Singer, "Liberation Theology in Latin America," *Modern Latin America*, Brown University Library, Available online at: https://library.brown.edu/create/modernlatinamerica/chapters/chapter-15-culture-and-society/essays-on-culture-and-society/liberation-theology-in-latin-america/ (accessed September 19, 2023).

7 "Standing Firm: The Land and Environmental Defenders on the Frontlines of the Climate Crisis," Global Witness, September 2023, 10. Available online at: https://www.globalwitness.org/en/campaigns/environmental-activists/land-and-environmental-defenders-annual-report-archive/ (accessed March 13, 2025).

8 Magdaléna and Noel Rojo, "Communality: A Response to Deforestation," *Outriders*. Available online at: https://content.outride.rs/en/communality-a-response-to-deforestation (accessed September 2, 2023).

9 "Constitución Política de Los estados Unidos Mexicanos," Article 2o. Available online at: https://www.diputados.gob.mx/LeyesBiblio/pdf/CPEUM.pdf (accessed March 13, 2025).

10 Magdaléna Rojo, "Mexico: Zapotec Water Rights and Self-governance—a Positive Precedent for Water Justice," *Minority and Indigenous Trends 2023: Focus on Water*, Minority Rights Group International. Available online at: https://trends.minorityrights.org/mexico/ (accessed September 1, 2023).

Chapter 7

1 Mark Weisbrot, "Telling the Truth about Guatemala—And U.S. Foreign Policy," *Fort Lauderdale Sun-Sentinel*, March 4, 1999.

2 Shannon Van Sant, "Autopsy for 7-Year-Old Migrant Who Died in U.S. Custody Shows She Died of Sepsis," National Public Radio, March 30, 2019.

3 Angel Canales and Graham Kates, "He Survived the 1,000-mile Journey to the U.S. He Died Days Later in Custody," CBS News, May 21, 2019.

4 Then known as Swipes for the Homeless.

5 Brian Stewart and Sophie Tatum, "Coronavirus Pandemic Exacerbates Challenges for Homeless College Students," ABC News, May 6, 2020. Available online at: https://abcnews.go.com/Politics/coronavirus-pandemic-exacerbates-challenges-homeless-college-students/story?id=70516465 (accessed August 30, 2023).

6 Naree W.S. Viner, "Overcoming Founder's Syndrome on the Road to Success," *Philanthropy News Digest*, May 27, 2020. Available online at: https://philanthropynewsdigest.org/features/career-insights/overcoming-founder-s-syndrome-on-the-road-to-success (accessed August 30, 2023).

7 Esther D. Kustanowitz, "Rachel Sumekh Looks to Boost Jewish Funders Network's Efforts to Fight Poverty and Hunger," *eJewishPhilanthropy*, March 22, 2023. Available online at: https://ejewishphilanthropy.com/rachel-sumekh-looks-to-boost-jewish-funders-networks-efforts-to-fight-poverty-and-hunger/ (accessed August 30, 2023).

8 Kustanowitz, "Rachel Sumekh Looks to Boost Jewish Funders Network's Efforts to Fight Poverty and Hunger."

9 Ethnically, Americans of Iranian heritage are often also Armenian, Arab/Iraqi, Azari (of Turkish heritage), and/or Kurdish, along with a host of other minority ethnic backgrounds. Religiously, Iranian Americans are often assumed to be Shia Muslim but many are irreligious, Jewish, Bahá'í, Christian, Sunni Muslim, or Zoroastrian.

10 While the first wave of immigrant were often individual students or professionals, the second wave consisted of political refugees, exiles, dissidents, and religious/political/ethnic minorities, often fleeing in family units.

11 Emily Sigalow, *American JewBu: Jews, Buddhists, and Religious Change* (Princeton, NJ: Princeton University Press, 2022).

12 Repair the World, "Interview with Rachel Sumekh of Swipe Out Hunger." Available online at: https://werepair.org/repair-interview-rachel-sumekh-of-swipe-out-hunger/ (accessed October 30, 2019).

13 Marshall Ganz, "Why Stories Matter," Sojourners, March 2009. Available online at: https://sojo.net/magazine/march-2009/why-stories-matter (accessed March 10, 2025).

Chapter 8

1 Peter L. Berger, "Secularization Falsified," *First Things: A Monthly Journal of Religion and Public Life* 180 (February 2008): 24.

2 Ulrich Beck, *Cosmopolitan Vision* (Chichester: Wiley, 2006).

3 Fred Dallmayr, "Cosmopolitanism: In Search of Cosmos," *Ethics & Global Politics* 5, no. 3 (2012): 171–86. Available online at: https://doi.org/10.3402/egp.v5i3.18618.

4 Howard Thomas Albert, *The Faiths of Others: A History of Interreligious Dialogue* (New Haven, CT and London: Yale University Press, 2021).

5 Azza Karam, "The Common Good, or Transactional Religion?" Inter Press Service, June 28, 2023.

6 Ibid.

7 Love Lazarus Sechrest, *Race and Rhyme: Rereading the New Testament* (Grand Rapids, MI: Wm. B. Eerdmans Publishing Co., 2022), 242.

8 Ramindar Singh and Quraish Patel, "Ela and Mewa Ramgobin Intent on Resurrecting the Gandhian Spirit," *India Today*, May 15, 1989.

9 Philip Bowring, "The Passing of a Reformer," *The New York Times*, January 5, 2010.

Afterword

1 Joan Didion, "In the Service of Immediate Cosmic Reform," *The New York Times*, March 14, 1971.

2 Gregory C. Stanczak and Donald E. Miller, *Engaged Spirituality: Spirituality and Social Transformation in Mainstream American Religious Traditions* (Los Angeles, CA: University of Southern California Center for Religion and Civic Culture, 2004), 43.

3 Stanczak, *Engaged Spirituality*, 20.

4 Liz Bucar, *Stealing My Religion: Not Just Any Cultural Appropriation* (Cambridge, MA: Harvard University Press, 2022).

5 Megan Rogers and Mary Ellen Konieczny, "Does Religion Always Help the Poor? Variations in Religion and Social Class in the West and Societies in the Global South," *Palgrave Communications* 4, no. 1 (2018): 73.

6 Charles Taylor, *Sources of the Self: The Making of the Modern Identity* (Cambridge, MA: Harvard University Press, 1992).

7 Rebeca Solnit, "'If You Win the Popular Imagination, You Change the Game': Why We Need New Stories on Climate," *The Guardian*, January 12, 2023. Available online at: https://www.theguardian.com/news/2023/jan/12/rebecca-solnit-climate-crisis-popular-imagination-why-we-need-new-stories (accessed February 26, 2025).

8 Marshall Ganz, "Why Stories Matter: The Art and Craft of Social Change," *Sojourners*, March 2009. "Public Narrative, Collective Action, and Power," in *Accountability through Public Opinion: From Inertia to Public Action*, ed. Sina Odugbemi and Taeku Lee (The World Bank, 2011): 273–89.

INDEX

www.ingramcontent.com/pod-product-compliance
Ingram Content Group UK Ltd.
Pitfield, Milton Keynes, MK11 3LW, UK
UKHW022030030826
474032UK00003B/63

9 781350 563452